Britain to America

MID-NINETEENTH-CENTURY IMMIGRANTS
TO THE UNITED STATES

William E. Van Vugt

University of Illinois Press • Urbana and Chicago

Publication of this book was supported by a grant from the
Ellis Island–Statue of Liberty Foundation.

© 1999 by the Board of Trustees of the University of Illinois
Manufactured in the United States of America
1 2 3 4 5 C P 5 4 3 2 1

This book is printed on acid-free paper.

Library of Congress Cataloging-in-Publication Data
Van Vugt, William E.
Britain to America : mid-nineteenth-century immigrants to the United States /
William E. Van Vugt.
p.   cm. — (Statue of Liberty–Ellis Island Centennial series)
Includes bibliographical references (p.   ) and index.
ISBN 0-252-02451-6 (acid-free paper)
ISBN 0-252-06757-6 (pbk. : acid-free paper)
1. British Americans—History—19th century.
2. Immigrants—United States—History—19th century.
3. United States—Emigration and immigration—History—19th century.
4. Great Britain—Emigration and immigration—History—19th century.
I. Title.
II. Series.
E184.B7 V36   1999
304.8'7041'09034—ddc21   98-25460
CIP

For Lynn

Contents

Acknowledgments   ix

Introduction   1

1 "A Motley Set"   7
2 Emigrant Farmers   21
3 Britons in American Agriculture   35
4 Immigrants from Industry and Crafts   60
5 Miners   78
6 The Welsh   96
7 The Elite: Merchants, Professionals, and Gentlemen   111
8 Women   122
9 Becoming Americans: Religion, the Civil War, and Institutions   131

Conclusion   153

Appendixes
  A. Sources   159
  B. Details of British Immigrants to the United States, 1851   165
Notes   175
Bibliography   207
Index   229
Illustrations follow page 34

Acknowledgments

It is a pleasure to acknowledge the many people who helped make this book possible. Ronald A. Wells of Calvin College introduced me to British-American studies in England many years ago, and he remains an inspiration in his teaching and scholarship. At Kent State University I was very fortunate to study under Robert P. Swierenga, who taught me how to conduct research on migration and directed my master's thesis on British immigration. His dedication to his craft and students was again evident when he read an earlier version of this manuscript and made valuable suggestions for improvements. Any errors or shortcomings that might remain are certainly mine alone. I owe a special thanks to Charlotte Erickson. Soon after I enrolled at the London School of Economics and Political Science to earn my doctorate under her direction, she accepted the Paul Melon Chair in American History at Corpus Christi College of Cambridge University and gave me the option of joining her at Cambridge or remaining in London. I chose the latter, in part because she generously offered to continue to be my advisor and mentor in both London and Cambridge. In more recent years I have continued to benefit from her wisdom, guidance, and unsurpassed mastery of the field. Her influence on the study of migration and economic history is well known, and this book is a tribute to her dedication and generosity. Dudley Baines was another important source of instruction and direction at the London School of Economics. I also benefited from the criticism of Philip A. M. Taylor, and Richard O'Reilly assisted with computer work.

In my research forays throughout Britain I have met many friendly and helpful people. David Morris of Richmond, Yorkshire, who has written a fine book on the migration of Yorkshire Dales miners to the Upper Mississippi River Valley, was gracious to me in his wool shop in Muker, where he provided useful advice and documents. Historian and guide Lawrence Barker of Healaugh in Swaledale took me to the top of the Dales to examine where miners worked before departing for America. In the several times we met, he enabled me to see the story of emigrant miners more clearly. In addition, a host of librarians and archivists throughout the country made my research trips as enjoyable as they were fruitful. Deserving special thanks are the staffs of the British Library, the British Newspaper Library in Colindale, the British Library of Political and Economic Science, the public libraries of Enfield and Southgate in north London, Cambridge Public Library, the Northamptonshire Record Office, the Lincolnshire Central Reference Library, the William Salt Library in Stafford, Sheffield Central Library, the Sheffield City Archives, the Yorkshire Archeological Society, Leeds Central Library, Leeds University's Brotherton Library, and Manchester Central Library. I am also indebted to the fellows of Corpus Christi College in Cambridge for inviting me to be a guest fellow during my research there. I could not have made these research trips without the logistical help of Leni and Adrian De Waard, Patricia and Steven Orme, and David Ash. My late father, Ernest Van Vugt, and mother, Phyllis Van Vugt-Bratt, supported me in more ways than I can count.

On the other side of the Atlantic, I have enjoyed extraordinary support from Calvin College. Besides a sabbatical leave and a Calvin Research Fellowship, the college has given me several travel grants for research trips in both Britain and America as well as funding for two students, Paul Fessler and Sharon Vriend, to conduct some of the research in county histories in the United States. Calvin College librarians Conrad Bult and Kathy Struck frequently amazed me with what they were able to obtain through interlibrary loans, and history department administrator Jane Haney assisted with the typing and preparation of the manuscript. Sam Anema assisted with computer work, and Michele Risany proofread the manuscript. I also enjoyed the hospitality and assistance of the Bentley Historical Library in Ann Arbor, Michigan, the Wisconsin State Historical Society Library in Madison, the Wisconsin Room at the University of Wisconsin at Platteville, the Mineral Point Public Library, the Dubuque County Historical Society, Lorus College in Dubuque, Iowa, and the Indiana Historical Society in Indianapolis. The Balch Institute of Temple University in Philadelphia supplied raw data from immigrant passenger lists, and geographer Gregory Rose of Ohio State University allowed me the use of his maps of immigrant settlement in the Old Northwest. Some data and analysis were published previously in the *Economic History Review,* the *Journal of Social History,* the *Welsh History Review,* and in *Immigration and Ethnicity,* edited by Michael D'Innocenzo and J. P. Sirefman (Greenwood Press, 1992). I thank the editors of these publications for permitting me to use some of this material in chapters 2, 4, 6, and 8, respectively.

Finally, I have had great support from Lynn Heemstra-Van Vugt. During the course of our five-year residence in England and nine subsequent research trips we shared many adventures and challenges. Lynn never wavered in her faith and encouragement, and it is with greatest pleasure and gratitude that I dedicate this book to her.

Britain to America

Introduction

In 1844 a twenty-nine-year-old farmer's son and aspiring preacher named Matthew Dinsdale left his ancient native village of Askrigg, nestled in the heart of the Yorkshire Dales of northern England, and after a storm-tossed, thirty-day passage arrived in New York. He then trekked to a small settlement called English Prairie in McHenry County, Illinois, where he enjoyed the company and support of old friends who had gone before him and paved his way with descriptive and encouraging letters. Dinsdale carried his credentials from the Wesleyan Conference in England and was soon assigned as a circuit rider for the Methodist Episcopal Church in the lead-mining region of southwestern Wisconsin and then the Lake Winnebago region, where he "grew familiar" with the Indians.[1] On his journeys he "virtually lived in the saddle" and met many other English immigrants. But Dinsdale did take time to do some lead mining at Mineral Point, alongside fellow newcomers from Yorkshire and Cornwall. He also had his eye on land.

Then, in late 1849, Dinsdale and some friends journeyed via Panama to the newly discovered goldfields of California. His primary aim was to preach at the rowdy mining camps, but that did not stop him from mining on the side. Indeed, within a couple of years he accumulated more than $4,000 in gold. He had gone to California to do good—and ended up doing very well.

During his early years in America, Matthew Dinsdale wrote long letters to his widowed mother and his brothers and sisters back in Yorkshire, who passed the letters around for friends and relatives to read. In them the agony of separation from loved ones is apparent. He begs for longer, more frequent letters. Matthew also added tantalizing descriptions of the advantages that Wisconsin offered to English immigrants such as himself. Although he was careful to tell his family that "I will not say anything to you about coming to this country, it is a matter that belongs to yourselves," he was no doubt delighted to read the reply of his brother Edward: The family "have thought that we should do much better in America than what we can do in England by the comments you give it is a much better Place." His younger brother John, John's wife Tirzah, and their two children joined Matthew in 1849, and the rest of the family made long-term plans to come later. Matthew made it easier for them by returning to Yorkshire in 1853, marrying a local lass, Mary Ann Mann, and then taking his family back to Wisconsin the same year. Additional relatives and neighbors from Askrigg joined them and purchased land nearby.

The Dinsdales prospered as English immigrants in Wisconsin. Matthew served several pastorates for the Methodist Church. He also bought land and opened a store in Linden. John Dinsdale started with eighty acres and a log cabin near Fennimore in Grant County and gradually increased his holdings to four hundred acres of improved land to become one of the area's most successful farmers. He was also remembered as a leader of his community.

The Dinsdales, of course, were just one family among hundreds of thousands of British immigrants who came to the United States during the middle part of the nineteenth century. Although the gist of their story can be reconstructed through unusually rich sources, they cannot be assumed to represent all or even most of the others from their country who preceded or followed them. The British newcomers were people of many very different stripes. Most were English, but many others were Scottish or Welsh, and not all shared the Dinsdales' agrarian background and desire to farm. Nevertheless, a number of features of their story pop up with remarkable regularity whenever the historical records allow a glimpse at individual migrants of the period.

Perhaps foremost is the fact that these people used a form of chain migration in which a family member followed friends or relatives already in America, became established with their help, and wrote letters back home to inform others of the details of the new land and how best to join them in America. In that way the Dinsdales seem typical of the great majority of British immigrants whose stories are known in some detail. They were also not wedded to a single occupation. The family combined farming, mining, preaching, and mercantile activity because it suited their goals and allowed them to fulfill at least in part what they had envisioned before they left for America. Their piety was not exceptional, and neither was the magnitude of their success after years of hard work. Nor was the fact that in spite of their gravitation toward other British immigrants they could assimilate more readily than other immigrant groups thanks to the language and essential cultural traits and traditions they held in common with most native-born white Americans. They were "invisible immigrants" in the sense that they could blend in readily with other Americans and engage more immediately in social and civic affairs.[2]

But such introductory observations only scratch the surface of the complex and fascinating history of British migration to the United States. This book is devoted to that history, particularly as it pertains to the middle part of the nineteenth century—roughly from the Panic of 1837 through the Civil War. Although that may not be a very long period of chronological time, it is a virtual era when one considers the scale and pace of social and economic change and development in Britain and America during those years. Britain was becoming the world's first industrial and urban nation, and while the United States was following Britain's example in the Northeast the rapid settlement of the Old Northwest provided unprecedented opportunities for farmers and rural artisans. In 1846 Britain repealed the Corn Laws and adopted free trade, which deepened the symbiotic relationship that Britain and America shared within the Atlantic economy. After a serious depression during the late 1830s and early 1840s and the social and economic misery associated with the middle "hungry forties," both British and American economies boomed until the Panic of 1857. Meanwhile, British migration to America greatly accelerated.

The key to this story is the fact that Britain and the United States were from 1820 to 1860 the two most interconnected countries in the world in terms of culture and economic growth. During this period Britain took almost half of America's exports, and America took about 40 percent of her imports from Britain. The two economies were so intertwined that historians cannot assess the growth of one country without looking at the other, and the flow of people westward across the Atlantic was one of the essential threads that tied the two nations together.[3] Thus, the migration of Britons to America occurred within the Atlantic economy. Inevitably, it was related to the fundamental socioeconomic developments of the Atlantic world.

This book is not a mobility study of immigrants in America. Rather, it is a history of British migration to the United States within its full Atlantic context. It is an attempt to do what Frank Thistlethwaite called for—treat "the process of migration as a complete set of experiences whereby the individual moves from one identity to another."[4] To accomplish this task, several questions about British migrants must be explored. Who were they, and why did they migrate to the United States? Where did they come from, and where did they settle? What kind of work did they do in Britain and America, and how did they differ from the entire British population from which they selected themselves? To what extent was their migration related to the social and economic adjustments that came with modernity, especially industrialization and urbanization? And what kinds of experiences did they have as both Britons and Americans? What, in short, were their stories?

Addressing these questions is challenging to say the least. That is one reason why comparatively little historical attention has been given to British migration. Marcus Hansen pointed out the irony long ago when he noted that "the English, who have contributed the most to American culture, have been studied the least by students of immigration."[5] The Welsh have been studied even less. The problem lies in the paucity of sources on British migration. Unlike other immigrant groups, the British generally did not form ethnic communities or produce ethnic publications as other groups did. An even more serious problem lies in the fact that the British government did not create extensive records and statistics on emigration to the United States, as did governments of other nations. Furthermore, statistics that are available are not always specific enough to be helpful. Not until 1875 and 1908, for example, did American and British officials begin to differentiate between English and Welsh migrants.[6] Because of the problem of comparatively meager historical sources, Hansen's observation will likely never become obsolete.

That is not to say that the history of British migration to North America has been neglected. Understandably, the early surveys used the most accessible sources, which happened to be government records that dealt almost exclusively with British migration to the colonies and dominions. Thus Stanley Johnson's *A History of Emigration from the United Kingdom to North America* (1913), W. A. Carrothers's *Emigration from the British Isles* (1929), and Helen Cowan's *British Emigration to British North America* (1928)—although all good surveys— were inherently limited, said little about migration to the United States (the migrants' favorite destination), and did not address many of the questions that interest modern scholars the most. Wilbur Shepperson's *British Emigration to North America* (1957) paid more attention to migrants bound for the United States, but he primarily focused on the small minority who participated in organized "projects and opinions." The great bulk of British migrants was ignored. Rowland Berthoff wrote the excellent and widely cited *British Immigrants in Industrial America, 1790–1950* (1953), but that was concerned only with industrial workers and did not address some of the most important questions about British and American socioeconomic history and migration.

A real breakthrough occurred in 1972 with the publication of Charlotte Erickson's *Invisible Immigrants* (1972), a treasure-trove of English and Scottish immigrant letters and an analysis that set new standards in the scholarly use of those documents. Welsh letters had already been edited and published in Alan

Conway's *The Welsh in America* (1961), and Maldwyn Jones made a significant contribution in "The Background to Emigration from Great Britain in the Nineteenth Century" (1973). Meanwhile, Erickson focussed on passenger lists to the United States, which required much labor-intensive research but yielded important information when used with British and American census materials. This work concentrated on the early and late periods of the nineteenth century and was published in several articles in *Population Studies* as well as in *Leaving England: Essays on British Emigration in the Nineteenth Century* (1994).

This was also the period when passenger lists and other sources were also used in two definitive works on British colonial migration: Bernard Bailyn's *Voyagers to the West: A Passage in the Peopling of America on the Eve of the Revolution* (1986) and David Hacket Fischer's *Albion's Seed: Four British Folkways in America* (1989). In addition, the lists have proved their worth in two works on the contributions of certain types of British industrial workers: David Jeremy's *Transatlantic Industrial Revolution: The Diffusion of Textile Technologies between Britain and America, 1790s–1830s* (1981) and Geoffrey Tweedale's *Sheffield Steel and America: A Century of Commercial and Technological Interdependence, 1830–1930* (1987). The passenger lists also provide many clues about the nature of the mid-century migration to America.

This book offers a comprehensive look at a critical period of British migration to America by exploring important economic, social, and cultural development on both sides of the Atlantic. It addresses questions that go to the heart of both British and American history. Because of the limited sources, all the questions one might have on the subject cannot be answered with absolute certainty. Some issues and themes yield only impressions, anecdotes, and ambiguities. Nevertheless, there are some important historical issues and questions that can be answered with specificity and certainty. Chapter 1 introduces the topic of British migration more fully, raises the questions to be addressed, and provides a general overview of the migrant population. Chapter 2 discusses the state of British agriculture at mid-century, the nature of the farmers who migrated to America after the repeal of the Corn Laws, and whether there was a causal relationship between repeal and British migration to America. Chapter 3 tells the story of how farmers, farm laborers, and others from Britain adjusted to American agricultural life. Chapter 4 looks at British immigrants from industrial backgrounds and addresses the critical question of whether there was a strong relationship between industrial change and migration from Britain to America. Chapter 5 is devoted to the miners because of their prominence in both British and American industrial history. Chapter 6 investigates the Welsh because they were a distinct group of British migrants and because of important unanswered questions regarding specifically Welsh industrialization and migration. Chapter 7 provides a look at the so-called elite migrants, including merchants, professionals, and those who considered themselves gentlemen. Chapter 8 considers British immigrant women, whom historians have all but ignored, and chapter 9 examines the forces of assimilation in America, including the role of religion, the Civil War, and immigrant institutions.

In this book, the people who left Britain for America are referred to as "emigrants," "immigrants," and "migrants," depending on the context of the discussion. The first term is most appropriate when viewing them in Britain, the second in America, and the third when viewing them in their full Atlantic context. These different terms illustrate how the migrants did indeed move "from one identity to another."

From Liverpool as I before have stated
We sail'd a motley set we surely were
With coals and iron was our vessel freighted
Scotch Irish Welsh and English were there
Going out to see if emigration
Was a recipe against starvation

There were ploughboys weavers blacksmiths tailors
Irish peasant and Welsh mountaineers
Together with a family of nailors
Scotch from the lowlands and some highland seers
Butchers bakers carpenters and joiners
There were also a lot of Cornish miners
—From "The Emigrant's Farewell," Thorpe Letters and Poems, 1839

"A Motley Set"

And so the motley British came to America. They never did form truly massive proportions, as did the Irish during the Famine or the Germans and Norwegians during the 1850s and 1880s. But some four and a quarter million Britons did come to the United States between 1820 and 1930 in three prominent "waves" or surges, the first from the mid-1840s to the mid-1850s, the second from roughly 1863 to 1873, and the third and largest from 1879 through the late 1880s. This book focuses on the people who formed the first of these waves—those of the mid-nineteenth century (fig. 1). According to official American immigration statistics, nearly a half-million (442,049) English, Scottish, and Welsh people entered the United States between 1845 and 1855, with fifty thousand or more arriving annually in 1849, 1850, 1851, and 1854. The actual numbers, however, were certainly greater.[1]

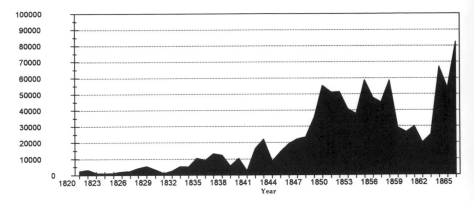

Figure 1. British immigrants to the United States. (*The Statistical History of the United States: From Colonial Times to the Present,* 1:106)

American officials tended to undercount British immigrants; in addition, many recorded as going to British North America through the port of Quebec soon crossed the border and joined the stream of those going directly to the United States. Roughly three out of four of Britain's emigrants during this period were bound for America. The Australian share rose in 1852 because of the gold rush there, but still it paled next to the United States as a destination (table 1). Who

Table 1. Number of British Immigrants to the United States[a] and Percentage Distribution of All Passengers Sailing from the United Kingdom, by Destination[b] (1846–54)

| Year | United States | | British North America | Australia/ New Zealand | Other | Total |
	Number	Percent				
1846	22,180	63.1	33.1%	1.5%	2.3%	100%
1847	23,302	55.0	42.6	1.9	0.5	100
1848	35,159	75.8	12.5	9.7	2.0	100
1849	55,132	73.5	13.8	10.7	2.0	100
1850	51,085	79.4	11.7	5.7	3.2	100
1851	51,487	79.5	12.8	6.5	1.2	100
1852	40,699	66.1	8.9	23.9	1.1	100
1853	37,576	70.0	10.6	18.5	0.9	100
1854	58,647	59.8	13.6	25.7	0.9	100
	442,049					

a. These are the official State Department figures for the total number of British immigrants. *Historical Statistics of the United States: Colonial Times to 1957,* 1:106.

b. These figures are for all passengers, both immigrants and travelers, leaving British ports. Calculated from the figures found in Appendix 1, *Thirty-third General Report of the Emigration Commissioners,* 1873, vol. 18.

the British immigrants were, and why and how they came to America, remain largely unanswered questions. Part of the answer lies in a brief comparison of Britain and America at mid-century.

Britain and America during the Mid-Nineteenth Century

"In the middle years of the nineteenth century the economic troubles of the preceding generation seemed to vanish as if by magic." Over the years, many major writers have echoed this frequently quoted analysis of Britain by the great economic historian Arthur Redford, and with some reason. The "hungry forties"—aptly named for the disastrous potato famine in Ireland and northwestern Scotland—were hard and bitter years for much of Britain. Industrial employment, agriculture, and real wages were depressed. Social tension increased in many of the northern mill towns as thousands were thrown out of work, and many people braced for the kind of social upheaval and violent political turmoil that was already gripping most of Europe. But the second half of the century got off to a much better start. The famine abated, textile industries boomed, and Britain led the world in a prosperous era of free trade. As the industrial economy shifted into high gear in the early 1850s, the nation entered what W. L. Burn has called an "age of equipoise": the period from roughly 1851 to 1867, distinct for its relative social stability and continuity. In the words of the social historian Asa Briggs, "Unlike the 1840s, the 1850s and 1860s were years of internal balance and widespread though not universal contentment."[2]

For Britain, the mid-century was a watershed. The Census of 1851 showed that it was the first urban and industrial nation in history. Only a fifth of the labor force was engaged in agriculture, and more than half of the population of twenty-one million lived in towns or cities of eight thousand or more people. For many writers, the year 1851 was especially significant. Macaulay called it a year "long remembered as a singularly happy year of peace, plenty, good feeling, innocent pleasure and national glory." Later historians concurred. The Great Exhibition of 1851, held in the fabulous Crystal Palace in Hyde Park as a showcase for the world's industrial and scientific progress (and which made Britain's preeminence clear to all), is often seen as a symbol for the prosperous quarter-century that followed it. In J. R. T. Hughes's view, it "foreshadowed an age of rapid expansion." In the eyes of others it "ushered in an age of prosperity which lasted virtually unbroken until 1873." The common notion was of a "Great Victorian Boom" that stretched all the way from 1850 to 1873, during which prices, profits, production, and prosperity rose steadily and significantly. Some writers see the publication of Spencer's *Social Statics* (1851) and Darwin's *Origin of Species* (1859), with all their confidence in the progress of humanity, as evidence of a "cult of progress" and a national mood of confidence. These historians agree that the mid-Victorians were happier and less troubled than the early or late Victorians.[3]

But what historians have yet to explain, and what this book addresses, is the fact that levels of British emigration rose sharply from the late 1840s through the early 1850s, precisely when the effects of the depressed hungry forties were receding, the industrial economy was growing, and opportunities for many workers were expanding (fig. 1).[4] One might plausibly suspect that the rising numbers of emigrants consisted of persons whose economic status had not improved or even had deteriorated, as was the case with some textile workers, ironworkers, and other skilled persons displaced by technological change. It is tempting to think of emigration as a safety valve for British workers threatened by industrialization, as was the case at certain times and places.[5]

Yet it could be that the increase in emigration was more a result of the beneficial side of industrialization and economic growth. Most people were becoming more able to bear the costs of emigration, and rising standards of living may have inspired some to seek an even better life in America. The fact that emigration rose during times of economic growth and opportunity in Britain does suggest the possibility that improved economic and social conditions induced many people to emigrate. Perhaps personal prosperity whetted the appetite and raised the expectations of some who then looked to America to fulfill their ambitions. After all, America's vast lands and economic and political freedom were legendary among British people, particularly the many whose neighbors, relatives, and friends had already moved there and had written glowing descriptions in personal letters. That positive forces were at play in the significant rise in emigration appears especially likely in light of what the American economy was like at the time.

While Britain was becoming industrialized and urbanized, the United States was still overwhelmingly agricultural and rural. Four-fifths of its labor force in 1840 was still engaged in agriculture. That general figure, however, hides America's regional diversity and dynamic industrial growth. By 1850, one-third of New England's workers and two-fifths of the mid-Atlantic's workers were engaged in manufactures, compared to a tenth of those in the Old Northwest and a mere twentieth in the South. As early as 1840, nearly all townships in southern New England had at least one manufacturing village with a cotton or woolen mill, an iron furnace, or some other establishment.[6] Thus British immigrants could find a wide variety of tempting opportunities in the United States—far greater than what Canada or Australia offered. In New England's textile mills, British machinists, engineers, dyers, managers, and operatives could find employment at comparatively high wages. In the coal mines of Pennsylvania and Illinois and in the lead, copper, and iron mines of Wisconsin, Michigan, and Illinois, British miners could use their skills and experience to earn two or perhaps three times what they would get for the same work in Britain. Some did even better in California's gold mines. Greater rewards for work also existed for British quarrymen in Vermont or New Hampshire, for ironworkers in Pennsylvania, domestic servants in America's towns and cities, or almost any kind of worker in any part of the country.

The United States was still experiencing what David Jeremy has called the "Transatlantic Industrial Revolution," whereby immigrants carried industrial methods and technologies from Britain to America. Although most of this technological transfer had already occurred, miners, machinists, engineers, potters, ironworkers, some textile workers, and others had skills that were still absent or in short supply in America. Higher earnings were there for the taking.[7]

And then there was land. It may be impossible now to comprehend what land meant to many during the nineteenth century. Some British immigrants in America later confessed to being "possessed" with the idea of owning land.[8] For many, land had sacred qualities. It gave life meaning and made it comprehensible. The Jeffersonian ideal that farmers on their own land reaped independence and virtue along with their crops was still alive and well, and it struck a responsive chord in the heart of many Britons. Inevitably, American land attracted many of Britain's emigrants. During the 1840s and 1850s it was possible to buy land in America for the cost of renting it for a year or two in Britain, and land was cheaper and easier to obtain in the United States than in Britain's own colonies. Government land was selling for only $1.25 per acre—good, improved tracts for only a few dollars more—as vast stretches of the North American continent were brought under control and cultivation, often at the cruel expense of Native Americans.

Furthermore, during the late 1840s and 1850s, a period of increased British immigration, the U.S. government passed a number of acts that greatly reduced the price of some land even further. Between 1847 and 1855, land warrants for sixty-one million acres were granted to men who had enlisted in the Mexican War and to veterans of previous wars, many of whom immediately sold these warrants for as little as 70 cents per acre. The Swamp Land Act of 1850 transferred to the states undrained federal lands that sold well below the government minimum, and in 1854 Congress reduced the price of land that had been on the market for some time. Land not sold for ten years was priced at only a dollar per acre. The longer it went unsold, the cheaper it was priced. Government land that had been on the market for thirty years or more was priced at a mere 12.5 cents per acre. Many of these cheaper tracts were composed of fairly good ground and only required some capital investment to make them profitable.[9] Thus, for white Americans and European immigrants, it was a golden age of agriculture. Land was typically easy to obtain, and hardworking farmers could expect profits. Britons took note and got in on the action, although little is known about their numbers, characteristics, and experiences.

Of course, the United States meant more than economic opportunity and land for the taking. Some identified their frustration with Britain's class system and comparative lack of participatory government as a reason for their emigration decision. One immigrant of 1850, George Tuffley, later explained that what attracted him to the United States was his early longing "to become a citizen of the country in which every voter had a voice in shaping the laws," and he claimed that within thirty minutes of his arrival in New York he found a justice of the peace and took an oath of allegiance to the government of the United States.[10] James Battersby clearly relished the egalitarianism of American society when in 1853 he wrote to his brother: "There is a great pleasure in working in this Country inasmuch as you feel as good as your employer and on a par with them, saying what you like . . . every one is alike, master and man."[11]

Yet it would be a mistake to think that purely political concerns were of primary importance, even to people such as these. Judging from the letters of others, the immigrants were not longing to participate in a democratic government so much as hoping to be free of government authority—especially, high taxes.[12] It is not always possible to distinguish between economic and other kinds of ambition, however. Acquiring land and farming it profitably was for many immigrants a source not only of economic security and independence but also self-esteem and the satisfaction of knowing that they were fulfilling God's will to subdue the earth. It was also, for many, the best way to secure a good future for their children.[13]

Although it is clear that the United States offered a better life to many people who were suffering hardship in Britain, it would be simplistic to say that migrants were being pushed out of Britain by distress or pulled to the United States by opportunities. Most would not have been able to distinguish between push and pull factors if asked to do so; the two forces were somewhat blurred in the context of each situation.[14] Although the timing of the increase in British migration to America had been influenced by the strength of the business and building cycle, individual decisions to emigrate ran deeper than that.[15] They involved careful, comparative assessment of what the two countries offered and deep and sober assessment of one's goals. Migrating also required a willingness to endure a rigorous and potentially dangerous voyage across the Atlantic Ocean.

The Voyage

The voyage from Britain to America during the mid-nineteenth century was an enormous undertaking that figured prominently in migrants' decisions to leave, especially for the vast majority who had to endure a cramped and stifling steerage compartment on a creaking wooden sailing vessel. By sail, the journey from Liverpool to New York took roughly five weeks, although bad weather could extend it to as much as fourteen weeks or more. The new transatlantic steamships that began to appear at mid-century made a tremendous difference. On them, the same journey took about twelve days and was safer and less traumatic, although hardly free of danger and discomfort.[16] For some migrants, the higher price of a steamship ticket was more than compensated for by the lesser time of lost wages.

Steamships also made it more thinkable to return to Britain in case America failed to measure up to one's expectations or if one merely wished to visit loved ones who had stayed behind. Many successful mid-century British immigrants made such return visits during the late nineteenth century—often more than once. Steamships made the world smaller so that emigration was no longer as great a step as it had been. It no longer seemed so irreversible. That the psychological barriers against emigration had fallen during the early age of steamships is evident in a letter written to Edwin Kimberley, an English immigrant in Wisconsin in 1853, from his relatives in Lincolnshire: "You say such a thing cannot be; that you might see us again, why there is going to be a line of Screw steamers run from England to America to commence in May next to go over the water to New York in 13 or 14 days, and the fare will be £6 . . . so don't talk about not seeing us again, we may perhaps pay you a prop[er] visit some of these days."[17]

Yet steamships were only beginning their takeover of the Atlantic passenger traffic. As late as 1856, 96 percent of all passengers landing in New York from foreign ports arrived aboard sailing ships.[18] The trip became less expensive during the 1840s and 1850s, as ships' captains and shipping companies began to tap the huge volume of people eager to leave Europe. Timber ships bound for America to pick up a cargo found it profitable to use poor emigrants who could scrape together a few pounds as human ballast, a situation that allowed impoverished people to flee Ireland during the famine but at the cost of appalling and frequently fatal conditions.

Although passage tickets were becoming cheaper, the financial costs of migrating were still considerable for people of limited means. During the mid-century period, steerage passages from Liverpool to New York fell to £3.10s (about

$17) or less, but provisions were not always included.[19] Then there were the costs of transportation to the port of embarkation and into the American interior (unless one intended to remain in the American port city), not to mention the wages lost during the voyage or the cost of living in America until employment was secured. It seems, therefore, that £5–6 ($25–30) was the absolute minimum required for an individual to emigrate to America, approximately £20 (about $100) for a family of four, even if the children were young enough for reduced fares. Wages of 10 shillings per week, by no means the lowest during the 1840s and 1850s, totaled about £25 ($125) per year, nearly all of which would be spent on survival, especially if there were a wife and children to support. For poorer people such as agricultural laborers, some of whom earned only 6 shillings per week, emigration would have appeared prohibitively expensive without some form of assistance.

The physical and psychological burdens of sailing were equally formidable. Just leaving a town or village to the port of embarkation and experiencing the "great lamentation" of parting from family and friends—"forever in this world" as most emigrants believed—was enough to make some reconsider their move. This particular trauma was lessened, though, for those who emigrated as groups of families and neighbors. Although there is no way to determine the proportions of mid-century British who did so, newspapers and diaries afford frequent glimpses of group migration, which seems to have been common. As one newspaper observed, "Nearly 50 persons at once started from the Midland Station in Lincoln for America . . . about 20 of the number came up . . . from the neighborhood of Boston."[20] The emotional support that came with group migration was no doubt necessary for many of these people to leave their home and board a ship bound for America.

During the late 1840s in particular, conditions on cramped and poorly ventilated timber ships were often terrible. Aside from sinking far from land, a typhus or cholera epidemic was likely the worst fate a ship could encounter. Of the 89,738 emigrants who left British ports for Quebec in 1847 (the worst year of the famine), 5,293 died of typhus on passage and 10,037 more died in Canadian hospitals—for a total of 15,330, 17 percent of those who embarked.[21] What one emigrant recalled in 1850 was all too familiar to others who had made the trip: "The scenes I witnessed daily were awful: to hear the heart-rending cries of wives at the loss of their husbands at the sight of corpses of their wives, and the lamentations of fatherless and motherless children . . . these were sights to melt a heart of stone. I saw the tear of sympathy run down the cheek of many a hardened sailor."[22]

Although not fatal, seasickness aboard a sailing ship taking five weeks or longer to cross the ocean was an ordeal one can scarcely imagine now. Typical observations of the kind of filthy hell that seasickness produced would include that of Benjamin Millward from Birmingham, who aboard the *Cornelia* in 1854 wrote, "The people are lying about in all directions, sick in scores. And I might say without exaggeration, they are in hundreds. . . . It is a pitiful sight to see them."[23] Joseph Hurst, who sailed to Philadelphia in 1847 as a cabin passenger, recorded in his diary, "The ship roll'd & tottered & her timbers creaked & shivered nay I did really think that at one time she was going down . . . the roaring of the waves together with the rolling of the shipe made it almost impossible to keep ourselves in our berths."[24] More than one emigrant reflected with gallows humor that "for the first quarter of an hour [upon leaving port] you feel afraid the ship is going down, and for the next quarter of an hour you feel afraid that it will *not* go down."[25]

For a minority of emigrants, usually some of those who could afford a private cabin, the voyage was not such a horrible experience, however. Some even claimed to have enjoyed the trip, as did Mary Harrison, who took seven and a half weeks to cross in 1842. Fifty years later she reflected, with perhaps more than a touch of nostalgia, that "she was sorry to see land, for she had learned to love the sea and did not wish to leave it." Others referred to their voyages as "pleasant." But one must wonder how pleasant they really were. Matthew Dinsdale recorded in his letters that his crossing was the most pleasant voyage ever, according to the experienced crew who took him to America, and yet he and his fellow passengers were wracked with prolonged and violent seasickness. For the great majority of emigrants, the experience was some mixture of terror, boredom, sickness, fatigue, adventure, and anxiety.[26]

The fear and misery that some emigrants experienced when shipwrecked, rescued, and taken back to England to try to immigrate anew are difficult to imagine. William Bosomworth's vessel sprung a leak and nearly sank on its emergency return to Liverpool, which extended his journey to America to eleven weeks. A collision at mid-sea nearly put an abrupt end to Arthur Longman's eight-week voyage, and Thomas Williams's ship reportedly took a full four months to cross the ocean in 1848. Thomas Liddle embarked on the *Corsica* at Liverpool in 1851 but was shipwrecked on the coast of Newfoundland. He lost everything except the clothes on his back, and it took him three more weeks to arrive in New York.[27]

One of the most dramatic voyages was that of John Shortney. The storms on his seven-week sailing were so bad that the ship was "all but wrecked" and every movable thing had to be cast overboard, including Shortney's luggage, which contained his clothes, money, and letters of introduction—"everything he possessed in the world except the suit he wore." Landing in New York with no resources and no place to go, he allowed chance to decide his fate by dropping his cane and going in the direction it pointed—westward.[28]

For those emigrants who had to bury family members at sea, the misery of seasickness and the fear of shipwreck were not the worst of it. Nor were the perils and hardships of emigration necessarily over once the voyage across the Atlantic had been completed. The Great Lakes were a watery grave for some Britons on their way to the Old Northwest. Others arrived safely in the port of New York but, inexplicably, never made it to their final destination. It is not surprising that some gave no thought to ever again crossing the ocean in a sailing vessel. For them, the dreadful voyage had made their migration irreversible. At least one who never intended to stay in America did so because of what she had experienced at sea, even on a steamship. Jane Chadwick was an apprentice dressmaker from Manchester who in her early twenties traveled with her aunt and uncle to visit America. In 1850 the party boarded the steamer *City of Glasgow*, which took only fourteen days to cross, but Chadwick was so ill on the journey that when the time came to return to England she refused to go "because she so dreaded the voyage." It was in America that Jane Chadwick decided to become an immigrant, and she proceeded to Atchinson, Kansas, where friends from England had recently settled and she could continue her work as a dressmaker.[29]

In short, the voyage was a truly formidable part of the migration decision and experience. The known rigors and dangers of the crossing undoubtedly kept the numbers of British emigrants from being even larger than they were. It is no accident that absolute peaks in European emigration were reached late in the nineteenth century after steamships had replaced sailing ships on the Atlantic and lowered physical and psychological barriers to the trip. Yet even during the mid-century's age of sail, huge numbers still managed to work up the courage necessary to come to America.

An Overview of Mid-Century British Migrants

At this point it is possible to make some new observations about British migrants as a group. First, their numbers were greater than official statistics claim. According to a one-in-ten sample ($n = 6,189$) of passenger lists of immigrant ships, an estimated sixty thousand British immigrants entered the United States by way of the five major ports in 1851 alone.[30] American immigration authorities appear to have undercounted British immigration in 1851 by roughly ten thousand people, or nearly 20 percent (table 1). Similar discrepancies have been detected for earlier years. Apparently, American officials, confronted with many passenger lists imprecisely filled in with "Great Britain and Ireland" in the "nationality" column, systematically overestimated the proportions that were Irish and hence significantly undercounted the number of British.[31] But even the ship-list estimates are conservative. An undeterminable number of arrivals in Canada crossed the border and were never counted as American immigrants. Assuming that the undercounting was fairly constant, the actual total number of British immigrants from 1845 to 1855 was closer to a million than the half-million counted by the authorities.

Another important, if expected, feature concerns the predominance of the English, who composed fully two-thirds of the British migrants whereas Scots made up a fourth and Welsh a twentieth (table 2). Their respective percentages in the British population were 81, 14, and 5. Thus, Scots were migrating at a higher rate than the English and Welsh, as they always had done, in large part because of a comparative lack of alternative employment with which to make adjustments in life.[32] Between two-thirds and three-fourths of the English, Scots, and Welsh were male (68 percent, 75 percent, and 62 percent, respectively).

In 1846 John Watson, a seventy-five-year-old Yorkshireman, boarded a ship and made the arduous voyage to Quebec, whereupon he moved to Ohio and bought 160 acres of land. But still the old man was not satisfied. He soon found greener pastures in Indiana and there passed the remainder of his long life.[33] Septuagenarians such as Watson were colorful but rare among Britons who entered America in the nineteenth century. In fact, persons over forty were significantly underrepresented in the migrant population. As has long been known about virtually all migrant populations, young persons predominated.[34] In 1851 those in their twenties migrated in proportions twice as great as the proportions they composed in the general British population. Children were somewhat underrepresented, and persons in their thirties were only minimally overrepresented. When compared to the earlier British immigrants, those of the mid-century period were younger on average, more commonly in their twen-

Table 2. British Immigrants by Sex (1851)

	Male		Female		Totals	
English	2,440	(39.4)	1,666	(26.9)	4,106	(66.3)
Scots	1,004	(16.2)	754	(12.2)	1,758	(28.4)
Welsh	201	(3.2)	124	(2.0)	325	(5.3)
	3,645	(58.9)	2,544	(41.1)	6,189	(100.0)

Source: See Appendix A for ship numbers and sources.

Note: The sex of sixteen immigrants could not be determined from the lists, so they were divided equally according to their nationality. Percentages are given in parentheses.

ties.[35] They had low dependency ratios and would spend most of their prime working lives in the United States.

By mid-century, British immigrants were younger than ever before (table 3). More were single as well. Roughly a third (two-thirds of all males aged fifteen and above) traveled alone, compared to only a fourth of all English and Welsh migrants (half of all males aged fifteen and above) in 1831. The figures for 1841 roughly split these differences.[36] The change from older and familial migrants to younger, more single migrants is usually seen as one of the characteristics of a shift from rural or folk migration to a labor migration, a change also identified in the migration of Germans, Swedes, Norwegians, and Danes during the later part of the nineteenth century.[37] Britons coming to the United States in 1851 were still far more familial than those of the late 1880s.[38] The trend to a labor migration, however, seems to have been well established already by mid-century—a generation before the trend occurred for other immigrant groups. That reflects Britain's earlier industrialization and urbanization.

The early trend toward a British labor migration is also evident in what little evidence is available about the migrants' origins. During the 1820s, 1830s, and 1840s, the heaviest flow came from more rural areas and nearly a quarter came from principal towns of twenty thousand or more. By the late 1880s more than three-quarters had come from principal British towns. The corresponding figure for 1851 is 69 percent, although there may be a bias toward urban origins for all of these years. Available data do not allow clear conclusions about the origins of all British migrants.[39]

It is easier to identify the migrants' destinations. According to the 1850 U.S. Census, the first to distinguish foreign-born inhabitants by country of origin,

Table 3. Age of British Immigrants (1851)

Age (Years)	Immigrants		1851 Census	
	English and Welsh	Scots	English and Welsh	Scots
0–14	28%	27%	36%	36%
15–19	10	10	10	10
20–24	21	25	9	10
25–29	15	15	8	8
30–39	15	14	13	12
40–49	7	5	10	10
50+	4	5	14	14
Number	4,431	1,758		
Total 6,189				

Source: See Appendix A for ship numbers and sources.

mid-century immigrants from Britain favored the states of the Old Northwest. In 1850 nearly half (48 percent) lived in the mid-Atlantic states, but that was the legacy of earlier immigration. Newer arrivals were heading west, as were many native-born Americans. The mid-Atlantic region, New England, and the southern region were being replaced by the states of the Old Northwest (especially Illinois, Wisconsin, Michigan, New York, and Pennsylvania) and some western states and territories as the main destination of English, Scottish, and Welsh immigrants. The greatest concentration of English immigrants in any state in 1850 was located in Wisconsin—6.2 percent of that state's entire white population. But between 1850 and 1860 Illinois experienced the greatest net gain in English immigrants of any state, followed by New York, Michigan, Wisconsin, and Pennsylvania.[40]

Work on the 1850 census manuscripts by Gregory Rose, a geographer, yields a clearer view of where the British tended to settle in the five states of the Old Northwest (fig. 2).[41] They had participated significantly in the earliest wave of white settlement in the region and showed keen interest in settling along the Ohio, Wabash, and Mississippi rivers, around the Great Lakes, and in the newly exploited land of Michigan, Illinois, and Wisconsin. Fertile, uncleared, or partially cleared farmland was available at low prices in these regions, and the lead-mining district of the Upper Mississippi River in northwestern Illinois and southwestern Wisconsin also drew concentrations of Britons. At the same time, coal-producing regions in eastern Ohio and southeastern Illinois and the iron-smelting and pottery works along the Ohio River absorbed many others. But by this time the British were also coming to cities in disproportionately high numbers, as seen in the counties containing Cleveland, Columbus, Cincinnati, Detroit, Chicago, and Milwaukee.

During the mid-century period most of these places were far less economically developed than Britain. Generally, they had lower standards of housing, lower per capita incomes, and inferior public facilities. Although the British and American economies were closely linked, they were at very different stages of development. To many British newcomers, however, the United States had the best of both worlds: everything from wild prairie and virgin farmland in the West and budding commercial agriculture in places such as Wisconsin to modernizing industries in the East. The United States surely held more options than Britain.

The vast sweep of social and economic change in nineteenth-century Britain and America is reflected in the kind of people who migrated. Agriculturalists were more conspicuous among British immigrants in 1851 than in any other year known. The same was true for servants. The proportions of laborers rose also significantly between 1841 and 1851. By mid-century they were as well rep-

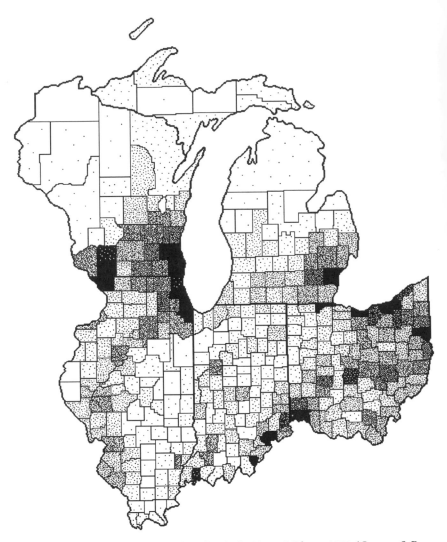

Figure 2. Each dot equals ten British settlers in the Upper Midwest, 1850. (Gregory S. Rose, "Indiana's Ethnicity in the Context of Ethnicity in the Old Northwest in 1850")

resented as they were in the 1880s, when British emigration had taken on the characteristics of a labor migration. Just as dramatic is the fall in the proportions of industrial workers between 1841 and 1851, although preindustrial craftsmen emigrated in fairly steady proportions. On the surface, it appears that mid-century migrants had more in common with those of the 1880s than with those of the 1830s, the major exception being the greater prominence of agriculturalists in 1851.[42]

Everything here wears a gloomy aspect—what will this Free-Trade lead to? I fear our downfall is sealed!
—James Finlay Letters, Ancaster Estate Papers, Nov. 30, 1848–May 31, 1849

Emigrant Farmers

No issue was debated with more heat and passion in mid-Victorian Britain than free trade, which was ushered in by the repeal of the protective Corn Laws in 1846. Industrial workers celebrated the cheaper bread that would result, although ugly food riots in protest of expensive bread continued to plague the western counties through the middle of 1847.[1] Industrial employers also welcomed free trade and cheaper bread because that gave them a convenient excuse to screw wages down still lower, precisely in the way Friedrich Engels had predicted in 1844.[2]

While industrial workers and employers welcomed free trade, the agricultural community was horrified by it. They feared that the loss of protection would allow foreign competition to ruin them forever.

Indeed, for American farmers repeal was a tremendous boon, for now they could tap the British market and profitably expand settlement in the Old Northwest.[3]

The impact of repeal on British agriculture has undergone various interpretations. The most informed contemporary observer was James Caird, a correspondent for *The Times,* who in 1850 and 1851 journeyed with an assistant through rural England to seek the "most trustworthy sources of local information" for an inquiry into English agriculture, the results of which were published the following year.[4] That famous report, which was carried out in response to farmers' complaints about low agricultural prices, contains detailed descriptions of each county's agricultural condition. Although noting the genuine difficulty of many farmers in some regions, Caird was convinced that improved farming methods offered a bright future to the nation's farmers in spite of repeal. Caird responded to Oxfordshire and Wiltshire farmers' urgent complaints that repeal had undermined prices and brought hardship by informing them that their distress was due to poor farming methods and low productivity.[5]

Later historians were not convinced. R. E. Prothero argued that free trade caused an "agricultural panic" and a period of "disaster" that lasted until 1853 and ruined farmers all over the country.[6] But only one historian, Marcus Hansen, saw a connection between free trade and emigration when he wrote that terror "gripped the English farmer when he realized that his wall of protection had been razed." It was this "widespread anxiety in regard to the future," said Hansen, that explains "the sudden revival of interest in emigration in 1848 and 1849." In 1849, "surprising numbers" of agricultural laborers and tenant farmers emigrated to the United States; in 1851, "thousands of yeoman farmers, tired of the struggle with low prices and high rents, left for America."[7] Hansen based those statements entirely on excerpts from the *Mark Lane Express,* a leading agricultural journal, and the *Emigrant Colonial Gazette,* which encouraged emigration. Given their readerships, such publications might have exaggerated the agricultural distress and link between free trade and emigration. They are also vague. Was the number of emigrant farmers unusually large at this time, or was it normal for "thousands" to emigrate?

According to the passenger lists of 1851, farmers were emigrating to the United States in greater proportions than in earlier or later years as Hansen had speculated. Nearly one-fourth of the employed male emigrants claimed an agricultural occupation, and nearly all of these were described as "farmers" at a time when only 6.5 percent of the male British labor force farmed.[8] An estimated five thousand British agriculturalists and their families migrated directly to the United States in 1851. Farm laborers, the most numerous of all members of

Britain's agricultural class, hardly appear on the lists, although considerable numbers of them did emigrate during this time (chapter 3).

Nearly a third (36.8 percent) of the farmers were under twenty-five; a few of the older ones emigrated as sons rather than as heads of households. It is likely that some were not true farmers and might have been more accurately described as agricultural laborers. But even accepting only those heads of household aged twenty-five and above as true farmers, an estimated three thousand farmers emigrated to the United States in 1851. With them emigrated nearly three thousand others, perhaps not true farmers but men who described themselves as such and at least had worked on farms.

It is also likely that many listed simply as "labourers" were actually farm laborers. Farm laborers often described themselves as laborers, and it is reasonable to suspect that careless or hurried enumerators found it more expeditious to list them as such. The distinction between the two was not always clear, and enumerators understandably did not see it as significant.[9] Such simplification can be seen in the marriage and birth certificates of those who eventually migrated to America and were featured in county histories. Of nine described as "labourers" on the certificates, three were known to have been farm laborers in England and five went to farm labor or farming in America either immediately or very soon after their arrival in America.[10] Such lumping surely occurred on passenger lists as well. Thus, the movement of British farmers and farm laborers together was even greater than the lists indicate. Farm laborers are hidden among the listings of both farmers and labourers.

As for the farmers themselves, newspaper reports usually described them as industrious occupiers of smallholdings, people who had managed to save some capital, or as farmers "of the best description."[11] The following excerpt from the *Lincolnshire, Boston, and Spalding Free Press* of July 2, 1850, is typical of this characterization and provides a number of useful details of emigration: "After harvest, it is expected that a great number of small farmers from the district east of Spalding will take their departure for the colonies or for America . . . the class now about to emigrate are small capitalists, possessing from £50 to £200, an insufficient sum for carrying on farming operations in this country under present arrangements."

From this account and many others a common theme emerges: Industrious small farmers possessing moderate sums of capital—£50–200 ($250–1,000)— were finding it hard to make a profit in Britain and so turned to other places, particularly the United States, where they hoped to gain greater rewards by working their own land. The smallness of such capital is noteworthy and consistent with the amounts taken by the emigrant farmers whose letters and biographies are available. They, too, were no doubt seeking the cheaper, unimproved lands of America, where they believed they could secure a greater return on their investments.[12]

Other evidence supports newspaper assertions that emigrant farmers were "men of capital." Of all the emigrants, farmers were the most likely to be traveling with wives and children. The average family size was larger than that of any other group, as was the percentage of families traveling with "extended" members (nephews, nieces, cousins, and other relatives).[13] Farmers were the most able to afford the greater costs of a family migration. They had at least some extra capital after selling their farm implements, livestock, and other assets and hence were not destitute.

One particularly illuminating, and typical, case is that of a Mr. Birtwhistle, a farmer from Wadworth, who in 1851 had stopped in nearby Doncaster with his family of "about sixteen members" on the way to Liverpool, from where the group was to sail to the United States. The *Doncaster Chronicle and Farmers' Journal* published his story on May 30:

> Mr Birtwhistle is reported to be a clever and skilful practical agriculturalist, and he has occupied the farm which he has just given up for upwards of twelve years, but finding that with all his energy and all his industry he could . . . scarcely "make both ends meet," he determined to relinquish his unprofitable occupation before his capital became exhausted and seek his fortune in "the land of the west". This is not the only instance which has occurred where tenant farmers in this neighbourhood unable any longer to bear up against the burdens by which they are so unjustly oppressed, have exiled themselves from their paternal home, and crossed the waters of the broad Atlantic, where with an untaxed and fertile soil they are able to become successful rivals in the race of competition with their brethren in the fatherland.

One of the most interesting facets of the report is that Birtwhistle emigrated "before his capital became exhausted," the implication being that he was motivated not so much by immediate hardship as by the threat of it. The fact that he and his household could afford sixteen passages is consistent with the evidence of larger family groups among emigrant farmers, and it suggests that he was still far from being a poor man. But the fear of becoming poor in England was very real to him because his capital was steadily draining away.

Birtwhistle's economic troubles appear to have been caused in part by taxation and the tithe, burdens cited by a number of other disgruntled farmers as well, among them a Mr. Worsley who in 1850 occupied a thousand acres. For the previous two years Worsley complained that "the tithe has much exceeded the

whole return of my investment."[14] Others claimed that rural Britain had a population surplus that was keeping the demand and rents for farms too high, which
prompted emigration.[15]

The most commonly reported root of farmers' distress and the most basic reason for extensive emigration was the low price of grain, seen as the result of free
trade.[16] Nothing in the newspapers suggests that farmers faring well in Britain were
emigrating to find something even better in America. Nor is there evidence that
British farmers were attracted first to towns before emigrating overseas, a common
pattern among rural emigrants from Norway.[17] Rather, they were said to be "hur-
rying away to the United states to escape from landlordism and pauperism."[18]

The perspective and objectivity of these reports, however, should be ques-
tioned. Newspapers were more likely to report the dramatic cases of distressed
emigration than the quieter departure of some farmers who may have been
motivated primarily by a desire for American land. There is also the possible
political bias of newspapers, which is not always easy to detect. The conservative ones may have exaggerated the "ruinous" effects of free trade in order to
defend the interests of the farmers and the landed classes. Yet the assumption that
all the many diverse reports of free-trade-induced distress and emigration were
biased would be a hasty and misleading generalization; not all can be dismissed
as political rhetoric. In fact, one newspaper known to be liberal, the *Cambridge
Independent Press,* also reported the desperate situation of grain farmers and their
cries for the return to protection.[19] Furthermore, the substance of these reports
is echoed in the estate papers of the Duke of Ancaster in Lincolnshire, where the
agent, James Finley, reported by late 1849 that the farmers had never been so
"dispirited" and that the following year "many" laborers and farmers were emigrating to America, "where they are not in the humour of Free Trade."[20]

Even if newspapers did overstate the relationship between repeal and agricultural conditions and emigration, the reports themselves and the fact that protection was removed may have had some psychological effect that spurred emigration. As far as the decision to emigrate was concerned, what farmers believed
or feared to be the economic impact of repeal may have been as important as
what was actually the case. And the prevailing agricultural message in journals
and public lectures as well as newspapers was that repeal had brought disaster
to England's farmers and that their future was bleak.[21] One farmer from "the East
of England, who has always been a liberal in politics" predicted in the *Northampton Herald* on February 1, 1851, that by the end of the year any five-hun-
dred-acre farm would suffer a "clear loss of at least £500." He also claimed to
know of "many instances" of farmers being forced off their fifty- to eighty-acre
farms, which had been held by their families for one hundred or more years and

had "just kept the tenants in comfortable circumstances." "All is swept away," he explained, "by foreign produce." Many similar cases were being reported for various other parts of the country.[22] Such reports may have persuaded some farmers, like Birtwhistle, to cut their losses and emigrate before they went completely broke.

Some newspapers went so far as to encourage emigration outright. As large numbers of Lincolnshire farmers were being "silently ruined week by week, by unprecedented depression in agricultural produce," the editor of the county's leading newspaper urgently warned those still solvent to leave before it was too late: "It is a last hope to these men to know that there is such a resource as emigration, and we only trust that they will look into it in time, and not sit down and suffer themselves to be ruined to the last farthing."[23] *The Times* saw little hope for farmers in a free-trade Britain and suggested sarcastically that "they had either better leave the country, or . . . buy a rope and hang themselves."[24]

The nature and severity of the agricultural distress in Lincolnshire is further revealed in the letters sent to the family of Edwin O. Kimberley, who emigrated from Pinchbeck (near Spaulding in southern Lincolnshire) to Green County, Wisconsin, in 1850. Kimberley purchased fifty acres of unimproved land and went through the initial stages of anxiety and regret while he and his family struggled to get established. The letters they received are from relatives and neighbors eager to get information and advice on how to join the Kimberleys in Wisconsin. The farmers referred to in the following letter were caught in a bind that was all too familiar to those finding it hard to adjust to the realities of post-repeal agriculture. They could not increase production, and their landlords were refusing to lower rents to compensate for the lower prices for grain. As Kimberley's brother reported, "The times are dreadfull with us Failures daily takeing place . . . & a maney more Quantities of People have given up there Farms because the Landlords will not lower the Rents . . . and the Times are dreadful bad indeed, & I am sorey to tel you I am in with most of them, & God only knowes weither I shall be able to pay my way for I am loosing money daily."[25]

Kimberley's aunt and uncle were also eager for information on how to join their nephew because "the times are so very bad in England . . . the people are Leaveing By hundreds It is truly Apailing [appalling] to go the spalding markets to see the public sales many distress sales others Bring goods from A Distance from their Creditors to raise Meanes to Leave the Country."[26] Later that year, others in the south of Lincolnshire wrote to Kimberley to say that "Their has been a great deal of distress about us lately people are being sold up daily one way or other . . . the Landlords don't feel disposed to lower their rents at present there are many people scarcely know how to scrape [?] along we think you just got out of the mes in time."[27]

Admittedly, newspapers and letters provide only impressions about the influence that free trade had on agricultural conditions and emigration at mid-century. The psychological effect of free trade, of course, can never be satisfactorily determined. But the available data and scholarship on grain prices and imports, together with additional evidence from the passenger lists and county histories, shed light on the important question of whether the economic effects of free trade were actually responsible for the unprecedented numbers of farmers who emigrated in 1851.

The extent and timing of both the rise in imports and the fall in prices (fig. 3) are striking. The emigrant farmers of 1851 left Britain at a time of unparalleled grain imports—more than four times the level immediately before repeal—and the lowest grain prices since the late 1700s.[28] Because grain farmers in 1850 and 1851 were selling their crop at only about three-fourths the price immediately before repeal and a little more than half of what they had received in 1847, it is understandable that they blamed free trade for low prices and took a dim view of a future without protection.

A number of scholars—notably Susan Fairlie, Wray Vamplew, and Jeffrey Williamson—have studied the relationships among repeal, grain imports, and grain prices. Although the relationship is not one of simple cause and effect, their conclusion is that repeal was largely responsible for the high imports and low prices of mid-century. Fairlie computed new data to demonstrate that home production actually declined after 1846, a finding that rules out the assumption by some earlier writers that rising output had lowered prices. Rather, rising imports, encouraged by the repeal of the Corn Laws, lowered grain prices because the demand for grain was inelastic. Fairlie solved the apparent anomaly between increasing imports and falling prices by pointing out that the low British prices were still far better than those paid on the Continent.[29] Vamplew found that some grain importers had devised elaborate mechanisms that sometimes allowed them to sell at prices comparable to those of the early 1830s. Nevertheless, he concluded that "the Corn Laws offered a significant degree of protection to British cereal producers," the removal of which in 1846 undercut the livelihood of many farmers. And Williamson's econometric analysis confirms the relationship between the Corn Laws, imports, and prices and the fact that tenant grain farmers and their landlords lost the most with repeal.[30]

Free trade certainly did not threaten to ruin all of Britain's farmers. As Caird had pointed out, many were thriving in the early 1850s. But their success depended on regional differences in agricultural practices. The use of advanced techniques made the key difference. With improved drainage, farm equipment, fertilizers, and crop rotations, farmers could maximize yields and compensate for falling prices.[31] Dairy and livestock farmers and more efficient farmers in-

Figure 3. Great Britain

volved with "high farming"—those with the capital and know-how necessary to adapt crops and operations to changes in the agricultural price structure—enjoyed special advantages. In particular, they turned their efforts toward raising more livestock and nongrain crops in order to overcome the effects of the disastrous grain market.[32]

Smaller grain farmers without the capital necessary to withstand a long period of losses or adapt to the raising of livestock or farming of other crops were differently placed.[33] As Vamplew put it, these "marginal farmers" were "squeezed out" by the low prices and the high costs of adaptation.[34] The question is whether these were the farmers who swelled the ranks of emigrants in 1851. Perhaps prosperous farmers seeking American land dominated the movement, a possibility that would suggest that no real link tied the repeal of the Corn Laws to the extraordinary number of emigrant farmers.

Some clues about the economic status of emigrant farmers can be gleaned from passenger lists. Between 1849 and 1854, 114 English farmers were listed with their county of origin, data that are revealing in light of Caird's 1850–51 survey (table 4). Not all of these data were drawn from the sample, and although one could wish that the origins of more farmers had been recorded, a definite pattern emerges that bears some consideration.[35] Furthermore, this distribution pattern is virtually duplicated by seventy-six people known to have been farmers when they migrated between 1847 and 1855 and whose county of origin was recorded in county histories.[36]

Table 4. County of Origin of Farmers (Heads of Household), (1849–54)

	Number	Percent
Severely distressed		
Yorkshire	33	
(North Riding = 3)		
(Not defined = 30)		
Lincolnshire	11	
Lancashire	6	
Surrey	4	
	54	47.4
Moderately distressed		
Suffolk	5	
Cambridgeshire	3	
Nottinghamshire	4	
Norfolk	2	
Essex	0	
Devon	1	
Buckinghamshire	2	
	17	14.9

Table 4. (cont.)

	Number	Percent
Minimally distressed		
Gloucestershire	3	
London	2	
Cumberland	3	
Leicestershire	2	
Staffordshire	2	
Cheshire	1	
Durham	3	
Derbyshire	2	
Sussex	1	
Gloucestershire	1	
Northamptonshire	1	
Oxfordshire	0	
Northumberland	2	
	23	20.2
Prosperous		
Bedfordshire	0	
Hampshire	0	
Berkshire	0	
Wiltshire	1	
Warwickshire	3	
	4	3.5
Not defined[b]		
Somerset	13	
Westmorland	2	
Kent	1	
	16	14.0
Totals	114	100.0

Source: Appendix A, table A1 and chapter 2, n35.

a. Grouping is based on Caird, *English Agriculture,* and it is open to reinterpretation. However, the difference between the "severely distressed" counties and the "prosperous" counties is clear in the survey. (The three cases from Warwickshire include one from Birmingham.)

b. Caird omitted Somerset, Westmorland, Kent, Cornwall, Hereford, Shropshire, and Worcestershire from his survey. The abundant cases from Somerset are misleading because ships leaving Bristol (the port favored by emigrants from Somerset) were more likely to have lists indicating the county of origin.

Nearly half of the farmers were from counties Caird identified as having the most serious problems for small farmers, especially grain producers. The farmers of large parts of Yorkshire, Lincolnshire, Surrey, and Lancashire (fig. 4), as described by Caird, faced difficulties in the early years after repeal and shared many

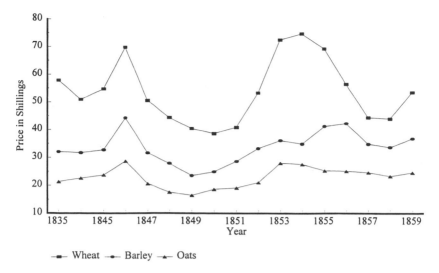

Figure 4. Imports and prices of British grain, 1835–60. (Brian R. Mitchell and Phyllis Dean, *Abstract of British Historical Statistics,* 98, 488)

of the characteristics of the emigrant farmers that were described in many newspapers. Lincolnshire—the county showing the second-highest detected agricultural emigration—had varied soil but much clay. Caird's analysis was that because of poor drainage and lack of capital improvement these "strong clays are by no means so well-managed . . . as in Essex and Suffolk." Hence, there was a "vast extent of land" in a "very backward state" that could not yield a bountiful wheat crop.[37] The same was reported for another major wheat county, Yorkshire, the most common county of origin. In the North Riding, much wheat and barley was being grown on clay. The West Riding's soil was described as "mostly clay" as well, and near Leeds much wheat and barley was also being grown with difficulty.[38]

As for Lancashire, "the great proportion" was held by small farmers without the "intelligence and capital" necessary to adapt to a more profitable form of agriculture. That might also be said of a number of other counties, but Lancashire also had the problem of extensive, poorly drained, clay soils. The typical course of crops in Lancashire was clover, wheat, turnips, and barley. It was the emphasis on corn planted in heavy soil that was handicapping Lancashire farmers and making adaptation expensive and return on investment very low.[39] Surrey, according to Caird, had a more varied soil than Lancashire, but undrained clays were dominant, especially in the extensive Weald of Surrey, where on "cold retentive clay subsoil" wheat farmers were almost universally distressed. Their "chief complaint" was of the low prices resulting from free trade, and then the tithe.[40] Thus, the four counties were distinctive in Caird's survey for being dominated by small farmers struggling to raise corn on heavy, undrained clay soils. They were also counties that appear on passenger lists with comparative frequency.

It would appear that the counties of moderate or minimal distress (the distinction is not always clear) had moderate or minimal numbers of emigrants. Suffolk, for example, consisted of three main divisions by soil type, and it was in the central southwest—some of the "worst heavy land in the country"—where "men of little capital" were "suffering from the pressure of the times."[41] But one can only guess whether the five Suffolk farmers who appear on the lists were from this distressed part of the county. Nottingham and Cambridgeshire, each with a few farmers, were similarly mixed in character.[42] Some farmers in counties such as Gloucestershire, Cheshire, Cumberland, and Durham also had problems but were solving them with increased investment from landlords and more extensive animal husbandry.[43]

Admittedly, farmers whose county of origin is known cannot be assumed to represent the entire population of emigrant farmers, nor can it be assumed that farmers leaving distressed counties were themselves distressed. Some were surely prosperous, even in the most distressed counties, and perhaps it is these who appear on the lists. A glance at the counties not represented by farmers on the lists, however, does lend weight to the view that prosperous farmers could not have been prominent in the movement. Virtually without exception, the counties not found on the lists were clearly the most prosperous counties, far removed from the detrimental effects of free trade.[44] Had prosperous farmers been dominant in the migration, one would expect to find the prosperous counties represented prominently in the lists; instead, they are the only counties not represented at all.

Bedfordshire had good soils, and Caird considered it a model county. He pointed to the county's landlords and farmers, who were investing heavily and farming with the latest methods, and urged those in less prosperous counties, "Go, and do thou likewise." The same was reported for Hampshire and Berkshire, where sheep and dairy cattle enabled farmers to prosper.[45] Although some small farmers near Northampton were not prospering, the county generally was dominated by larger farmers benefiting from their landlords' investments in capital improvements.[46]

Thus, several prominent features common only to the counties of detected emigration may be identified. Much of the land was heavy, poorly drained clay in which little capital had been invested. There was also a conspicuous absence of mixed farming, and the heavy reliance on growing corn on these soils in the wake of repeal undermined many small farmers' chances of profitability.[47] Meanwhile, the farmers and landlords of counties of little or no detected emigration either did not have these problems or were meeting them head-on with investments and improvements, especially in drainage and mixed farming.

Caird's detailed descriptions of Lincolnshire, Surrey, and Lancashire contain additional clues that help to explain why these counties appear to have lost the greatest numbers of farmers to the United States during 1851. Sometimes old-fashioned practices contributed directly to the movement of farmers. Especially onerous and odious to the farmers of Lincolnshire and Surrey was "compensation for unexhausted improvements," the custom whereby an outgoing tenant received from his successor payments for short-term improvements left behind, for example, dressings of manures, ploughing, planted crops, or accumulations of hay and straw. This was considered a "heavy tax on the farmer's capital" and a "demoralizing" custom. Tenures were short in these counties, partly because the custom was a means of recouping at least some losses in bad times, thereby providing an incentive to move.[48] In Surrey, where most farmers had only yearly tenures, relations between farmers and their landlords were said to be among the worst in the country. It seems probable that the farmers of Surrey were less committed to their land than those in Bedfordshire, whose tenures were of twenty years or more.[49]

The lack of capital investment in the land was one cause for low yields and unprofitable corn-farming in counties of detected agricultural emigration, but that was not always due to a lack of capital itself. Many of the large landlords, especially in Lancashire, possessed capital but were disinclined to invest in farming, preferring to reap high profits from land used by railways and industry. They showed scant interest in meeting farmers' needs for intensive investment in land.[50] That lack of commitment must have sapped morale, for if the land was neglected grain farmers could never expect to counter the effects of Corn Law repeal and secure prosperity.

It appears, then, that unprecedented numbers of British farmers emigrated to the United States at mid-century. Evidence points to the repeal of the Corn Laws and the consequent fall in grain prices as the best explanation for exceptionally high migration. The majority of emigrants seems not to have come from areas that were abreast of the latest methods and capital improvements, so it is likely that the "best of the English farmers" did not lead the agricultural migration. Rather, it appears that the extraordinary movement may have been dominated by undercapitalized grain farmers, many contending with undrained clay, who were unable to increase production or adjust to more profitable forms of agriculture and thereby compensate for the low grain prices.[51] Many were quite young and no doubt the tenants of smallholdings. They were apparently not among the most distressed or ruined farmers, for they still could afford to emigrate with their families. As those most affected by the end of protection, however, they no doubt feared the ruin that was being widely reported at the time.

Not all emigrant farmers were fleeing hardship or even the threat of it, however. Some prosperous farmers were among the emigrants, ones whose migration seems to have been prompted mainly by American opportunity and a desire to fulfill rather high expectations (chapter 3).[52] For those who had contemplated migration to America for some time, repeal may have determined the timing of their decision to leave Britain rather than the decision itself. Furthermore, the Crimean War caused grain imports to taper off, and prices soon climbed, temporarily exceeding their previous levels and affording some relief to Britain's grain producers.[53] The distress-related migration of British farmers was thus short-lived, but that combination of improved circumstances could not have been foreseen. In the eyes of many small farmers on poor soils, foreign competition brought to an end the days of good prices and profitable farming and made inevitable changes to farming at home. To many British farmers at mid-century, America was a haven where change could be avoided, where it would be possible to farm their own land profitably, and where they could take satisfaction in the likelihood that their children would have a promising future.

The *City of Glasgow* of Liverpool, the first steamer to carry British immigrants in steerage compartments regularly to America. The ship sank in the Atlantic in 1854 and carried 430 people down with her. (From *Gleason's Pictorial*, September 6, 1851)

An emigrant ship leaving Liverpool, 1850. The dramatic scene of emigrants leaving behind loved ones on the docks is recounted in many immigrant letters. (From the *Illustrated London News*, July 6, 1850)

"As I Was"

"As I Am"

This set of engravings is from Vere Foster's *Work and Wages,* a popular emigration pamphlet published in London in 1855. Although an idealized depiction, such dramatic improvement in America was not uncommon for British immigrants during the mid-nineteenth century.

"Land-Ho—Scene on Board an Emigrant Ship." This somewhat idealized scene captures the sense of hope and anticipation that British immigrants had upon their arrival in America. (From *Harper's Weekly,* June 3, 1871, 509)

The idyllic residence of Joseph Allen, a poor farmer who emigrated from Lincolnshire in 1851. He settled in Oakland County, Michigan, where he gradually built his large, successful farm. (From *Portrait and Biographical Album of Oakland County, Michigan,* 1891)

Thomas Birkett left his native Cumberland as a miller in 1852. He settled in Washtenaw County, Michigan, where he rose from miller, to mill owner, banker, and real estate investor. (From *History of Washtenaw County, Michigan,* 1881)

William Broadhead left Thornton, Yorkshire, as a poor handloom weaver in 1843 and became one of the leading businessmen of Chautauqua County, New York, where he owned several textile mills, a clothing store, and an axe factory. (From Georgia D. Merrill, ed., *History of Chautauqua County, New York,* 1894)

Charles Bailey rose from handloom weaver to woolen mill manager in Yorkshire and then emigrated to even better things in Herkimer County, New York, where he was hired to set up Jacquard looms. Eventually, he and his family established their own successful knitting goods company. (From George A. Hardin, ed., *History of Herkimer County, New York,* 1893)

Shake Rag Street, Mineral Point, Wisconsin, a street scene that could have come from Cornwall itself. (Courtesy of the Mineral Point Room, Mineral Point Public Library)

A prosperous-looking Cornish family and dwelling in Mineral Point. (Courtesy of the Mineral Point Room, Mineral Point Public Library)

The elaborate balcony on this house indicates the prosperity achieved by this Cornish immigrant family in Wisconsin. (Courtesy of the Mineral Point Room, Mineral Point Public Library)

The Gold Rush. The Road Sweeper off to California

"The Gold Rush. The Road Sweeper off to California" (1849). The California Gold Rush attracted people from all corners of Great Britain and those already in America. (From J. Leech, *Early Pencillings from* Punch [1864])

As to the farming buisness it [is] carried on a little different in some respects there is not half the work to raise a crop that there is in England for the land is naturally rich potatoes grows in abundance without manure.
—Isaac Taylor, Dec. 20, 1848

You say you have bought a farm of 50 acres—unfenced and no house upon it and not broken up. I am afraid you have over done yourself.
—M. Squire to Edwin Kimberley, July 23, 1850

Britons in American Agriculture

The rising wave of British immigration to the United States during the mid-nineteenth century was formed in part by unusually high numbers of farmers, many of whom were small tenant farmers without the capital necessary to increase production and adjust to free trade and falling grain prices. But that does not mean that the prospect of owning a large farm in America was not an equally important inducement for farmers to migrate. During the antebellum period Britons from all backgrounds succumbed to land fever and tried their hand at farming in America. If tailors, weavers, lawyers, and merchants found American farmland an irresistible attraction, then how much more so did Britain's farmers and farm laborers?

Britain's farmers usually faced a different agricultural and commercial environment in the United States and had to make adjustments in order to thrive. In particular, the "advanced methods" of "high" or "scientific farming," which often proved vital for success in Britain after the repeal of the Corn Laws, were labor-intensive because of extensive manuring, crop rotation, and drainage requirements. Such methods were entirely appropriate for Britain but less so for the mid-century United States, where labor was scarce but resources abundant. Shifting from English methods to American ones was not always an attractive option. One observer noted in the 1830s that of all immigrants the English had the most difficult time adjusting to American conditions, in part because of a stubborn belief in the superiority of their own farming methods.[1]

Many had reason to be scornful of prevailing American methods—initially. From the English perspective, American farming methods appeared careless, wasteful, and shabby, and the American tendency to farm the soil to the brink of depletion violated what some might have called a moral obligation to farm responsibly and not abuse the land. As one person from England observed, "The Yankee farmers are the most careless in their operations of any agriculturalists I ever saw. They would not lay in their manure, as they said it would fill their fields with weeds."[2] To neglect manuring was unthinkable for most British farmers. In fact, many Lincolnshire farmers valued their cattle primarily as "manufacturers of manure."[3] But economic reality usually forced English immigrant farmers, as it did other immigrant groups, to lay aside their old methods and adopt American ones.[4] For the English, that usually meant less emphasis on manuring and a lowered ratio of labor to land.

Such adjustments, however, were not always necessary right away. In some places in America, English farmers found it possible to succeed splendidly with their old methods. Members of an English (mostly Lincolnshire) farming colony in Floyd County, Indiana, for example, who in the 1840s and early 1850s had settled on rich lands next to navigable rivers, were able to retain their labor-intensive methods, which required "severe manual toil," and farm so profitably that some native-born farmers followed their example.[5] Here was a notable reversal of the general pattern that British immigrants adopted American farming methods.

Even those who had to abandon some of their agricultural strategies still made important contributions to American agriculture and the development of the Old Northwest. The widespread fear that the "best of Britain's farmers" were leaving for America may have been more politically motivated than true in the sense that struggling tenant farmers with little capital rather than more prosperous farmers were dominating the movement. Yet in another sense Britain was yielding some of her most energetic and ambitious farmers to America; largely literate, they were willing to uproot themselves and endure a strenuous voyage and eager to work their own land for profit.[6]

Many immigrants earned reputations for being progressive or scientific farmers who kept their holdings unusually tidy and orderly and introduced Americans to advanced and innovative methods. They were also lauded for "elevating the standards of agriculture" and establishing the model farms of their counties. In Lafayette County, Wisconsin, a number of English farmers arrived in the late 1840s and "began to practice those thrifty and thorough methods of cultivating the soil which make their own country a garden spot the world delights to see." These farmers "thoroughly understood the business in a scientific way," and it was reported that many others in the area adopted their methods.[7] At least one observer noted that the reason the English "rank among the most skilled farmers in the world" and had "complete knowledge of husbandry" was because their country's limited land resources had enforced "prudent habits."[8]

That, at least, is the picture that emerges time and time again in county histories. One must be skeptical of such sources because county histories were not in the business to criticize people. Still, it is striking that so many mid-century British immigrant farmers were recognized in their communities as progressive or scientific farmers, accolades not used as often to describe other immigrants or native-born farmers. Milo Quaife, a historian, agreed with this recognition as it applied to British immigrants in Wisconsin.[9] That should not be shocking. England, after all, was the origin of many of the inventions, methods, and breeding experiments that produced the agricultural revolution of the seventeenth and eighteenth centuries. Particularly during the half-century following Independence, America appears to have received much of its inspiration for innovative agriculture from England.[10] Early clovers, for example, were called "English grass," and advanced farming in America was based on what were commonly termed "English methods" of agriculture. These methods, pioneered by the English and Dutch, were based on an efficient blend of livestock farming and mixed crops. Instead of mining the soil through repeated plantings, as was typically done in America, English farmers maintained fertility by rotating crops with nitrogen-fixing legumes and soil-conserving grasses and collecting manure for fertilizer. Contemporary observers in western Wisconsin knew that English farmers who hauled manure onto their fields raised the best crops in the region.[11]

The English were also known for their expertise in drainage techniques, which they had perfected by the 1840s because England's need for drainage was so extensive.[12] John Lyth, a brickmaker and apprentice earthenware maker who left York for New York state in 1850, became the pioneer of drainage pipe manufacturing in the United States, and to promote his business he taught local farmers and gardeners how to lay tile and derive the full benefits from drainage.[13] Newspapers published in the Old Northwest featured articles on British drainage methods, which the English appear to have introduced to the Illinois prairie.[14]

The British farmer's reputation for being expert in breeding livestock dated back to Robert Bakewell's times. Various English breeds of hogs were common on American farms, and British immigrant farmers of the mid-century period were frequently credited with introducing new breeds of other livestock into the country.[15] John Zuill, who came to Wisconsin from Stirlingshire, Scotland, in 1845, was known as the most successful championship breeder of cattle in Rock County, and additional championship breeders from Britain arrived in Wisconsin during the late 1840s.[16] Quaife even concluded that "the impetus to cattle breeding in Wisconsin is to a considerable extent due to efforts of British-American farmers" and that "so far as high priced and valuable quadrupeds go, Wisconsin is a British commonwealth."[17] The same might have been said for other parts of the Old Northwest. After George Davis emigrated from England to Lake County, Indiana, in 1857, he crossed various breeds of hogs to produce the new Victoria breed, which won him numerous prizes at the Chicago Fat-Stock Show during the 1880s.[18]

Finally, some British immigrants helped to dispel Americans of a prejudice against prairie soils—one based on the faulty assumption that land without trees was not fertile enough for profitable farming. As early as 1817 Morris Birkbeck and George Flower chose a section of Edwards County, Illinois, for their settlement and took the fertility of that prairie land for granted. Other English immigrants arrived in Illinois later and helped to open the prairie to cultivation.[19] In 1850 a small English colony led by Francis Greenwood was among the first to settle on prairie lands in Benton County, Indiana, although they found the flat terrain and extremes in weather hard to endure.[20] As significant as these contributions to American agriculture were, the British generally had to adopt American methods. More assimilation than acculturation occurred in British farmers who migrated to America during the mid-nineteenth century. They were, after all, already in the process of becoming Americans.

Clearly, they were diverse in their levels of skill and what they could contribute to American agriculture. The same can be said about their amounts of capital. Comparatively few were as affluent as John and Margaret Webber, who left Somerset in 1849, came directly to Winnebago County, Illinois, and quickly purchased three improved farms of about six hundred acres.[21] Still, it was common for newly arrived immigrants to purchase sizable acreage outright, although often it was land that needed significant clearing and improvement. Less spectacular and more typical was the ability of Dorset yeoman farmer Edwin Allen, who as the illegitimate son of an English gentleman had moderate assets with which he was able to purchase eighty acres—thirteen of which were improved—immediately upon arrival in Waukesha County, Wisconsin, in 1845. Allen and his wife still had to spend their first year in a miserable claim shanty that measured ten by twelve feet but purchased an additional sixty-four acres during their second year.[22]

On the other end of the spectrum, a considerable minority of farmers arrived in a state of virtual poverty and financial desperation, and free trade was not necessarily the root of their problem. Thomas Hopkins was a "master farmer" and "in good circumstances" in England until he lost his crops to drought and his livestock to distemper. In the face of such disaster he decided to emigrate while he still could and arrived in Wisconsin in 1851 with only $4.50 in his pocket. Resorting to road work until he could send for the rest of his family, he eventually was able to purchase nearly six hundred acres of land, and by the 1880s his stock was worth about $12,000. Thomas Borland, a prosperous livestock farmer on nine hundred acres that he rented from the Duke of Argyle in Ayrshire, had a nearly identical experience when pleuro-pneumonia struck his cattle and drove him into bankruptcy. He then decided to emigrate to Michigan in 1853 with "very little means" and after working as a farm laborer there for a few years was able to purchase his first forty acres.[23]

In this manner the labor shortage that existed in much of the Old Northwest provided the poorer immigrant farmers from Britain the opportunity to acquire the capital and knowledge about American farming that allowed a successful transition to local agriculture. That usually involved performing farm labor for wages, then renting a farm, and eventually purchasing land. Some also found it necessary to engage in various forms of sharecropping to become established before purchasing land, and perhaps most bought land that needed some clearing and improving.[24]

The exact proportions of British immigrants who purchased uncleared or minimally cleared land cannot be determined. If the county histories for Dane and Jefferson counties, Wisconsin; Jo Daviess and Winnebago counties, Illinois; and Hillsdale County, Michigan, are any guide, between a fifth and a half of British immigrants who took up farming in these counties between 1845 and 1855 purchased land that needed extensive clearing. How many more did the same but did not have that fact recorded is unknown, but the numbers may have been high.[25] These proportions were lower in the more eastern and well-developed counties, but British pioneers were nevertheless unhesitant in taking on the daunting challenge of clearing land in America. Nor were they reluctant to imitate native-born Americans and preempt land by squatting. That the English were the most numerous of all immigrant squatters in Wisconsin and Minnesota reflects the fact of their common language, which facilitated grabbing the best land. But the English and Scots were also among the squatters least likely to persist on their lands once they had gained title of them.[26] That is best explained by their inexperience in carving a home and farm out of the virgin forest.

Clearing land was a herculean task that few if any had experienced in Britain and that most would find they had underestimated. British immigrants on wooded land typically cleared fewer than five acres per year. Not surprisingly, those with sufficient capital or skills in some trade frequently hired others to perform the backbreaking tasks of bringing their land under cultivation.[27] Few could afford to hire much labor, and those who attempted to clear land were susceptible to the mental anguish of fearing that perhaps they were not up to the task. Immigrants like Stephenson Bewick, who could not cope with clearing his eighty acres of timberland in Ohio, eagerly returned to England after he was offered employment there. Eight years later he emigrated again to Wisconsin, this time to settle on the prairie.[28]

In addition to underestimating the difficulties of clearing unbroken land, some English immigrants were initially disappointed. Although they had eyed America's abundance of cheap land, they had not anticipated some of the drawbacks of America's agricultural market, particularly the low prices being paid for crops. As Matthew Dinsdale noted of former compatriots in southwestern Wisconsin in 1847, "Some Englishmen find great fault with this country because they cannot turn what they raise into gold and silver at their own door. They err by viewing things comparatively that are quite different. No one ought to expect to purchase land for five shillings an acre and sell wheat for eight shillings a bushel."[29]

In spite of the surprising disappointments that some British immigrant farmers endured in America, especially the shocking reality of clearing land and the low prices for farm produce, the migration was ultimately a positive one that relatively few seem to have regretted for long. Migration to the United States was an increasingly attractive option for British farmers, particularly after the repeal of the Corn Laws pressured them to increase production and expanded America's grain market in Britain. The same was true for farm laborers, who were subject to the same combination of pressures and inducements.

Farm Laborers

While farmers in Britain rented or owned land, made investments and took risks, and reaped profits or suffered losses, farm laborers performed the more mundane tasks at the mercy of the farmers and the local labor market for wages. Although the line between farmer and laborer was sometimes blurred (because poor farmers could fall to the rank of laborers during hard times and laborers could rise to become farmers in good times), there usually was a significant social and economic gap between the two. That gap was a powerful incentive for laborers to consider becoming farmers in America.

The social and economic situation of British farm laborers in the mid-nineteenth century has challenged historians for some time. In one of the first important accounts, Wilhelm Hasbach wrote a powerful and sympathetic book on agricultural laborers that included a chapter entitled "The Demoralization of the Labourer." Hasbach used James Caird's least optimistic descriptions and probably exaggerated the worst effects of the Old Poor Law and such other evils as the gang system and payment-in-kind, for a most discouraging assessment of a nineteenth-century farm laborer's position in general. Furthermore, he believed that Caird had overestimated the average wage rates and failed to consider fully the effects of winter unemployment. In Hasbach's eyes, the trend toward farm mechanization and the increased intensity of the cultivation of the soil lowered the demand for laborers and thus their level of economic livelihood. It seemed clear to him that eighteenth-century laborers had a better life than their nineteenth-century descendants.[30] Thus Marcus Hansen did not startle anyone when he wrote that "surprising numbers" of farm laborers joined tenant farmers in the migration to America when the repeal of the Corn Laws challenged their financial security.[31]

But just as historians have reevaluated the situation of Britain's farmers after repeal, so, too, their view of the laborers has changed. The older view is now seen to be overly sympathetic and misleading, especially because it ignores regional wage variations.[32] W. A. Armstrong has suggested that before 1850 a laborer's standard of living did not decline as Hasbach and others believed. Rather, it fell relative to the living standards of the other agrarian classes and some industrial workers. Although there were no doubt many instances of poverty and rural degradation, especially during the years following the Napoleonic Wars when discharged soldiers glutted the labor market and agricultural prices plummeted from their war-inflated heights, the condition of farm laborers had improved considerably long before mid-century.[33]

More recent research offers new statistical evidence that unemployment among laborers was no higher in the 1840s or 1850s than around 1820 and that it may have been considerably lower, although one might expect high unemployment in 1820 because of the lingering effect of demobilization after the war.[34] Other writers stress the importance of the seasonality of agriculture and the fact that during good harvests labor shortages compensated for the labor glut of the winter months. One, E. L. Jones, has maintained that any glut of farm labor that did exist in the 1840s changed to a "partial, but structural shortage" of labor during the 1850s, mainly because industry was attracting workers from rural areas with high wages and drying up many of the traditional sources of casual agricultural labor.[35] Undoubtedly, the trend of internal migration to urban areas improved the lot of farm laborers. Between 1851 and 1871 their number fell by about 22 percent, and some areas were often hard-pressed to find sufficient laborers at affordable prices.[36]

What, then, can be said about the migration of these farm laborers to America? As noted in the previous chapter, passenger lists scarcely mention their presence, although that cannot be taken at face value because ship captains apparently did not feel the need to distinguish farm laborers from unskilled laborers on the manifests. Furthermore, it was noted that some of the younger "farmers" and farmers' sons were probably more accurately farm laborers. They are likely hidden among the farmers, especially the laborers on the lists, because other evidence leaves no doubt that large numbers of farm laborers did leave for America during the mid-century period.

British newspapers occasionally observed the emigration of farm laborers. The *Plymouth Journal,* for example, reported in the spring of 1851 that "a large number of small farmers and farm labourers, with their families, are daily arriving here, to emigrate." And by the early summer of the same year another newspaper reported that "agricultural labourers, small shopkeepers, and mechanics are emigrating from Lincolnshire in droves."[37] Although the exact number who were farm laborers is uncertain, it is clear from other reports that these numbers were significant for some parts of the country. The *Bristol Times* stated in June 1851 that so many had emigrated that farmers all over Britain feared "an insufficiency of labourers to gather the harvest." Later in the year, another newspaper reported that the "emigration of farm laborers, lookers, shepherds, &c from the island of Sheppey, Kent, is going on to such an extent as to inconvenience the farmers, graziers, &c, to a rather alarming degree."[38] It appears that the view that England's "partial, but structural" shortage of agricultural laborers during the 1850s due to laborers leaving the countryside for industrial towns in Britain should be modified to include those who also emigrated overseas.[39]

Many farm laborers emigrated because their wages were too low to support a family. Some even suffered falling wages at this difficult time. Although Caird reported that 6 shillings was the lowest weekly wage rate anywhere in the country, laborers in East Sussex were reportedly getting only 5.[40] Even those making considerably more were finding it impossible to make ends meet because of seasonal unemployment, which Caird and modern writers seem to have underestimated. The "general cry" among those farm laborers emigrating from Sheppey was that "we cannot live here for the wages given—9s or 10s a week; and then, during . . . the winter, not even obtain a day's work for from five to six weeks altogether."[41]

The detailed notes to the 1851 census confirm that large numbers of farm laborers emigrated from some places because of low wages and poverty. All of the parishes in the subdistrict of North Petherwyn near Launceston, Cornwall, for example, experienced a significant decline in population between 1841 and 1851. The census enumerator ascribed the decrease to "the low rate of wages obtained by agricultural labourers, inducing many of them to emigrate." The same story was given for Mexborough in the West Riding of Yorkshire. "Many agricultural laborers from Mexborough have emigrated beyond [the] seas," the census observed, because of the general agricultural depression that was holding wages down. For the parishes of Hinckling and Hoveton St. John near Tunstead, Norfolk, the decrease in population was attributed to the "depressed state of agriculture . . . having driven many labourers to emigrate and others to seek employment on the railway works . . . near Hull." Similar reports were made for Devizes, Wiltshire; St. Buryan and Helston, Cornwall; and Askrigg in the North Riding of Yorkshire. Most of these areas are located in some of the poorest, lowest-wage counties of the time.[42]

The depressed conditions and low wages pushing farm laborers to emigrate had several main causes according to observers writing in local newspapers—and taxation was one of them. A number of Devonshire farm laborers emigrated from Ashburton because "the present enormous and unjust taxation of the country . . . [was] pressing on the agricultural community of Devon."[43] They were no doubt referring to taxes on the farmers' earnings, which reduced what they could pay their laborers. Britain's relatively high taxes were one reason why low taxation in the United States was reported with such enthusiasm in emigrant literature and "America letters."[44]

But the most widely reported causes for agricultural distress at mid-century and for miserably low wages were free trade and falling grain prices. Those farmers finding it difficult to adjust to free trade and compensate for the lower prices by raising production had little hope of paying their laborers good wages—or those to which they were accustomed. Self-serving as it was, a group of Essex farmers went so far as to apologize to their laborers in *The Times:* "We, the neighboring farmers, deeply deplore our inability to continue the present rate of wages to our worthy labourers; the fact is we cannot afford it. Free-trade has brought us into close competition with foreigners."[45] More alarmingly, on the Ancaster estate in Lincolnshire free trade had reportedly forced farm laborers' wages from 13 shillings per week in 1847 to 10 per week in 1850, and the laborers vented their outrage through incendiarism. Great Steeping northwest of Boston suffered four cases of arson in only five weeks in 1849, and the estate agent for the Earl of Ancaster recorded that "many labourers have already left for the United States and many more talk of going. Parish Officers are dubious about helping them as some will probably leave their families behind."[46] Some Lincolnshire farmers were unable to offer employment at any wage rate. "Labourers of the best description," said one report, were emigrating from the Boston area to New York in the spring of 1851 because they "could not obtain labour in consequence of the low price of agricultural produce."[47]

At first glance, it may seem surprising that so many impoverished laborers were able to get to America. Fortunately, a number of detailed personal accounts reveal their means and strategies for their migration. Samuel Hadaway, for example, struggled as a farm laborer in Kent for only 2 pence a day before he became "entirely destitute" and had to go to the poorhouse. Somehow he was able to borrow £10 to finance his emigration, and he landed in New York in 1849 at age nineteen with only 1 shilling. After eight months of farm work in Wayne County, New York, he repaid the borrowed money, and within fourteen years he was farming his own land in Michigan.[48] But few could borrow that kind of money to emigrate. Some received poor law assistance from the government through landlords or local charities, however only a small fraction of Britain's emigrants were assisted in such ways. Even then, that assistance was almost invariably restricted to those bound for the colonies.[49]

The system of one person emigrating alone through the pooled savings of several people and then sending back remittances for passages for other family members was common among the Irish, Italians, Poles, and other groups. Newspapers confirm that many British farm laborers arrived in that way. Emigrant laborers from Sheppey accepted remittances from relatives who had gone before them, for it was said of them that "it is beyond doubt the principal part of them, particularly the elder branches of families, both fathers and mothers, have had the money remitted to them from their sons and daughters who have gone before them." These sons and daughters had likely purchased passage tickets with their families' pooled savings. As young and healthy immigrants in America they worked hard, lived frugally, and remitted their savings to their families, for whose arrival they made preparations. Another reporter observed that "fifty to a hundred agricultural laborers of the best sort" were preparing to leave Litttleport and Southery near Ely. They left their wives and children "till money can be sent for their passage hereafter." The creation of migration chains and use of remittances was apparently common among Lincolnshire laborers as well. Commenting on the large numbers of recent emigrants, many of whom were farm laborers, a local newspaper reported that "those who have gone are sending through the Spalding Agent and other sources, means to their parents, relations, and friends, to follow them, and those who are now going will follow their example."[50]

Even some of the poorest farm laborers managed to get to America during the mid-century. They usually had to scrimp and save for years through long-term planning before buying a passage ticket, but in America their continued frugality, ambition, and very hard work eventually paid off. Some were people of extraordinary drive and ambition who endured long years of hardship to achieve their goals in America, and their stories are worth reconstructing insofar as they reveal the substance of their migration experience. A representative case is that of John Daniels, a farm worker from Devonshire, where farm workers were among the lowest-paid in the country. There Daniels toiled on a farm for a shilling a day to accumulate his passage money, which appears to have taken about ten years. By the age of twenty-five he had saved enough, and in 1851 he sailed to New York. There, he found farm work for only $40 per year, not much more than his wage in Devonshire. He also found an American-born wife, and by saving most of his wages he managed two years later to move to Hillsdale County, Michigan, where he bought forty acres of "wild woodland." Like other English pioneers in this time and place, Daniels first lived in a "rude log shanty" and lived a very hard life. He took ten years to clear his farm, which he sold and with the profits bought eighty acres of "unbroken forest," which he also gradually cleared and in retirement handed down to his son. Through sheer determination, long-range planning, and a willingness to clear two farms, poor English farm laborers such as Daniels fulfilled their ambitions on the rapidly developing American frontier.[51]

In the remarkable story of Jonathan Clark are additional details of how impoverished farm laborers successfully migrated from Britain to the Old Northwest and how the ability and willingness to adapt to new situations and endure temporary setbacks were often crucial for success. Clark was put to farm work at age eight in West Walton, Norfolk, where he earned a mere 2 shillings per week as a shepherd boy. He then "went out to service" on another farm at age twelve, but through the age of nineteen all of his earnings went to support his widowed mother and younger brothers. Then, for one year he was allowed to work toward the purchase of a single passage ticket, and in 1848, at twenty, he sailed to New York and arrived in Chicago, "penniless and friendless, but resolute and ready for whatever came." Clark found a miserable job hauling wood during the severe winter of 1848, during which he severely froze his feet and was cheated out of his wages by his dishonest employer. He was luckier the following spring when he found farm work and then became apprenticed to a carpenter. Within two years he was able to send passage money to the family he had once supported in England, a classic example of chain migration and of how poor emigrants were able to adapt to situations and pursue new occupations in America.[52]

Notwithstanding the poor circumstances of emigrant farm laborers, they were generally not victims of economic hardship and leaving England as a last resort. For example, Thomas Varley, a farm laborer near York who was unable to sign his name on his marriage certificate six years before he emigrated to Illinois in 1850, later recalled that his move was inspired not so much by hardship but by determination "to seek his fortune in America." Even so, he had to leave his wife and children behind, and after he arrived in the United States with but 2 shillings he worked as a farmhand in Will County for four years before he could afford to send for them. After their reunion, the Varleys rented land for four years and then purchased unimproved land. Thomas then got the basic education that he lacked in England, such that in his later years he was known for being "fond of reading."[53] Another illiterate emigrant farm laborer, John Froggat, left Worksop, Derbyshire, in 1849, landed in New York with $60, and with his wife Mary rented land for three years near Buffalo and then came to Dane County, Wisconsin. As true pioneers they started out in Wisconsin with a log cabin on forty acres, which they gradually enlarged to 540 acres, and developed a successful cattle-breeding operation. Froggat was rightly remembered as one "whose unaided efforts have made him a substantial member of the community."[54]

That was the typical way in which British farm laborers managed to become farmers in the United States. There are many colorful examples, a few of which illustrate long-term patterns of adjustment to American agriculture and farm ownership as well as the resiliency and determination that carried people through. Thomas Greenow, who arrived from England in 1852, worked as a farmhand in America for several years, rented land for sixteen more, and finally purchased his own land in Ontario County, New York. Farm workers who were determined to purchase land quickly had to settle for small plots, as did David Hallock, who bought only ten acres about eight years after his migration in 1852 although he sold it within three years to buy forty acres. By working as farm laborers and then renting, buying, improving, and selling small tracts of land for bigger ones, British farm laborers accumulated enough sweat equity to become substantial farmers in the United States.[55]

Not all were stuck in abject poverty, however. Cornish farm laborer John Burden, who was illiterate when he married Mary Ann Metters in 1842, managed to take their seven children with him when he emigrated to Wisconsin in

1857, although he had to borrow $12.50 to move his family from Milwaukee to Palmyra in adjacent Waukesha County. Ten years later Burden owned 232 acres and a large flock of merino sheep and was out of debt.[56] Even more impressive was the success of John Walters, a farmhand who left Monmouthshire in 1852 at age thirty-two because he knew he could improve his financial condition in America. He was able to purchase 160 acres within just a year of his arrival in Henderson County, Illinois. Farm laborers such as Walters had the capital that made a rapid transition from laboring to farming possible. With drive and ambition they were motivated more out of the desire to seize opportunities than to escape hardship. That drive set them apart from many of their fellow laborers who remained in Britain.[57]

Many farm laborers had experience in a variety of labor and thus acquired an adaptability that served them well in America. That was true of James Turner, whose path from farm laborer to farmer was long and convoluted. At the age of eight he was sent out by his widowed mother to be apprenticed to a Devonshire farmer, for whom he worked thirteen years, learning "all the labors of farming operations." Then for eleven years he worked more lucratively on the roads and at a lime kiln before returning for two years to the farmer to whom he had been apprenticed. All the while, Turner had thought of "trying life in a foreign country," and in 1853, at the age of forty-one, he migrated to Peoria, Illinois. There he found farm work, sent for his two brothers still in Devon, and finally after the Civil War bought forty acres of "wild prairie land" at $10 per acre, which later proved to be the core of one of the choicest farms in the area. Turner's hard-won success was attributed to the fact that he had been well trained in England as a farmer's apprentice and that he exercised "persistent toil and excellent management of his affairs."[58]

Many other farm laborers displayed an ambition and acquisitiveness that prompted their migration, although they had a hard life in England, too. James Fell, son of a farm laborer in Appleby, Lincolnshire, was working in the fields by age eight. But, as was later recorded, "the opportunities afforded a farm laborer in England were not sufficient to satisfy the ambitions of young Fell," and he emigrated in 1851, "hoping to better his condition." Unfortunately, the ship that he boarded at Hull was overwhelmed by smallpox by the time it reached Quebec. Fell himself caught a light form of the disease, but as soon as the ship's quarantine had elapsed he labored at whatever he could find in Canada and Rochester, New York. Then he managed a farm for eleven years in Chatham County, New York, after which he bought forty acres in Will County, Illinois. He later extended his farm to 160 acres. Fell's story is closely echoed by many others who were similarly motivated, primarily, it seems, by ambition, perhaps a sense of adventure, and a determination to become more than a farmhand.[59]

But this optimistic account of the migration of ambitious farm laborers making free decisions to come to America must be balanced by the fact that free trade depressed wages and stirred many to emigrate because of severe difficulties. Furthermore, Stephen Fender is right about the "psychology of emigration": It was important for migrants to believe that "they had made the choice to go of their own free will."[60] It is certainly possible that some laborers later exaggerated their ambitions and free decisions while downplaying the extent of the premigratory difficulties. That remains one of the deep psychological questions that will never be fully answered. But if some sources downplay the distressed background of emigrant farm laborers, the possibilities that attracted them to America were real at mid-century. Even allowing for the potential bias of the sources, not all farm laborers were distressed and desperate. A varying mixture of distress and ambition lay behind their migrations.

What enabled and encouraged even poor farm laborers to emigrate and face the difficulties of the voyage and adjustment, of course, was the fact that in the United States farm labor was generally paid so much more and the cost of land was so much less than in Britain. Energetic farm workers in the prime of life, such as William Wetherall, earned the equivalent of $40 to $45 per year in Yorkshire in the mid-1840s and thus had little hope of ever buying land there. But in Michigan, British farm workers were earning nearly twice that rate during their first year and then three times that rate within four years.[61] It has been estimated that under very good circumstances they could typically accumulate $500 in about five years.[62] Some exceeded this remarkable performance, however. Angus McLean, who emigrated from Argyleshire in 1858, accumulated $800 in savings after only six years of farm work in Winnebago County, and then he bought an improved farm for $30 per acre.[63]

As long as these immigrants could get to a farm that needed labor, they could gain a foothold, accumulate some capital, and then start renting a farm. Then, through persistent toil and gritty determination they could eventually bring in enough money to purchase land—usually in small, unimproved tracts. By improving it and selling at a profit, larger acreage could be purchased, improved, and expanded—all for a successful and satisfying culmination of a life that started as an underpaid laborer in Britain. With frugality, sufficient capital could be accumulated in a reasonable time. Enough farm laborers realized that dream to encourage still more to come.

Farmers' Sons

As many as a third of the immigrant farmers were probably the sons of farmers rather than independent farmers in their own right. They worked under the authority of their fathers and did not necessarily have a future as farmers in Britain. Those who emigrated to the United States during the mid-century period came, like the farmers themselves, from a wide range of backgrounds and situations and had varying amounts of capital. Samuel Foster was obviously not going to inherit his father's "large estate" in Somerset on which he was "engaged in farming," so in 1845, at age twenty-three, he came to Waukesha County, Wisconsin, and within ten years had an impressive farm of his own.[64] For him and others like him, being the sons of large farmers had advantages. They usually had more capital than farm laborers and a well-rounded agricultural experience. The same was true of Thomas Butler, who was raised on his father's estate near Chester, where he had been put in charge of complex farming operations. By age twenty-six he was able to take his wife directly to Morgan County, Illinois, and within about five years he purchased an improved eighty-acre farm.[65]

But most migrant farmers' sons were the sons of poor farmers, mainly tenants, whose prospects in Britain were bleak. Robert Willis was the son of a Somerset farmer whose means were "quite limited," and his life in England was like that of any poor agricultural laborer until he emigrated at age thirty-two in 1850. Willis had to leave his wife and two daughters in England for three years until he earned their passage money by doing farm work in New York state, and then in 1855 he was able to buy eighty acres in Fond du Lac County, Wisconsin.[66] The privations that Willis endured were common to many other farmers' sons who emigrated during this time, including Walter Gray of Lanarkshire, Scotland, who arrived in the United States in 1849 with only 50 cents in his pocket and endured the trials and hardships of pioneering on the wild Illinois prairie land that he eventually purchased.[67]

Other farmers' sons similarly lacked any parental financing and were no better off than an average farm laborer. George Silverwood left his native Yorkshire in 1848 and reached Milwaukee without a penny to his name, but immediately he went to work clearing land for pioneering farmers farther west until he was able to purchase his own 125 acres of uncleared land in Jefferson County.[68] Some, like Samuel Bater, a son of a Devonshire farmer, had "no means" and had to borrow money to emigrate.[69] Once in America, these young men had to work for years before they could even rent a farm, much less buy one. Enoch Stafford, raised on his father's farm in Nottinghamshire, left for America in 1851 with little more than his farming knowledge, started as a farm laborer in Illinois, and then rented land for another ten years before he could purchase his own. After he left his father's farm in Lincolnshire in 1851, George Dixon had to work at farm labor for a full fourteen years in Cook County before he could buy cheap farmland in Newago County, Michigan.[70] Thus, farmers' sons who emigrated did not necessarily have appreciable advantages for their migration. Most resembled emigrant farm laborers more than emigrant farmers.

Predictably, the bulk of emigrant farmers' sons were seeking farms of their own in the Old Northwest, although many found it either necessary or advantageous to do nonagricultural work before engaging in farming. Philip Nicholas, for example, left his father's farm in Cambridgeshire in 1852 and went directly to Brownville, Pennsylvania, with $1 in his pocket to work in a foundry there for 75 cents per day. Seven months later Nicholas found farm work in Ohio, and within two years he was able to purchase eighty unimproved acres of land in Van Buren County, Michigan. Similarly, John Bedford, son of a Lincolnshire farmer, emigrated in 1852 to Illinois, but after working as a farm laborer for three years returned to England, only to emigrate again to Illinois the following year with his new English wife. This time he worked as an engineer, after which he resumed farming, "the occupation to which he had been bred."[71] Still others were apparently intending to leave agricultural life altogether, as though farming had no appeal to them despite being raised on farms. For example, George Hardie, son of a Scottish farmer, emigrated in 1852 at age twenty-eight and went directly to the copper mines of Michigan's Upper Peninsula. He proceeded to become a mine captain at various mines and eventually retired comfortably to his fine suburban home in Waukegan, Illinois.[72]

Novices and the Agrarian Myth

The farmers and farm laborers who left Britain during the mid-century period to farm in America were joined by a wide variety of others who had the same aspirations and determination to farm their own land. Many were artisans who likely had some familiarity with agriculture, but others were from industrial or professional backgrounds and may or may not have had prior experience on the land. Thus, considering the large numbers of the immigrants who were farmers or farm laborers, as well as the fact that a large although indeterminable portion of the others were also intending to farm in America, it is reasonable to estimate that well over half of British immigrants to the United States during the period would either farm or attempt to farm. The pull of America's land was that strong.

It should not be surprising that Britons from urban and industrial backgrounds successfully took up rural and agricultural lives in America. First, many of these people had originally left farms in search of work in Britain's cities and industries and did not necessarily shed their love for the land or their desire to become farmers once they entered cities and factories. But even in the cities, well into the 1840s, Britain's urban and industrial people were not completely divorced from the land. They were in frequent and intimate contact with it and held a profound cultural desire to own it. Artisans, for example, traveled deep into the British countryside when they "tramped" for work, and they often had to take up farm labor, which provided them some basic farming knowledge and sometimes a desire to become farmers themselves.

Furthermore, Britain's industrial workers were often recruited to perform farm labor during peak harvest times, and hence the transition to farm life in America was not a totally alien concept. Up to the middle of the century and beyond, Britain's cities were not fully urbanized in the modern sense of the word. Even London and Manchester had open spaces and were near the countryside. Industrial workers and their children could and did walk into the surrounding countryside, where they could observe agriculture and nature. In the cities, there was much allotment cultivation, complete with pigsties and chicken coops. Land and farming still represented a deeply held cultural ideal, a sense of freedom and independence and an escape from harsh industrial life. In America such a transition was realistic and commonly made. For those who had actually been raised on farms before entering industrial or urban work in Britain, emigrating to a life of American agriculture was, paradoxically, a return to their roots.[73]

Yet it is also true that a fair portion of Britons bound for American farm life had little or no prior experience in agriculture. These were not people who had been victims of the repeal of the Corn Laws, although some may have been acting out of a revulsion for what industrial life was becoming or what they feared it would become in the future. At the same time, they were likely moved by an idealized sense of what American agriculture offered them. Some were duped by the agrarian myth that American farming consisted of an idyllic life of carefree self-sufficiency. Many, after experiencing the reality of pioneer life, would leave agriculture, gravitate to towns and cities, or return to Britain.

Evidence on those who were beaten by the myth and reality of pioneer life is hard to come by, but many found themselves so ill-prepared for agrarian life that failure was practically inevitable. In the northwestern part of Flushing Township in Genesee County, Michigan, was an "English Settlement" consisting of recent arrivals from England, some of whom admitted to being "entirely new at the [agricultural] business, and knew nothing about chopping, milking, etc., and the consequence was, some of their experiences were laughable in the extreme." Thomas Hough, for example, first overpaid someone to yoke his newly purchased oxen and then had to keep them yoked night and day because neither he nor his English friends knew how to release them or how to work with oxen. Allowing oxen to starve nearly to death and getting lost in the forest were other perilous, not to mention embarrassing, moments for these parvenus.[74] James Hardy, a linen manufacturer from Barnsley, Yorkshire, "found it awkward work to swing the ax" in Waukesha County, Wisconsin, where he settled in 1842.[75] Similarly, members of the English colony in Floyd County, Indiana, were also not "adept with an ax" and resorted to allowing native Hoosiers do the clearing in exchange for cordwood.[76] Samuel Pearce, an apprenticed chemist and druggist from Clavering, Essex, emigrated in 1847 at age twenty-three to Du Page County, Illinois, where he farmed for two years. "Becoming satisfied that he was not adapted to the life of an agriculturist," however, he went to Chicago and resumed his drug trade and practiced medicine.[77]

Then there was the case of Thomas Stoddart, a musical instrument maker and stationer in Fifeshire. "Hearing of the glories of the great West . . . he concluded to come to the land of promise" in 1849. At age thirty-two, he and his family, together with thirty-six other Scots, emigrated to the United States. The Stoddarts proceeded immediately to Waupan, Wisconsin, settled on eighty acres, and plunged into farming. To his dismay, "It didn't agree with him; he couldn't get along with the steers and other wild animals; ploughing didn't suit him, neither did pitching hay." Apparently renting out his farm, Stoddart then clerked in a store for $10 per month, was appointed postmaster of Chester, and then sold his farm for $3,500 in gold, after which he returned to his true calling of making instruments. Stoddart Organs gained "a wide and just celebrity. . . . like their maker, [they were] honest, sound and reliable."[78]

Although it is impossible to estimate the numbers of novices who entered American agriculture and the proportions who succeeded, it is nonetheless clear that there were enough successes to nourish the agrarian myth and encourage more participants. It is also remarkable that Britons of such widely diverse backgrounds picked up agriculture for the first time in America and managed to become successful, even fabulously successful in contemporary British terms. Stonemasons, doctors, linen workers, sailors, grocery clerks, railroad conductors, wagoners, druggists, hatters, blacksmiths, engravers, merchants, and others joined in the pursuit of American land and succeeded to some degree. They prepared themselves well by gaining as much knowledge about America as they could and by making realistic judgments about what awaited them on an American farm. They also made long-term plans, although the lure of America's land was strong enough to make sudden converts of some upon arrival. Fitz Robins, for example, immigrated to Illinois in 1843 to use his skills as a carpenter and wagonmaker. Observing the opportunities that the fertile Illinois soil offered, he "abandoned his calling to give attention to agricultural pursuits" and bought an uncleared farm in 1845.[79]

The key to many novice agrarians' success as American farmers was the wise retention of their old line of work. In 1850, for example, Birmingham gunmaker

George Tuffley arrived in Platteville, Wisconsin, where for five years he practiced his craft. Then, with no prior agricultural experience, he purchased government land for only 50 cents an acre, expanded his holdings to four hundred acres of woodland within two years, acquired practical farming skills, and eventually became one of the most successful farmers in the county.[80] Many others continued to blend their old occupation with farming until they became fully established. Good examples include forty-six-year-old London attorney William Petherick and his wife, Rosina Anne, who emigrated with their six children to Sun Prairie in Dane County, Wisconsin in 1849 and purchased forty acres on which they pursued their dream of being farmers of their own land. At the same time, William obtained a license to practice law in the state and federal courts and did so with considerable success. He also earned the reputation of being a "man of broad culture." He likely knew his fellow countryman William Slatter, who had attended Oxford University, also emigrated in 1849 to farm in the same township, and must have stood out as a man of culture and learning.[81]

Another example of how nonagricultural people retained skills in order to fulfill their ultimate goal of farming is that of Capt. Joseph Bouch, a sailor from Lincolnshire who rose to become the master of a trading vessel that plied the coastal waters of England and the Mediterranean. Bouch emigrated to Chicago in 1851 at age thirty-five and bought his own schooner in 1853 and a farm in 1855. He continued to sail the Great Lakes and was instrumental in building the first harbor at South Haven, Michigan, but in 1869, at fifty-three, he sold his vessels and moved onto his farm.[82] Such reliance on past occupations and willingness to delay farming was common among British immigrants without agricultural backgrounds. It is also part of the story of John Porter, son of a Scottish physician, who in 1848 left his clerkship in a grocery and drygoods store in Blackburn, Lancashire, and came to Peoria, where he resumed work as a clerk for a merchant for another four years. Then in 1852 he picked up farming and enjoyed formidable success. By the time he died in 1878 he owned 240 acres of wild land and had brought it under "fine improvement." It was not prior agricultural experience but "only by the quiet force of persistent and unremitting toil" that this former clerk made such a successful transition to American farming.[83]

In still other ways British immigrants of nonagricultural backgrounds secured farms in America and in the process displayed an ability to be flexible in their plans and adapt to new situations. Some found it practical to pick up an entirely new occupation, and many blended farming with some form of remunerative labor until they could devote their full energies to it. Working in the pineries of Michigan during the winter months enabled former grocery store clerk Robert Nightingale to become a farmer in Illinois, as it did for a number of other British immigrants.[84] More would go to northern Michigan's iron and copper mines instead. Henry Nayler, who left Yorkshire for America in 1858, learned the blacksmithing trade in Wisconsin, practiced it for ten years, and then at age sixty-four bought and worked a farm of 154 acres.[85]

It was also common for Britons to plunge right into American farming, apparently without prior agricultural experience or any intention of ever doing nonagricultural work again. A fair portion of them fully realized their goals. A representative case is that of Joseph Anderson, foreman in a Glaswegian foundry, who emigrated to New York state in 1850, took up farming, and raised his sons to be farmers as well.[86] Similar cases include a Staffordshire engraver, a London railroad conductor, a stonemason from North Wales, a Lincolnshire grocer, and Joseph Stubbs, a poor druggist's apprentice and grocer from Lancastershire who dreamed of owning land in America. Stubbs arrived in Wisconsin in 1845 with only $25 (which he subsequently lost by making a bad loan) and married in Milwaukee. Within three years, at twenty-one, he bought eighty acres of wild land on which the couple endured the extreme rigors and dangers of pioneering on the frontier. Stubbs and his wife Mary had to struggle to raise their first log cabin and fourteen children, but eventually they owned four hundred acres.[87]

These stories and others show the power that the agrarian myth had on the imagination of Britons of almost every conceivable background and that success of mythical proportions did occur from time to time. They also indicate a certain tenacity, determination, and energy on the part of the migrants, because coping with such change demanded nothing less at a time when the shock of emigration had not fully worn off. At the same time, there was likely never a better place or time for nonagrarian immigrants to become farmers than in the Old Northwest during the 1840s and 1850s. So much affordable land was available, and prices for agricultural produce were usually high enough to make a decent profit. During the early 1850s in particular, grain farmers in Illinois enjoyed a string of bountiful harvests that brought them "unbounded prosperity," and during the Crimean War grain prices climbed as the blockade of the Black Sea constricted grain exports from the Ukraine and English wheat crops fell shorter than expected.[88] In addition to these advantages, commercial agriculture was rapidly developing in the Old Northwest as growing towns and cities became linked to farming areas by emerging transportation systems and provided growing markets for farmers. Novices willing to acquire basic agrarian skills and knowledge about American farming and who worked very hard ("like slaves," recalled Henry Lye) could succeed beyond their expectations.[89] There was so much to gain. The immigrants certainly heard of some of the people who had gone before them with little or no money but eventually owned an estate that in

Britain only noblemen possessed. The risks were acceptable, for in the event that farm life proved unsatisfactory one could still hope to sell land for a profit and follow some other path.

America's vast lands were also a place where bitter failures occurred and regrets were expressed, even when migrations had been based on the supposedly reliable information of immigrant letters. Evidence for such failure was less likely to survive than that for success, but a Leeds clothier, William Brown, recorded in 1849 that in America he had seen many who "have been tempted to leave their comfortable homes in England to go and join their relations, who were in fact only obtaining a miserable existence in the back settlements of America. I have seen many disappointments of this sort," Brown continued, "some of whom, having been comfortable before, when they saw miserable shanties where they expected mansions, immediately returned when they had the means; but by far the greatest number would amalgamate their finances with their relations and go spend the remainder of their miserable lives, buried in the forest."[90] Newspapers occasionally reported failures that sprang from poor planning. As one recorded, "Many cross the ocean without having well considered the capabilities of the particular land they have chosen, and with something of the idea that once they alight upon the happy shore, prosperity and wealth must inevitably attend upon their footsteps."[91]

Many British immigrants who pioneered the Old Northwest endured such primitive conditions and hardships that they deeply regretted their migration, at least until they had established homes and farms and begun reaping the benefits of their growing communities. Duncan Hossock, who left his native Inverneshire in 1855 and experienced all the classic privations of pioneer life in LaPeer County, Michigan, cleared his land by himself while he lived in a crude shanty. His food consisted of potatoes and the "occasional luxury of a hedgehog."[92]

Some British immigrants nearly starved in the American forest, and many more felt endangered by wild animals and Indians.[93] Their experiences could be nightmarish. William Shanks, who left Renfrewshire in 1846, came to Milwaukee via the Great Lakes, and then to Columbia County by ox team, a journey that took about three weeks. For nearly half the distance his wife walked behind with her two-year-old daughter on her back—so rough were the roads. That first summer they were so sick with the ague that they did not finish their log cabin before winter, when they were hit by storms so fierce that they had to live on meager rations to survive. For a six-week stretch they were isolated by the deep snows. Even in better weather, loneliness and isolation nearly overcame them.[94] Such conditions drove Emily Fox to leave her Sussex-born husband Samson and their primitive farm in Allegan County, Michigan, and go back to her relatives in New York.[95] The group of English who settled on the prairie soils of Benton County, Indiana, likewise found the "bleak prairie and the winter winds" too much to bear, and after they "had a good cry" and wished they had remained in England they left for a more hospitable location.[96]

The most spectacular failures and widespread regrets by British immigrants in mid-century rural America occurred among participants in the several grandiose and ill-conceived attempts to establish organized English colonies. The most ambitious of these schemes was that of the British Emigration Temperance Society, which was organized in Liverpool in December 1842 and commenced settlement in Mazomanie, Dane County, Wisconsin, the following year. The product of an idea hatched in a Liverpool temperance coffee house by employees of a nautical instruments firm—whose imaginations were fired by their contact with world travelers—the society had elaborate plans and lofty intentions. It would not only enable poor British laborers and artisans to acquire farms in America but also reduce Britain's industrial labor supply (and thereby raise industrial wages), promote temperance, and turn a profit to boot. Through weekly contributions of a shilling, members could purchase a share in the company, and when enough capital was raised for purchasing and developing frontier land in Wisconsin those members wishing to emigrate entered a lottery that determined who would go. Each winner would receive an eighty-acre, improved farm and a house furnished by the society, although ownership would occur after paying rent from the farm income. With the energies of sober and industrious immigrants working their own land, and anticipated commercial traffic along the nearby Wisconsin River, where plans for centrally located mills had been made, the society seemed bound for success and profit. Possibilities seemed endless.[97]

Out of nearly a thousand members, an impressive 691 Britons—mostly tradesmen from Yorkshire and Lancashire—came to the Mazomanie area between 1843 and 1850 and established small towns such as Heyworth and Gorstville (in honor of the society's founders) in what was then "almost an unbroken wilderness." The nearest settlers were ten miles away. Thirty miles distant was Mineral Point, which by 1850 had a community of about seven thousand Cornish immigrants although the two settlements had little in common and kept apart. Through this scheme a large number of English immigrants filtered into unsettled parts of Wisconsin during the mid-nineteenth century, where for many years they retained their English manners and customs. Forty-four of the original migrants were still living in or around Mazomanie at the end of the century.

The British Temperance Emigration Society can be seen as at least a partial success. By 1847 it claimed assets of more than $18,000, it had purchased 9,600 acres, and a large percentage of its members had emigrated and settled on good land, some of them permanently. Some, like David Harrop, who married the daughter of founder Robert Gorst and eventually owned two large farms, were surely satisfied with their fate.[98] Yet true to the nature of such schemes, problems soon surfaced, and dissension and distrust grew. As early as 1846, complaints were leveled against the agents, fifteen farms were abandoned, and the society began to dissolve into a series of bitter lawsuits. It did not help matters that most settlers had little or no farming experience, that many had virtually no money upon their arrival and hence found it difficult to make their payments, or that houses and mills remained unbuilt. Tempers flared as the society's agents threatened to dispossess settlers who could not pay their rent. Gorst himself became "so disgusted with the people" who arrived from England that he urged the officers in England to dissolve the society. Later he bitterly regretted ever having organized the project. Outside observers such as the Conference of the Primitive Methodist Church, with whom most of the Society's emigrants were affiliated, were scornful of the entire scheme and warned others not to take part in it. The church observed that "most of the members have been disappointed" and that "about a dozen houses and farms . . . have been deserted, the owners being starved out." By 1851 the society's activities in immigration were over, and the organization was soon terminated. The goal of establishing an English agricultural colony dedicated to temperance remained elusive, although many immigrants, perhaps as many as a thousand in all, did get to America through the society's scheme.[99]

Other schemes to establish English colonies in Wisconsin include attempts by socialists in Waukesha County. One consisted of a small group of thirty-one Owenites who were originally industrious mechanics. The group dissolved into jealousies and infighting after only a few years of work. The second was organized as the Utilitarian Association in London in 1843 and bought a mere two hundred acres near Mukwonago. It split apart after a year, primarily because the immigrants were townspeople and not cut out to be pioneers in a strange land and because members failed to work sufficiently under its socialist organization.[100]

Another notable English emigration scheme of the period was the Iowa Emigration Society led by George Sheppard, editor of the *Eastern Counties Herald,* a major newspaper of the Lincolnshire region. After a visit to the United States in 1843 he became convinced that a properly run emigration scheme could benefit England's working classes by settling some of them on twenty-acre farms on the American frontier, thereby reducing the labor supply in England and raising wages. These were the same hopes that drove the British Temperance and Emigration Society. The settlement scheme was based in part on the cooperative settlement ideas of French socialist Charles Fourier. Sheppard's newspaper provided all the necessary publicity and encouragement. In May 1850 the first group, consisting mainly of tradesmen, left Hull for Liverpool and arrived in America after a seven-week voyage.

Sheppard now had to travel ahead of the group and find suitable land in Iowa. Eventually, he came to Clinton County, where he established Sheppardsville (now Welton). In letters to the *Herald* he described the land in idealized terms as a place perfect for agriculture and having "a close resemblance to the finest parts of the Yorkshire Wold," yet the reality was something quite different. The settlement was too small, and it lacked timber. The land was average at best, in need of extensive drainage, and too distant from markets to be as profitable as Sheppard had envisioned. Furthermore, the California gold rush had raised the costs of supplies. Many members angrily expressed dissatisfaction with the destination to which Sheppard had led them. Some, disgusted, returned to England and blasted the society's reputation. Part of the problem was that expectations had been raised too high by an idealized vision of frontier life. People steeped in the agrarian myth were now confronting reality. From a different perspective, the secretary of the society complained in the *Herald* on January 23, 1851, that "the English make the worst kind of settlers; they grumble and growl at everything—comparing all things with the state of things at home—forgetting that this is an entirely new country."[101]

Like the members of the British Temperance Emigration Society in Wisconsin, most Iowa Emigration Society settlers were disgusted with what they found in America. Their site was too small and remote to support craftsmen and merchants, and many moved to better locations as soon as they could. When Sheppard left Iowa for Washington and then Canada, the community at Sheppardsville soon "faded from the Iowa scene" and from the interest of people still in Lincolnshire.[102]

A number of similar British emigration schemes were hatched during the mid-nineteenth century. One, the Staffordshire Potter's Emigration Society, will be described in the following chapter because it provides an intimate glimpse of the attempt by a specific group of poor industrial workers to get to America. But the difficulties and failures that some British immigrants experienced on American farms, as individuals or as members of an emigration scheme, should not overshadow the success with which the majority entered American agriculture. The emigration of British farmers and farm laborers during the mid-nineteenth century is a powerful example of the Atlantic economy at work and of the symbiotic nature of economic change and development in Britain and America. The repeal of the Corn Laws helped create adverse conditions that stimulated agricultural emigration from Britain; it also enhanced the attractions of the

United States by giving grain farmers in America a new access to British markets and thus new viability. The very changes that had squeezed out some of Britain's farmers created openings for them in the Old Northwest.

The general success of British newcomers to American agriculture was, however, far from unmitigated. While depending heavily on the help and advice from family members and old friends who had preceded them, many nevertheless were severely tested by primitive conditions and strange surroundings. The work was harder than they had imagined, and the need to adopt strange, new American agricultural methods and attitudes proved they had to become truly American farmers—not British farmers in America. Yet among the thousands of newcomers there were quite a few who could show the Americans a thing or two about drainage, breeding livestock, and how to create a model farm out of raw or minimally improved land.

The surging numbers of English immigrants who came to the United States during the mid-century period to farm—including the significant numbers reacting to difficulties that arose from the repeal of the Corn Laws in 1846—were a motley group of people. They are hard to characterize, but their zeal and energy, dedication and resourcefulness are impressive, as is the extent of their success, especially that of individuals who had little or no farming experience. Those who left industrial backgrounds to become American farmers are particularly interesting, in part because some experienced what emigration to America could mean in its ideal form—a rejection of harsh industrial life, a return to the land, and the achievement of personal renewal and independence. Of course, not all immigrants from industrial backgrounds would attempt farming in America. Industrial immigrants were also a "motley set."

A fair day's wages for a fair day's work, or, EMIGRATION!
—Motto of the United Branches of Crate-Makers and Packers, 1844

Immigrants from Industry and Crafts

The same ships that brought farmers and farm laborers from Britain to America during the mid-nineteenth century also brought many people with backgrounds in a wide variety of industrial and preindustrial craft occupations. That is not surprising. Britain at mid-century was the world's only urban and industrial nation, with unparalleled technological achievements and a growing lead in most types of industrial manufacturing. Accordingly, its labor force was the most diversified in the world. So were its emigrants, especially those who chose the United States over the colonies.

Although the United States was in earlier stages of economic growth than Britain, and much of its energy focused on pushing the frontier westward, the young nation did have modernizing industries in which workers could earn in two days what took them a week to earn in Britain. In a country that was literally expanding, artisans had many more niches to fill. While Britain's economy flourished during the mid-Victorian boom, the American economy offered even wider opportunities.

The common language and culture that British immigrants shared with their American hosts greatly facilitated their entry into the American labor force and accelerated their rise to supervisory positions. But it was their skill and experience that made them especially attractive. Most American employers not only welcomed skilled Britons warmly but also recruited them actively. Representatives from American textile and iron and steel companies frequently went abroad to bring back workers who had needed skills, especially after Britain lifted its ban on the emigration of skilled artisans in 1824. In America, British immigrants could capitalize on their reputation for being skilled and disciplined workers. The Joseph Hurst family, for example, arrived in Philadelphia from Manchester in December 1847 without having prearranged their employment, but as newly arrived Britons they were recruited on the docks to take up work in nearby textile mills. To seal the deal, they were enticed with good housing.[1]

British immigrants did not always deserve sterling reputations, however, and some American employers suffered for assuming that they did. That was the experience of John Curtis, an Ohio abolitionist, free-trade advocate, and associate of the British member of Parliament Richard Cobden, who with Curtis was investing in American enterprises, including textile mills. With obvious frustration Curtis reported to Cobden from Ohio in May 1844 that "we engaged an Englishman who had good recommendations and who made large professions of ability to erect a small establishment for manufacturing [silk] and to superintend its operation but he proved entirely incompetent and we were obliged to throw his machinery away as worthless."[2]

Some British industrial workers disappointed American employers with their intractability, their sense of independence, and even militancy, which surfaced when the immigrants grew dissatisfied with their wages, with the high costs of living in America, and with the arbitrary reduction of working hours. Many in New York City and New England factory towns came to realize that higher American wages came with an unpleasant price—a frantic work pace that left many exhausted and discouraged at day's end.[3] The early tendency of dissatisfied British workers to organize and fight injustice was another unpleasant surprise for some American employers. In later years especially, such militancy caused some employers to avoid hiring the "troublemakers" and in their stead hire the more docile immigrants pouring in from southern and eastern Europe. Some British industrial immigrants also brought with them a strong affection for beer and a tradition to hold "Saint Monday" as a holiday for recovering from a weekend of binge drinking—all of which tarnished their reputation for being disciplined workers.[4]

Yet in spite of such isolated problems the more positive reputation of British workers endured and was reinforced by the great majority who delivered what employers expected of them—and more. Skilled British immigrants had much to offer to America. They, in turn, had much to gain, whether working for an employer, for themselves in a craft, or as a farmer on their own land. What often proved necessary was a flexibility and willingness to adapt to America's precise employment needs and environment, much in the same way that immigrant farmers had to adapt to America's agricultural environment (chapter 3). Some British immigrants of the antebellum period in New York City were too specialized in their trades and reluctant to change and make the most of American opportunities.[5] These would account for some of the failures who eventually returned to Britain or lived out their lives in poverty. But most British immigrants, especially those who left the eastern cities and settled westward in either new agricultural areas or the villages and towns that served them, showed an uncanny ability to make occupational changes and go with the flow of the migration experience.

During the industrialization of the mid-nineteenth century there were two general categories of skilled workers: preindustrial craftsmen not experiencing technological change and industrial workers who had experienced change and at times technological displacement. Among the latter, textile workers were the most prominent, nearly 9 percent of Britain's male labor force in 1851. But in that same year their percentage among immigrants to the United States was only 3 percent, for an extremely low index of representation of 33. Therefore, it is noteworthy that an estimated 650 adult male textile workers migrated from Britain to the United States in 1851 alone and that roughly half were weavers. One would have expected even more given the huge numbers of textile workers in Britain.[6]

With such low proportions of immigrants from the textile industries, the mid-century marked a transitional period in the history of British industrialization and migration. Between the 1820s and the early 1840s textile workers came to the United States in more significant numbers, mainly because many handloom weavers felt threatened by power looms.[7] As late as 1847 many textile workers emigrated because of a depression in the industries of Lancashire and Yorkshire.[8] But in mid-December 1847 a major revival in industry was reported for the region of Manchester, and soon other mill towns were also seeing brighter days.[9] By 1851 British textile workers were the least likely workers to migrate to

America, even though many still faced technological displacement.[10] Whether that was due to a lack of means, as one writer has suggested, or to a lack of need and desire can be answered by taking a closer look at the textile workers who did emigrate.[11]

Immigrants in Textiles

Most immigrant weavers from Britain were handloom operators. They were generally older than other immigrants—a quarter were forty and over—and thus had likely entered work before the widespread conversion to power looms.[12] Perhaps they intended to resist change at this late stage in their lives by emigrating. In his study of Preston, Lancashire, at mid-century, Michael Anderson found that "most of those who did migrate later in life did so because they had to," particularly distressed handloom weavers.[13] Younger emigrant weavers were likely handloom weavers, too, if only because they were males. The 1851 census reveals that males within the textile labor force were the last to mechanize; in Oldham in 1851 males worked handlooms and females worked power looms.[14]

Why, then, were the numbers of emigrant handloom weavers so limited? Emigration was an affordable option to most, especially those with a family income. Male handloom weavers facing lower wages and unemployment at mid century commonly sent their wives and children to textile factories in order to avoid poverty.[15] It also appears that weavers used family incomes to emigrate. More than half in 1851 traveled with family members who were likely wage-earners, a proportion much higher than that for any other group.[16] Thus, rather than poverty being an issue, it seems more likely that their incentive to emigrate was low.

At mid-century, New England's expanding textile mills offered little to Britain's male weavers. By the 1830s New England's mills had already made the shift to power looms and the women and children who operated them.[17] Matters were different in Philadelphia. Because of worker resistance to mechanization and a steadily profitable market for finer handloomed products, Philadelphia retained a handloom industry, and some six thousand weavers were employed there as late as 1859. Only half of the city's textile machines used steam or water power in 1850.[18] Here was a place where Britain's handloom weavers might preserve their old form of work if they wanted.

Many apparently did. Half of the weavers whose city of destination was indicated on 1851 passenger lists were going to Philadelphia; of those whose state of destination is known, a quarter were going to Pennsylvania.[19] Their letters make it clear that some intended to weave only long enough to accumulate the capital necessary for farming.[20] But again, even the incentive of owning land had relatively little effect by mid-century, because surprisingly small proportions emigrated. Weavers were accepting change in Britain rather than avoiding it in America; work for men expanded in Britain's factories.[21] That was even more true for the other textile workers, especially spinners, who were even less likely to emigrate. They had experienced the greatest change in technology in the previous decade, when many adjusted to larger spinning mules and self-acting machines and textile workers emigrated in more significant proportions.[22] By mid-century, Britain's growing textile factories seem to have been absorbing potential emigrants rather than producing them through industrialization and technological change.

Those textile workers who did migrate during the mid-century period were an interesting and diverse group, judging from twenty-three who emigrated between 1845 and 1855 and later appeared in U.S. county histories.[23] There is little evidence that they were victims of technological displacement or unemployment and had emigrated as a last resort. Rather, most seem to have been ambitious, resourceful people who were rationally using what they had to improve their future by going to the United States. That was true of John Schofield, a handloom weaver who had also managed to open a small general store. Although he was "doing well," he "wanted to do better and decided to try his fortunes in the United States."[24] Thomas Anderton, a Lancashire cotton bleacher, emigrated because he had "heard much of the advantages which the New World offered to young men."[25] Similarly, Edward Fisher was born and reared in Wales and then as a young man moved to Nottingham, where he prospered as a lace maker. Yet in 1845 he migrated to Madison, Wisconsin, and with the funds he brought with him became a successful money lender and speculator in real estate.[26] Most arrived in America with meager savings. Perhaps typical was Charles Bennett, a Devonshire fuller and clothdresser who disembarked with only a half-sovereign to his name.[27] But they did arrive with a capacity to succeed in America's industry or on America's farmland.

The most famous British immigrant with a background in textiles was young Andrew Carnegie, who arrived as a boy with his family from Scotland in 1847. By the end of the century he was the richest man in the world. Less spectacular but still noteworthy was William Broadhead, a Yorkshire weaver with some mechanical skills who migrated to New York state in 1843, clearly out a sense of ambition and adventure. As with many of the other textile immigrants, he used a network of information and people to get started in America—in Broadhead's case, an uncle who had preceded him. Broadhead eventually established nine weaving factories in Jamestown in Chautauqua County that employed eight hundred operatives and became a leading force in the area's economic and civic development.[28] The arrival in 1857 of Charles Bailey, a Yorkshire weaver expert with various types of looms, is significant because it marks a transfer of textile skills: Bailey was hired to set up Jacquard looms in a mill at Little Falls, New York.[29]

Others who remained in textile work in the United States rose to become proprietors of mills and were later described as capable people who were "thoroughly acquainted" with all the details of the business.[30] Such men were generally awarded the most privileged positions in the mills of places such as Central Falls, Rhode Island. For women, however, conditions were not much better than those in Glasgow or Manchester, especially as cheaper Irish labor flooded in during the 1840s and 1850s.[31]

Yet many if not most did not remain in textiles. Roughly half of those found in county histories became farmers, usually within a short time of arrival. Although these proportions cannot be applied to all British textile immigrants, they indicate that the prospect of becoming an American farmer was an important reason why many came. As James Caird noted of Yorkshire's textile workers, "All classes engaged in the woollen manufacture seem to have a taste for land."[32] Although some of these who did come to America to farm recalled being severely tested during the difficult process of clearing land, most eventually succeeded as farmers.[33]

The story of John Spencer, a weaver from Clitheroe, Lancashire, illustrates how one immigrant weaver laid the network through which many other weavers arrived and took up American farming. In Lancashire, Spencer's "independent and spirited nature" got him into trouble with his foreman, who blamed him for some mishap, discharged him, and threatened to blacklist him. But Spencer could see in this adversity an opportunity to fulfill his long-held desire to settle in America. After landing in Massachusetts in 1842 and working in the mills of Fall River, where he easily found work with other Lancashire weavers who had preceded him, Spencer took up the cooper's trade and tramped westward. Near Manitowoc he found "the land he had dreamed of" and purchased 160 acres. He was so happy there that he persuaded friends and neighbors in Lancashire to join him and helped them obtain nearby land, where a small community of former Lancashire residents eventually became established. Although not formally educated himself, Spencer donated land for a schoolhouse and helped erect it, and when circuit riders were not available to preach in the local Methodist Church he "filled the pulpit very acceptably." The English community founded by Spencer prospered and retained its English character until the second and third generation drifted away and sold their property to later immigrants.[34]

The long road from British textiles to American farming was one that relatively few Britons took at mid-century. As Britain's textile industries boomed and

America's pulled in Irish workers, the migration of weavers and others in the industry slowed to what was, in proportional terms, a trickle.

Ironworkers and Engineers

The other group of industrial workers subject to technological change—iron-workers and engineers—were more likely to emigrate than the underrepresented textile workers but not nearly as likely as farmers or laborers. An estimated 440 engineers emigrated directly to America in 1851, as did about 660 ironworkers, among whom the most common were founders, boilermakers, and watch and instrument makers. What is most surprising is that puddlers and founders—who not only performed the heaviest, most back-breaking tasks but also were likely to be affected by technological change—were among the least inclined to emigrate. Only engineers were overrepresented. Even the combination of highly skilled watch and instrument makers, millwrights, and boilermakers outnumbered foundry workers. Twenty years earlier, puddlers, founders, and other metal workers were the dominant members of this immigration group.[35] Clearly, industrial emigration from Britain had changed by mid-century.

Like textile workers, foundry workers did not have much incentive to migrate—even to Pennsylvania. The Keystone State was the location of America's largest, most diverse iron industries. The latest technology was used in the eastern part of the state, whereas older, traditional technology prevailed in the west. Thus Pennsylvania normally offered opportunities to all kinds of ironworkers—those whose skills and work experience were traditional and probably outdated in Britain and those with the latest skills.[36] In the late 1840s, however, the railway boom in England and America collapsed, and cheap rails flooded the American market. The fall in English rail prices halted the construction of rail mills in Pennsylvania, and the hardships extended beyond the world of the railrollers. Pennsylvania's pig iron industry was also hard-hit; by the end of 1849 production had fallen by 35 percent. Not until 1852 did a second railway boom revive the industry and offer fuller employment.[37]

While opportunities for ironworkers were declining in America they were growing in most parts of Britain, especially those not so heavily dependent on rail production. By mid-century Britain was producing about half of the world's pig iron, and the industry was entering its fastest growth period ever in order to meet the various demands of a growing economy.[38] The discovery in the 1830s of Scotland's famously rich Black Band ore (extremely productive when smelted in James Neilson's new hot-air blast furnace), together with the opening of Cleveland's rich ironstone deposits in 1851, allowed tremendous expansion of

Britain's iron industry in the northeast.[39] That growth occurred partly at the expense of the South Wales industry, which still depended heavily on rails and found the new competition hard to bear. Significant numbers of Welsh ironworkers did migrate to the United States during the late 1840s, largely because of these difficulties (chapter 6). Overall, as in the textile industries, expanding opportunities for ironworkers and engineers in Britain absorbed potential emigrants.[40]

The surviving evidence on those ironworkers and engineers who did come to the United States at mid-century is scanty, but a few generalizations are apparent from the stories of eleven known ironworkers and fourteen known engineers and machinists who emigrated between 1845 and 1855. Ironworkers, engineers, and machinists were also inspired to move by an ambition cultivated by promising reports about what was achievable in the United States. Perhaps most identified with Scotsman Peter Kinnear, an apprenticed machinist who had a strong love for his native land but whose ambition "to make a name and place among men was stronger still," causing him to leave Dundee in 1847. James Sheriffs, a Scottish ironworker, also recalled that he had become "inspired by the glowing accounts of the opportunities" of America before he left Banff in 1848 and became a foundry superintendent in Menomonee, Wisconsin. After that he established the successful Sheriffs Manufacturing Company in Milwaukee.[41] Other ironworkers "had some means" when they arrived in America, but none mentioned hardship as a reason for migration.[42]

Another common characteristic of these people was the considerable experience and skill they had acquired before migration. They appear to have been extremely employable in Britain. Nearly all of the ironworkers, engineers, and machinists in county histories had served full apprenticeships. Some had been journeymen, and several had been foremen or superintendents. Henry Elliott, a Scot, had gained experience as an ironworker and machinist under the supervision of locomotive inventor George Stevenson and then became superintendent of a locomotive works before he left in 1854. He joined his son, who had also mastered the trade in Britain and migrated five years earlier. Together they established a successful family business in Illinois.[43] Several others had clearly mastered their craft before migrating and in America earned local reputations for being the most skilled in their field.[44] They had carefully weighed their future in Britain with that in America and opted for the latter.

One particularly important group of workers who were attracted to American industry at mid-century and had an impact far greater than their modest numbers would suggest was composed of specialized workers from Sheffield's crucible steel and toolmaking industries. Sheffield had long tapped the expanding American market for many types of iron implements, but at early mid-century American manufacturers were tapping the skills of Sheffielders by luring some of the best workers across the Atlantic with high pay and lofty managerial positions. Enough Sheffielders came to the United States between the early 1830s and the 1850s to push U.S. industrial technology forward, and soon Americans could compete with Britain in the production of most kinds of crucible steel and tools. Sheffielders helped produce the first cast steel direct from pig iron at Jersey City and Pittsburgh in the 1840s after several American businessmen traveled to England to learn Sheffield methods and returned with workers they had recruited. Particularly with the production of cutlery, saws, files, chisels, razors, and other related tools, skilled immigrants from Sheffield proved indispensable to the rapid development of America's industries, although Americans then refined the processes in order to save labor costs and simplified the product to meet specific demands of the American market.[45]

Although the immigration of the skilled Sheffielders to American industry had significant results, their numbers were small in comparison with other groups. Ironworkers and engineers did not migrate in high numbers at mid-century; what drew nearly half of those who appear in the county histories was American farmland. Although somewhat less inclined to take up farming than the textile immigrants, the ironworkers, engineers, and machinists who became farmers displayed a similar pattern of working at their trade as long as was required to save the necessary capital. Welsh rolling mill worker Thomas Downton worked in American mills for a full twenty-seven years after his emigration in 1850 before he finally bought and worked a farm, which he brought under a "high state of cultivation" in spite of an apparent lack of farming experience.[46] Others did have such experience and proved themselves capable of taming uncleared land as true pioneers.[47] The mid-century period was likely the most propitious time for British ironworkers and engineers to pursue an agrarian or industrial life in the United States, yet the numbers who did so were not great.

Technological changes associated with industrialization were not important inducements for emigration at mid-century. Ironworkers, especially textile workers, were among the least likely to migrate, no doubt because of a low American demand for these skills at mid-century and a high British demand for labor in growing and changing textile factories and ironworks. Emigrant engineers and specialized iron and steel workers and toolmakers were more numerous because they had greater opportunities and a wider range of settlement in America than those bound for foundries and mills. Economic distress was not an important cause for their migration. Their skills continued to be in demand in Britain, but some migrants were in pursuit of American farms. Whatever the advantages America offered skilled industrial workers generally, they were not strong enough to lure extraordinary numbers from Britain's expanding textile and iron industries, not even those threatened by technological change.

Immigrants in Preindustrial Crafts

British craftsmen were not undergoing the kind of technological changes that most industrial workers were at mid-century, and yet as a group they were more likely to migrate to America. These preindustrial workers composed nearly a third of both the immigrant population and the whole British population in 1851 (table A2, Appendix A). Among them, building trades workers (half of whom were carpenters and a fourth of whom were masons) and miners (chapter 5) migrated in more significant proportions.

Britain's building trades workers generally shared in the economic growth of the period. Their nominal wages rose by some 40 percent between 1840 and 1866, even though they were also working fewer hours per week.[48] Most of this improvement, however, occurred during the 1860s. Wages rose slowly in the late 1840s, when building activity was still low in Britain although rising slightly.[49] As for their economic conditions and migratory decisions, these emigrants' origins are especially important. If they were from rural parts of the country they were likely affected by rural depopulation.

The story of Britain's rural depopulation and the consequent decline in rural markets for the goods and services of craftsmen is especially relevant for the mid-century period. During the late eighteenth and early nineteenth centuries, Britain's rural population grew even as industries and cities sucked in rural people. Naturally, such growth required greater numbers of craftsmen to provide necessary goods and services, which sustained rural craft economies. At some point before the middle of the century, however, continually greater proportions of people were leaving rural areas for towns and cities. So many parishes had shrinking populations that the entire populations of some counties suffered a net loss between 1841 and 1851.[50]

Along with depopulation came the breakdown of isolation and the rise of urban competition for rural markets as continued strides in technology and transport allowed cheaper factory-made goods to be sold in towns and villages. It was inevitable that many or most rural industries and markets for craftsmen were either destroyed or reduced to negligible proportions.[51] One early writer, Peter Anderson Graham, in 1891 visited the villages he had known as a boy and talked with the oldest inhabitants who had remained there. He found that "when railways began to penetrate the rural districts the hopes of such people were very high. It was imagined that every stagnant little market town would be awakened up into new life and prosperity. The exact contrary happened. No sooner did people get accustomed to trains than they carried their custom to the largest towns. . . . Nearly all the little towns—with population under five thousand say—are in decay if they depend for prosperity on the adjacent country."[52]

Building trades workers were particularly hard-hit by rural depopulation. Graham was struck by the frequency with which cottages were "ruined, empty, and crumbling." As populations slowed or fell, so did local demand for housing, minor construction, and even repairs. As Graham concluded, "Country masons and carpenters suffer more severely [than others]. A glance at any semi-depopulated district is sufficient to prove how much employment they have lost. Building is at an entire standstill. . . . Where there is a difficulty in finding tenants, cottages which otherwise men would be employed to repair are allowed to get worse til pulling them down is the inevitable end."[53]

Such extensive depopulation and declining fortunes for building craftsmen in rural Britain contributed to the significant flow of building trades workers to the United States. Evidence provided by the thirty-five English building trades workers who provided their county of origin on the ships' lists, plus the twenty-one who provided their town of origin, is inconclusive, but it does lend support to this hypothesis. Almost half came from agricultural counties, and relative to other groups they were associated with smaller towns and villages rather than the large cities (tables B6, B7, Appendix B). The mainly rural origins of the emigrant building trades workers are indicated also by those who later appeared in the county histories, although again the evidence is sketchy. Only three of the twenty-four cases found gave a city as their last place of residence (London or Glasgow), six gave a small village, and most of the rest (not providing a more precise origin) came from decidedly rural counties such as Cambridgeshire, Lincolnshire, Somerset, Westmorland, Norfolk, Devonshire, Warwickshire, and Cornwall.

In America, the immigrants' rural aspirations seem to have continued. Of the twenty-four immigrant building trades workers found in county histories, about half took up farming, sometimes in conjunction with a building trade, after accumulating the necessary capital. Some were farmers' sons who had learned a building trade or had at least some experience in agriculture before emigrating and then continued a dual occupation after emigration. Samuel Clark, for example, was a carpenter and joiner who had "always worked at his trade in connection with farming," and he continued to juggle these two occupations after emigrating from Norfolk to Illinois in 1848.[54] Farming was in the blood of these people.

Most who eventually turned to farming arrived with very little capital, worked at their trade, and then devoted full attention to agriculture, as though being a full-time farmer had been their long-term goal all along. Their skills gave them leverage with which to enter American agriculture. They had options and flexibility that could prove invaluable during their early years of settlement. A typical case is that of John Campbell, a mason from Blair Atholl, Scotland, who left for Illinois in 1851 and bought unimproved land in Will County soon after his arrival. He carried on as a mason so that he could hire others to clear his land for him. Eight years later, the hardest work behind him, Campbell turned to farming his newly improved land and became extremely successful at it.[55]

Immigrant building trades workers enjoyed advantages in the fact that construction jobs were often easy to find in many parts of the United States, in stark contrast to the many parts of Britain undergoing rural depopulation. They could often find work immediately upon their arrival without prearranging employment through the help of a network.[56] Yet it is likely that most wisely used the assistance of other British immigrants already in their area of chosen settlement to minimize the risks of migration and maximize their chances of success. Carpenters and stonemasons going to southwestern Wisconsin and other areas where large numbers of British immigrants had settled were able to prearrange employment through letters or at least find work through the large community there.[57] For those willing to join the hoards of Forty-Niners trekking to California to mine gold, the rewards for work could be staggeringly high. On his first day in California, Faithful William Chapman earned $16 as a carpenter, although the high costs of provisions reduced his total earnings considerably.[58]

Immigrants in the Wood, Food, Shoe, and Metals Trades

Compared to the miners and building trades workers, other preindustrial workers did not migrate in considerable numbers. Those in food processing (who were mostly butchers, bakers, and millers) and woodworking (cabinetmakers and wheelwrights) were underrepresented. So were clothing workers (shoemakers, tailors, and needlewomen), while metalworkers (nearly all of whom were smiths) were only minimally overrepresented. Thus a trend is evident. Fewer of the migrants were craftsmen, at least insofar as they were enumerated in 1831, 1841, 1851, and in the 1880s. By mid-century their numbers were moderate, and negligible by the late 1880s (table A2, Appendix A).

The comparative paucity of these craftsmen is particularly interesting in light of the rural nature of craft industries and their declining importance in the British economy. As a group, craftsmen traditionally relied on the business of rural communities. Shoemakers in rural areas, for example, were known to enjoy their greatest demand after the harvest, when money was available for workers to purchase new boots and shoes for their families.[59] Blacksmiths and wheelwrights were especially dependent on the needs of farmers, although increasing numbers were being employed in cities too.[60] As with the building trades, rural depopulation and the rise of modern transportation undermined the livelihoods and opportunities for traditional crafts in many parts of rural Britain.[61] Craftsmen in the wood, clothing, food, and metals trades were especially vulnerable to competition that railroads brought from urban and industrial areas, and yet they were not inclined to emigrate. America was not a significant safety valve for these displaced persons, as has been assumed.

One explanation may be that America's capacity to serve as a safety valve was not that great by mid-century. It is true that all of these workers were still in some demand in the American economy, certainly more so than during the 1880s. It is also true that some British immigrants learned trades such as blacksmithing upon their arrival and prospered.[62] But by mid-century there was apparently a greater need for such workers to plan their migration carefully and ensure employment first by acquiring information about a particular area's demand for their skills, as it was common to do.[63]

One of the more popular emigrant guides, published in 1851, contained valuable and apparently accurate, unbiased information and warned skilled craftsmen of the consequences of emigrating without first doing their homework:

> The artisan who goes to America with the expectation of being employed in his own trade, should be a *firstrate workman.* . . . A good skilled artisan, however, is valuable here as well in America; and before he leaves the old country, he will do well to consider whether his trade, if it be a failing one on this side of the Atlantic, may not be utterly useless on the other side. . . . An intelligent artisan will generally have some brother of the trade who has gone before him, and can give him information. If he has not some such means of acquiring distinct knowledge of the remuneration of his profession before emigrating to the States, he had better stay at home, as he may find that his occupation is overdone, or that he is far excelled by the local workers, and will be obliged to descend to the rank of the unskilled labourer.[64]

The tone of this advice seems contrary to generally held notions about nineteenth-century America's thirst for skilled craftsmen and the ease with which they could enter American life.[65] Around mid-century, that demand had become increasingly satisfied in many areas. That was less true in the building trades and mines, industries that continued to expand generally throughout the century. But the fact that laborers were far more overrepresented than craftsmen supports the idea that mid-century America had more to offer laborers than skilled craftsmen.

If the low numbers of craftsmen in the wood, food, shoe, and metals trades can be explained in part by the limitations of America's opportunities, then limitations in the dislocation and disruption associated with declining rural populations and markets might also provide some explanation. Some found it relatively easy to adjust at home to the changes that accompanied rural depopulation. Shoemakers, for example, took on more repair work, and blacksmiths were particularly able to exercise flexibility in attracting customers.[66] In contrast, building trades workers were harder hit by declining rural markets. They also had wider openings awaiting them in the American economy and consequently were much more likely to migrate.

Craftsmen near growing towns and cities could make a short move and find work there.[67] Those from more rural and isolated parts of the country, however, faced a more formidable and wrenching long-distance internal migration and could see America as an acceptable option. They likely account for many who emigrated at mid-century, when most craftsmen, compared to other groups, had rural origins. Roughly 60 percent of woodworkers and food processors came from agricultural counties, for example, and were among the least likely to declare themselves originating from the larger cities (tables B6, B7, Appendix B), and nearly half traveled in family groups that included relatively large numbers of dependent children. Woodworkers were typically older than other preindustrial emigrants and had the largest percentage in the 25–34 age range as well as the 55–64 range but nearly the lowest percentage under 25 (tables B8, B9, Appendix B).

That woodworkers were the most familial and mature of all craftsmen may be significant. They seem to have waited to emigrate, perhaps because more time was normally required to become an accomplished and established wheelwright or cabinetmaker than for most other craft occupations.[68] If age does reflect work experience, then most woodworkers no doubt emigrated with skills and some experience already acquired. They may have been inspired to emigrate by declining rural markets in Britain, by the possibility of owning land in America, or both.

Some of the speculation about emigrant craftsmen can be reduced by turning to those whose life stories were later recorded in county histories. In addition to the twenty-four building trades workers, also identified were twelve shoemakers, ten millers, eight blacksmiths, and seventeen other preindustrial craft emigrants. A few widely shared characteristics emerge. Not surprisingly, many eventually took up farming, which was likely their long-term goal and reason for emigrating. That applies, however, mainly to shoemakers (nine of twelve cases eventually entered agriculture) and building trades workers (half of whom became farmers). Yet only two of the ten millers, two of the eight blacksmiths, and under a third of the rest did the same.

Shoemakers and some building trades workers generally had more to gain from entering agriculture than did blacksmiths, millers, and others who were in a good position to establish their own businesses and "do better" than the average farmer. The importance of millers to newly opened farming areas can hardly be exaggerated, for their occupation transformed subsistence agriculture into market agriculture and pushed the American frontier toward more advanced stages of development.[69] Thus the rewards for capable millers were usually high—high enough to keep them in their line of work. Most immigrant millers who appear in county histories continued their line of work in the United States, quickly became foremen, and then mill owners in their own right. Among the most successful was Thomas Birkett, a master miller who left Cumberland for Michigan in 1852 and quickly gained considerable wealth and power. Once in Michigan, Birkett first worked as a miller, then took charge of a mill that he eventually purchased, and then gradually acquired a number of other mills. Later he organized and owned the Dexter Savings Bank, of which he was also president. Birkett also speculated in southern pine lands with a pair of U.S. senators and bought a three-hundred-acre farm with more than two miles of frontage on Portage Lake in Michigan. He also purchased large businesses in the northern part of lower Michigan. This was a remarkable life's journey for the "humble tradesman" from Cumberland.[70] Similar although less spectacular steps toward success were achieved by at least four of the other immigrant millers, and a few others were content with owning one mill or entering farming.[71]

Shoemakers showed much greater interest in taking up farming. Most seem to have emigrated specifically to acquire capital for farming and did so without any apparent farm experience. In what seems to be a typical case, John Wood left Brighton, Sussex, for Rock County, Wisconsin, in 1852. He continued to work at his craft until 1855, when he bought eighty acres and began farming under trying conditions and without any experience. During the winter months he had to fall back on his trade in the nearby town of Albany to make ends meet, but gradually he improved his land, expanded his farm to 120 acres, and became a successful American farmer.[72] The pattern was familiar to other immigrant shoemakers from Britain, although the rise to farmer was often much slower. John Youngs, who left Norfolk the same year that John Wood left Sussex, worked as a shoemaker for a full twenty years in New York state before turning full time to farming, and Henry Tuck from Bradford, Yorkshire, took up farming more than thirty years after his emigration in 1845.[73] Some chose to stay with shoemaking and became dealers, but for most the lure of farming in America was too powerful to resist.

Shoemakers share another important feature: They were surviving at their trade in Britain but wanted more out of life. That was clearly true for Samuel

Fowler Smith, whose life history is exceptionally well documented.[74] Smith was one of four shoemakers who lived in the small village of Walton, Yorkshire, which had only about 240 people in the 1830s. Although he was able to work steadily at his craft in Walton and surrounding areas, he saw a hard future in England, only minimally above poverty. He also perceived a social stigma against shoemakers and knowing that, as a well-read, ambitious young man, he was "capable of something better," especially after his brothers sent him encouraging letters from America, he left for Indiana in 1835. Although Smith was determined to find a new line of work in America he initially fell back on shoemaking and had to "re-learn" his craft when he was forced to use wooden pegs instead of the shoe nails he had used in England. Then he found an opening in the wheelmaking business and eventually became the leading partner in the nation's largest wheelmaking establishment in Indianapolis.

Other shoemakers also displayed an ambitious personality and a sense of adventure. Robert Scott from Fifeshire was "not . . . satisfied with his future prospects in Scotland" before he emigrated to Illinois in 1852. Another Scottish shoemaker, Matthew McMillan, emigrated in large part because he desired to "see something of the New World, of which he had heard so much."[75]

Although blacksmiths and various other immigrant craftsmen showed less interest in taking up American farming than did shoemakers and building trades workers, a minority became farmers in the same kinds of ways: by remaining at their craft as long as necessary before renting or purchasing land and by working very hard to cultivate it. But most remained at their craft for good and became operators or owners of their own smithy, tailoring shop, butcher shop, or whatever. Blacksmith Robert Morris of Anglesea, Wales, performed his skills at various places throughout the United States before being put in charge of the railroad blacksmith shop of North La Cross, Wisconsin, and George Turner, a journeyman blacksmith who left Nottinghamshire in 1854, took a similar position before following an opportunity to open his own manufacturing business, in his case making railroad spikes and iron fencing.[76] Even then, the attraction of owning land was sometimes irresistible. Some became owners of farms that they rented out while running their businesses, and many had children who became farmers. But the success that these British immigrant craftsmen enjoyed in the United States was enough to keep most of them content in their trade.

Some British craftworkers came to the United States through organized emigration schemes, one of which was particularly important for the way it targeted a specific group of artisans: the potters of Staffordshire. The Potters' Joint-Stock Emigration Society and Savings Fund was organized by the Staffordshire Potters' Union and an act of Parliament in 1844. The union had been supporting unemployed potters at considerable expense, and leaders looked at both sides of the Atlantic and reasoned that it would be better to assist their migration to America, "where lands were cheap and where industry would surely be rewarded, thus relieving their country of surplus labor, and enabling those that remained to obtain better wages."[77] Funds were raised through the sale of stock to workers, and families were selected by ballot, apparently from among both unemployed and employed potters who were in difficult circumstances.

By 1846 the society had selected 1,640 acres near the town of Scott in Columbia County, Wisconsin, only twenty miles from the colony being established by the British Temperance Emigration Society (chapter 3). Each family was to be given twenty acres on which to farm and make pottery. The scheme, like others of its kind, seemed to have a promising start because idealized visions of America encouraged wide participation and enthusiasm. The drawing of the ballots was a festive occasion, complete with choral-singing, dancing, and band music. During the Easter week of 1847 forty-four winners left for Liverpool. Bands played, and several thousand people came to wish them luck and bid farewell. By the end of the year, 134 persons were settled on what was now called Pottersville, but inadequate planning and funding and the unrealistic hope of farming profitably on only twenty acres of cheap land doomed the plan from the start. Many immigrants found themselves in a state of destitution, and "starvation seemed to stare them in the face."[78]

Although the society tried to prevent the spreading of discouraging reports and opened the scheme to workers of other trades, continued financial problems reduced it to dissolution and bitter lawsuits. As it turned out, the society did not properly purchase the land, and members were squatting on Indian land, from which they were forced to leave. Such mismanagement, which was reported in English newspapers by 1851, illustrates the poor planning of the scheme and how it could not possibly have succeeded. Some potters returned to England, but most remained, took up land nearby, and "in due course of time became substantial citizens." Once in America, most were able to dig themselves out of poverty and become prosperous farmers. The principal motive of some emigrant potter-farmers was to escape distress in England, but their overall numbers were not great.[79]

As the mid-nineteenth century passed, the surge of British migration to the United States had less and less to do with technological displacement or any other adverse effect of industrialization. By 1851 it was farmers, some preindustrial craftsmen, and laborers who swelled the emigrant ranks, not the industrial workers of 1841 and earlier. Some rural building trades workers were no doubt suffering from the steady flow of people to cities and industrial centers. Some Welsh miners also reacted to troubles in their industry by emigration (chapter 6), but that cannot be considered as a true craft migration. Their numbers were not so extraordinary, and many sought land rather than to escape hardship. The many "labourers" were composed of a mix of farm laborers and unskilled laborers, the latter also likely making positive moves and intending to take advantage of America's higher wages and wider scope for employment. Outnumbering all other occupational groups, and generally single and younger, these migrants constitute a significant "labor element" and thereby distinguish the British from other ethnic groups arriving in America during the period.

By mid-century those industrial workers who did emigrate included many who were not likely affected by adverse industrial change. Foundry workers were greatly outnumbered by engineers and highly skilled machinists who were in demand in Britain. Handloom weavers were proportionately fewest in number, and the existing evidence suggests that they were motivated as much by land in America as by distress in Britain. Industrial workers generally emigrated in such low proportions that Britain's expanding industry seems to have been absorbing potential emigrants by mid-century. The expanding economy meant that industrial emigration from Britain was limited, generally not of a distressed nature, and not widely used as a safety valve.

Who pities the man who goes down
Into the deep, dark dungeon
Where the sun never shines by day,
To earn his morsel?

Who pities the man who goes down
After kissing his wife and child
Good bye for the last time,
Like many a brave man has done?
—Poem of Cornish miners in Wisconsin

Miners

No nation is more closely associated with mining than Great Britain. The ancient Phoenicians and Greeks got much of their tin from Cornwall, and the Romans their lead from Yorkshire.[1] The coal industry also blossomed early in Britain, where people in the thirteenth century were already turning to coal for their heating and cooking fuel and craftsmen used it to produce iron implements. As the mines went deeper, the skills and technology of mining evolved and allowed still greater rates of productivity. By the early nineteenth century some British mines plunged nearly a thousand feet below the earth's surface and stretched far underneath the seabed.

Britain's hunger for coal especially was insatiable. Production grew to meet not just the escalating demands of industry, railways, and steamships but of domestic use as well. In addition, coal was being exported in growing proportions, especially from 1870 on.[2] Inevitably, demand for coal generally pressed the labor supply, so much so that it was often necessary to recruit miners from the general labor market and pay them wages that were high by the standards of the time. Although the wages were surely not high enough to compensate them for demonic working conditions and an early grave, coal miners did earn significantly more than necessary for subsistence. Those in Aberdare in 1850 earned as much as 30 shillings per week when regularly employed, and miners sometimes earned even more in the northeast, where many of them lived in free, colliery-owned housing or received rent allowances in addition to their pay. But because they were paid on a piece-rate basis miners' peak earning power declined with age, and fluctuations in coal prices and the caprices of management made earnings unpredictable.

During the mid-century period, as Priscilla Long has remarked, "The world of the coal miner was largely a British world." Thus British miners of coal and mineral ores introduced the skill of craft mining to the United States and contributed enormously to the industrial revolution there. They brought their tools, know-how, and culture to America's mining regions. During the 1850s alone, nearly thirty-seven thousand British miners migrated to the United States. The figures do not take into account those who returned to Britain, but neither do they include those who entered the United States via Canada.[3]

In 1851, when a little over 5 percent of Britain's male labor force were miners, almost 7 percent of Britain's immigrants to the United States were miners. The ratio is similar to that calculated for emigrant miners in the early 1840s and late 1880s.[4] Because all of these years were ones of noticeably high British migration to the United States, a characteristic feature of that migration seems to be the movement of disproportionate numbers of miners.

Although their numbers were high, miners' overrepresentation was still modest in comparison to that of farmers and unskilled laborers. Moreover, considering the British miners separately as English, Scottish, and Welsh, an important distinction emerges: Only Welsh miners were overrepresented as migrants (chapter 6). The English and Scottish were slightly underrepresented, in large part because the coalfields of Northumberland and Durham were booming at the time and pulling in more prospective English and Scottish emigrants than Welsh. These proportions do not include all of the English hard-rock miners of mineral ores, many of whom were going to Wisconsin by the cheapest possible route—the port of Quebec—and were not counted as immigrants.[5]

Roughly a quarter of the miners were described specifically as coal miners, and fewer than a fifth were quarrymen. The rest are described simply as "miners," although most were likely coal miners because the limited data on their origins and destinations associate them with the coal regions of Britain and the coal regions of Pennsylvania (tables B4 and B10, Appendix B). The distinction between coal and hard-rock miners was not always significant, however. Miners' skills were transferable, and they often switched back and forth between coal and minerals when it made sense to do so. Hard-rock miners entering the United States at mid-century were a considerable socioeconomic and cultural force.

Hard-Rock Miners

Most immigrant hard-rock miners were tin, copper, and manganese miners from Cornwall or lead miners from the Yorkshire Dales. They were seizing opportunities in the Driftless Hill region of the Upper Mississippi Valley in northwestern Illinois, western Iowa, and especially southwestern Wisconsin (Grant, Iowa, and Lafayette counties), as well as in Michigan's Upper Peninsula, where iron was first produced from Lake Superior ore in 1846. Towns such as Galena, Illinois, Dubuque, Iowa, and Platteville, Mineral Point, and Shullsburg, Wisconsin, grew with the influx of British immigrants and the mining and smelting skills they brought with them. To this day, their descendants and culture figure prominently in those areas.

Cornish and Yorkshire miners entering the United States at mid-century were following in the footsteps of countrymen who had preceded them by a decade or more, shortly after the Winnebago Indians were brutally expelled to the West. Cornish tin miners were in the Galena lead district of Illinois as early as 1820, and a Cornishman was in Shullsburg in 1827. By the mid-1830s Cornish miners began arriving in significant numbers in what was still a wild frontier land. In effect, the early immigrants became a base for subsequent British immigrants, and by the 1840s extensive migration chains of people and information had been laid between Cornwall and Yorkshire on the one side of the ocean and the mineral region of the Upper Mississippi River Valley and Upper Michigan on the other.

But it was still a bridge that required courage to cross—and not just because of the daunting journey. The rough mining culture and the perceived threat of Indian attacks and wild animals could be shocking. It caused some miners' wives, like Mary Bennet, to plead to return to Britain.[6] Such concerns did not significantly stem the flow, however, and 13,114 British-born people were living in the Driftless Hill region by 1850, including an estimated seven thousand from Cornwall. By 1860 that number had more than doubled.[7]

In this wild and starkly beautiful part of America the Cornish were soon famous for discovering new mines, and especially for developing preexisting mines to their fullest potential. The Cornish knew how to mine deeper into the hard rock and follow the mineral veins. Many hit the jackpot by exploiting lead mines after their discoverers had hit solid rock and abandoned them for lack of expertise. People in southwestern Wisconsin assumed that when a Cornishman abandoned a mine there was no more lead to be had. Most of the Cornish were noticeably short in build because they had spent so much time bent over and toiling away in the cramped tunnels of a mine shaft.

Along with their skills, knowledge, and experience, the Cornish brought considerable technological improvements such as the safety fuse and new smelting devices like the Scotch hearth furnace. The first British miners in the region were especially important for bringing new industrial techniques of lead production. Among them were smelter Richard Wallers, who established the first blast furnace in the United States in Platteville, and John Watters, who built the first furnaces in Dubuque. It is no wonder that the Cornish filled more than their fair share of the leading positions in the expanding industry. Many of these newcomers later became prominent men, entered state legislatures and other political offices, and were remembered as the builders of their communities.[8] At the same time, Yorkshire Dalesmen also filtered into the region and made an impact. Most originated from the lead-mining areas of Swaledale and Arkengarthdale, although some had spent a year or more in the coal mines of Pottsville, Pennsylvania, before proceeding westward, an example of how the distinction between coal miners and ore miners was not always clear.[9]

The considerable magnitude of the migration of Britain's hard-rock miners to America was prompted by structural economic changes in Britain and sustained by the great rewards achievable in the Upper Mississippi River Valley and then vividly reported back in Britain. By the 1830s some of Britain's tin and lead mines were approaching exhaustion just as new mines were discovered in Spain. That caused lead prices to drop and rendered Britain's less productive mines unprofitable. Copper and tin mining did recover in Cornwall after the depression in the 1840s, and lead mining recovered somewhat in Yorkshire by 1850. But even in better times mining conditions were barely tolerable.[10] Declining wages, greater danger in ever deeper mines, and mine closures themselves convinced many Cornish and Yorkshire miners that only poverty or virtual poverty awaited them in their villages and that emigration now made more sense than ever. In some places the departure was dramatic. The population decline in St. Stephen, Cornwall, during the 1840s, for example, was attributed specifically to the stoppage of work at the local manganese mines and the departure of workers.[11]

Yet emigrant miners were not driven purely by economic despair, for they were delighted to find that one could become an entrepreneur in America with little or no capital. In America the cost of a mining lease was simply a percentage of the ore that was raised. Such wide opportunities for immediate independence and gain were powerful attractions and incentives that those in Britain could only dream of. Cornish immigrants often formed unrealistic expectations of getting rich quick and then returning to Cornwall. For many, such expectations were fuelled by a willingness and even determination to travel and see the world. As one Cornishman explained, "Wages, indeed, are only one consideration out of many; for we are a race of gypsies, and love . . . change and travel for themselves." The desire to "see the unknown places of the world" was a part of Cornish nature, which partly explains the fact that Cornwall had the highest net emigration rates of all counties in England and Wales in the last half of the century.[12] So strong was the tradition of Cornish migration to America that people in western Cornwall commonly referred to the United States as "the next parish."[13] For such people, the increasing hardships in Britain became the occasion to move and satisfy their wanderlust.[14]

Simple poverty and hardship do not in themselves explain the Dalesmen's migration, either. The quest for greater political equality moved some.[15] Edward Alderson, who left Arkengarthdale for Illinois in 1839 with a group of fellow miners, wrote back to his family in 1841 and revealed what may have been among the miners a commonly held reason for coming to America, one that was both economic and political in nature: "This is the country for a poor labouring man. A man can get a better living with working half the time than he can do in the old country with working all the time. He can get a parcel of land at the low rate of a dollar and a quarter per acre, then he can raise his own grain . . . and keep all kinds of stock, as many as he has a mind to. . . . The English men in general had rather work for themselves as they generally make more money and another thing they are their own Boss they can work when they please."[16]

Naturally, such glowing letters attracted more miners from the Dales. Indeed, Alderson's brother Jonathan was so impressed that he and his wife joined Edward in the next year. In 1843 Jonathan wrote to his sister his own account, which again reveals aspirations that went beyond mere economic gain: "Here we have no Crown, no Duty, no Bishops, yet I have not seen a begar running from door to door. . . . We sit in our humble little cot free of rent, we can turn on the perarie horses or cows free, and . . . have as much hay as we please. No gamekeepers. We work when we please and we play when we please. We have no stuarts [stewards] to boo [bow] to and no gentlemen. We are all as heigh and independent as another."[17]

As illustrated by the Alderson brothers and so many others, the extensive information network was widely used by immigrant miners from Britain. In his early study of the Cornish, based on interviews with the immigrants themselves, Louis Copeland found that "most . . . were induced to come by the glowing accounts of the mines that were sent home by some relatives or friends who had preceded them."[18] Chain migration involving detailed letters of information and assistance from relatives or former neighbors already in America was also a factor. Cases of miners following family members to America abound. Many left the same village or dale as a group, traveled together on the same ship, and shared the trek across America to the Upper Mississippi River Valley, where they settled as a transplanted community. Group migration of that nature lessened the feeling of insecurity and lowered the psychological threshold against emigration.

It is through such chain migration that a community of miners and farmers left the area of North Molton, Devonshire, and established itself at a place appropriately called Devonshire Hollow in Lafayette County, Wisconsin, during the mid-century period.[19] For this community, migrating from British mines to American ones was hardly a leap into the unknown. Many had prearranged employment and accommodation through former neighbors or family members who had preceded them and had enjoyed the support that came with group migration. The encouragement and reality of opportunity could hardly have been more tangible. The need for skilled miners in the Wisconsin lead region was widely advertised in Britain through various emigrant publications, letters, and newspapers, as was the fact that British immigrants tended to rise quickly to positions of authority within the American industry. With fresh opportunities in mining and farming in a region of America that already contained communities of British immigrants, and with mining opportunities declining for most hard-rock miners in Britain, the flow of miners continued to surge.

Social Life in America

Mid-century immigrants from Cornwall, the Yorkshire Dales, and other parts of Britain carried unique social and cultural traits that left a deep and lasting impression, wherever they settled in America. Unlike other miners in the Upper Mississippi River Valley, British hard-rock miners tended to bring along their families, and they did not always find it easy to fit in with the rougher, native-born mining population dominated by young single men. Jonathan Alderson warned his sister and brother-in-law that "the only fault" he could find with his new home in southwestern Wisconsin was "the wickedness of the people," their foul language, and his impression that "a man's life is no more valued than a dog. Every man carries his jackknife or pistols."[20]

When they first came to the Upper Mississippi area in the 1830s the miners found a rough and ugly place that was neither natural nor civilized. The hills had been stripped of trees and replaced with filthy piles of refuse, rocks, and garbage. Squatters seemed all too willing to protect their rights with guns or fists. Dilapidated log huts and shanties were scattered along the town site, and on Sundays worshippers in the new Methodist Episcopal Church in Mineral Point—organized by the Cornish in 1839 and made of logs until rebuilt by Cornish stonemasons—often found it hard to compete with the noisy din of drunken carousers in the adjacent tavern.

The Cornish loved their beer, too, but rarely did they get drunk and cause disturbances. Typically they would leave the mines at Saturday noon and gather to drink beer and smoke their pipes as they had done in their native land. The Cornish were remembered for being quiet, good-natured men and women who were deeply religious, peaceful, and law-abiding citizens who counteracted the lawlessness of these early times. They and other English miners and their families were thus an early source of domestic values and stability on the mining frontier, and they helped transform the rugged mining frontier into a more developed state. Not all were perfect citizens, of course. According to the records of the Primitive Methodist Church, some of the English newcomers were themselves "addicted to Sabbath-breaking, drunkenness, and gambling."[21] Overall, however, the British newcomers were a positive social transformational force. In mining towns such as Mineral Point, the Cornish in particular attempted to replicate as much as possible their old life and in doing so made lasting marks on the region's cultural fabric.

They brought a distinct dialect and words and pronunciations that persisted long after the heyday of mining. Like many Yorkshiremen, the Cornish had an unusual way of using the *h* at the beginning of certain words. They tended to drop it out and put it in where it did not "belong" for others. Cornish people would refer to their "'ome sweet 'ome," for example. Or, if asked to spell *saloon*, a Cornishman would reply: "With a hess, a hay, a hell, two hoes and a hen." Now, some descendants recall conversations with old-timers that would go something like the following: "I was a h'usher at a wedding, and at the reception I must 'ave 'ad 'alf dozen of them there 'ighballs."[22]

The idiosyncratic usage of *h* was combined with words carried over from the ancient Cornish language, which shares Celtic roots with Welsh and Breton. For the Cornish in southwestern Wisconsin, smoke was called "smeech"; chimney, "chimbley"; and houses, "houzen." Near was "nist," and lunch was "croust" or "a bit o' crib." Mine was "bal"; are not, "art en"; and yes was given as "iss" or "iss you."[23] That way of speaking lasted in parts of Wisconsin until as late as the 1940s, to the extent that American newcomers would remark that it was as if they had entered a foreign country. The Cornish were Old World people and still attached to folk tales and beliefs. Some still believed in pixies, fairies, and giants. Those who became lost were called "pisky laaden" (one who was led astray by pixies) and could find their way home only by wearing some clothing inside out. Such were the folk influences brought by the Cornish.[24]

More permanent were the buildings the Cornish erected that still grace the mining regions of the Upper Mississippi River Valley. Built out of local limestone and in the same style as houses in Cornwall, they stand as monuments to the deep impact of the Cornish and other English immigrants on the area. The Cornish also brought along certain foods, including clotted cream. The most familiar is the pasty—a potato, onion, and sometimes meat pie that was savored in the mines, perhaps after being heated in a shovel over a mining lamp. So popular were they that they are still proudly featured as a delicacy in the old mining towns of the Upper Mississippi River Valley, the Upper Peninsula of Michigan, and in Cornwall itself. Less popular to outsiders was stanning pie, baked with a whole mackerel or some other kind of fish, whose head pokes through the crust to give the pie an eerie, almost devilish, appearance.

Occupational Adaptation

The successful adjustment of Cornish and other British miners in America's lead region was made possible by their professional expertise. Perhaps equally as important was their remarkable occupational flexibility. Many if not most had some proficiency in both farming and mining and could successfully turn their hand to either occupation when they wanted or needed. No doubt a majority intended all along to become American farmers. The mining communities of the Yorkshire Dales developed out of villages originally devoted to arable farming, and for these miners turning to farming in America was a return to their roots.[25]

Some have claimed that Cornish immigrants never intended to become American farmers—that the decline of mining virtually forced them into farming and that the transition was made only with great reluctance and difficulty.[26] Undoubtedly that was true for some. But there are also many examples of Cornish and other English immigrants who combined mining and farming in Britain and eagerly established their own farms in America, including many Cornish who came to the lead region for the specific purpose of acquiring a farm.[27] In the Upper Mississippi River Valley they found an ideal place for settlement, one that was rich in minerals and rewards for their skills and had an abundance of cheap, fertile farmland that resembled parts of England.[28] There they could continue to combine occupations, if they chose, when lead prices were high and then gradually shift to farming as they accumulated sufficient capital. They knew the shift would inevitably occur as the region's mines reached exhaustion. Wisconsin's lead production peaked between 1845 and 1847, and by 1850 agriculture had replaced mining as the main occupation in the lead region. The transition was not a hard one for British immigrants, many of whom became successful and even prominent agriculturalists.[29] Miner-farmers such as Cornishman John Baker proved to be better farmers than their American neighbors who "bled the soil dry."[30]

The notion that the immigrants dreaded giving up mining for farming seems odd in retrospect. Few Cornish miners lived to the age of sixty. In Swaledale, where the average person who was not a miner lived past that age, lead miners and smelters lived, on average, fewer than forty-seven years.[31] Because mining in the Mississippi lead region was also hard and dangerous, it must have been a relief for immigrant miners to turn to a life of agriculture on their own land after a few years of mining to acquire the necessary capital. The difficulties and hardships that some encountered as farmers, especially during the hard times following the Panic of 1857, perhaps caused some to look back nostalgically on their more lucrative days as lead miners, but their striking capacity and willingness to change location and occupation demonstrated an ability to adjust to new situations in America.

The occupational changes the immigrants made during the course of their lives were often extensive and complex, but common patterns emerge from the many surviving family histories and indicate a remarkable resourcefulness and adaptability—and often an eagerness to set aside mining for farming. A good representative of the Cornish is William Peny, whose family had a long tradition in both mining and farming. In Cornwall, Peny himself was a miner and owned a small farm. He put his son to work on that farm, then to work in a quarry, and then at the age of sixteen in the mines with himself. But the elder Peny, dissatisfied with his life in Cornwall, sold out and emigrated to Jo Daviess County, Illinois, in 1849. His son joined him the next year, although three years later he went to the copper mines of Lake Superior, where he often worked a thousand feet below the surface. Four years after that he returned to Illinois to mine lead, and two years later he quit mining altogether and turned to farming. First he rented land and then in 1870 he purchased eighty-six unimproved acres, which he gradually developed and expanded.[32] Such a familiarity with both mining and farming allowed people like the Peny family plenty of scope for succeeding in American life.

Both the occupational and geographical mobility that the Cornish exercised in the United States during these years was often amazing. Judging from the surviving accounts of the miners in the lead region of the Upper Mississippi, it is clear that many were adventurous and rugged types who were hard to please and willing to take risks to become satisfied with life. They were not desperate victims of hardship in Britain. Many had mining experience in Scotland, South America, and Australia, and most had participated in the California gold rush or at least one mining trip to the Lake Superior region. Many also went to Montana, Nevada, Arizona, Colorado, other western states, and even Mexico. Some made regular visits to the West for thirty years after leaving Cornwall. Narrow escapes from Indians, Rocky Mountain blizzards, and other western perils were common experiences.[33] They were full participants in the saga of westward expansion. As carriers of the expertise that made the expansion of the mining industry possible, they contributed in no small way to the economic development of the West—or to the dispossession of Native Americans—as they moved time and time again across America.

The frequency with which the immigrant miners moved throughout the American west and Old Northwest was surprising, although a certain logic and purpose lay behind it. Many, like John Jackson, moved frequently because that was the best way to maximize the earnings with which to develop their farms. A miner by the time he was nine, Jackson emigrated at age twenty-five, two weeks after his marriage in 1847. First he mined iron in New Jersey for two years, then for three years he worked as foreman for a gold-mining company in Virginia, and then in 1852 he moved to Hazel Green, Wisconsin, where he purchased a small farm. But Jackson soon turned to mining there, too, until he left his family to work as a foreman for a New York company in the copper regions of Michigan. He next went to Virginia City, Nevada, via Panama, where he became a foreman in gold and silver mines and earned money that he invested into his expanding Wisconsin farm. In these ways Jackson juggled mining and farming in diverse parts of America for almost thirty years, and then at age fifty-four he devoted his full attention to the farm. There, he continued to pursue his hobby of collecting geological specimens, which he preserved "with great affection."[34]

For most immigrants, mining was not just a means of acquiring capital for farming. It was a convenient alternative to farm work when that option became desirable or necessary. As in Cornwall and Yorkshire, mining was the best way to earn money during the winter, when farming operations slowed. Thomas Reed, a Cornish farmer who was "ambitious to better his condition," emigrated directly to Jo Daviess County in 1851 and settled on a farm. Every winter he mined lead, "finding it very profitable," although he devoted summers to improving his farm.[35]

Just what kind of earnings English miners made in the lead mines of Wisconsin depended on luck, skill, and hours of work; the majority worked for themselves by paying 10 percent of their ore to the government for mineral rights. But what Ralph Ashworth earned was apparently not that extraordinary. After emigrating in the late 1840s to New Diggings in Lafayette County, he wrote to his wife in Lancashire to say proudly that he had made 25 shillings in seven hours of work, although he was averaging from 15 to 18 shillings per day above expenses. He was able to send his wife 50 sovereigns, with which she could join him after their long year of separation.[36] Earnings in that range more than compensated for the higher costs for American goods. Some miner-farmers even found it practical to stick to mining and pay others to clear their land. Cornishman Alexander Panluna mined for five years in Galena and then bought nearly 150 acres of virgin land. But he hired a man to do the back-breaking work of clearing it. Panluna continued to mine until 1881, when finally, at sixty-five, he abandoned mining for farming. In this case, mining was preferable to clearing land and a way for a man of limited means to acquire a large, improved farm.[37]

Of course, not everyone from Cornwall who was in American mines was preparing for farm life. Some mined with their eyes on entrepreneurship, as did Joseph Tangye, who grew up in Cambourne learning the blacksmith trade and then mined copper and tin until he emigrated in 1853 at the age of twenty. First he worked the copper and lead mines of Chestnut County, Pennsylvania, before proceeding to Shullsburg, where he mined for nine years. Then Tangye became a clerk, went to Scales Mound, Illinois, and established his own store, which became the largest in the town. Another Cornish immigrant, William Perry, mined for more than thirty years in Cornwall and Wisconsin before opening his own store. Such long-term adaptive patterns were common among the Cornish.[38]

British immigrants pursued other types of occupations in the Upper Mississippi Valley at mid-century. By 1845 the *Mineral Point Democrat* was reporting the area's dire scarcity of skilled mechanics, positions the British were especially able to fill. The English dominated the boot and shoe, blacksmithing, and carpentry trades in New Diggings and figured prominently in other trades in the region as well. Some of the Cornish in Iowa County were not miners but stonemasons, merchants, doctors, tin-dressers, and tailors.[39]

Not all British immigrants prospered as hard-rock miners in America. The surviving sources are clearly biased toward immigrants who were successful, those who adjusted to American life and stuck around to tell their tale. People who failed or became disenchanted with America either moved on or returned to Britain. The case of Cornishman Richard Wearne is a good reminder that some British miners failed miserably in the Upper Mississippi River Valley. Wearne appears to have been one from Cornwall who risked a decent life there for an even better one in America and lost the bet. Arriving in Milwaukee via Montreal in 1848, Wearne, his wife, and their eight children walked the entire distance to the lead region, living on the game they could kill. On their homestead in Peddlar's Creek (now Linden) in Iowa County, the family suffered the full rigors of pioneering life in squalid surroundings, and for years they regretted their hasty and ill-planned decision, apparently unable to reverse it. Wearne's agony is palpable in an entry he wrote in his diary a year and a half after the migration: "I . . . regret much for leaving so good and respectable a life at home for such a toilsome grievous life as this. Many comforts to be enjoyed at home not to be found here; foolish I was to leave my situation and give away my property for as little as nothing for such a place as this. But now it is too late."[40]

Unfortunately, there is no way to determine how many immigrant miners failed and eventually moved on, but certainly the mobility, eagerness, and success with which British miners pursued opportunities in new places in America predominated, as is most dramatically seen in their experience with the California gold rush.

The California Gold Rush

No group of people were struck harder by gold fever in 1849 than British immigrants. The California gold rush drew in people directly from Britain as soon as word of the discoveries crossed the Atlantic. As early as March 30, 1849, the *Lincoln, Rutland, and Stamford Mercury* reported sarcastically that "two or three wise people in Lincoln have sold off their goods for the purpose of going to the land of gold [California], to get rich, or to die a few years before in all probability they otherwise would do. No mania is too wild not to find followers. Hundreds of the California gold hunters will end their aspirations in becoming delicious morsels for the wild beasts, even if they should escape fever."

But the gold rush had its most powerful effect on those already mining lead in the Upper Mississippi River Valley or copper and iron near Lake Superior. British miners in the Susquehanna and Schuylkill coal valleys of Pennsylvania also joined the gold rush in droves. Those immigrants had recently made the arduous voyage across the Atlantic and traveled into the American interior, where they were cashing in on their experience. No strangers to uprootedness and the pursuit of brighter mining opportunities, they could see a trek to California as just another step in their migration. Thousands rushed westward when they heard what was possible in Eldorado.

The great intensity of the exodus of British miners from the Upper Mississippi River Valley to California is partly explained by the fact that most lead mines were becoming less productive. Some were nearing exhaustion. Thus the timing of the gold rush was perfect. Nearly half of some seven thousand from Cornwall in Wisconsin left for California. Of these, roughly half soon returned to Wisconsin, where most had left family members behind.[41] As one eyewitnesses in Iowa County recalled, gold fever had strange and devastating results:

> The effect was magical; the large floating population, attracted by the glittering ore forsook their lead diggings and disposed of all their available assets to defray the expenses of a trans-continental trip. A hegira of unparalleled proportions set in, and all business was paralyzed. . . . Every branch of trade was prostrated, and the mechanic and merchant, the miner and smelter, suffered alike in the general ruin. The fever of emigration . . . developed into an irreversible contagion. Panic-stricken, all classes fled toward the West, deluded by the mirage of wealth that beckoned them on the golden fields.[42]

At the height of the exodus, sixty teams and two hundred people left Mineral Point in just one day. Platteville, with its large Cornish and Yorkshire population, was "largely depopulated" as merchants, craftsmen, even professional people, joined miners in the westward march. Land values plummeted all over the lead region as people sold their land for almost nothing to raise the means to get to the goldfields. As local economies collapsed, many merchants felt compelled to pull up stakes and follow the miners to California, further crippling the local economy.[43]

The gold rush sapped the vitality of the area to such an extent that the Primitive Methodist Church, to which most immigrant miners from Britain belonged, feared that the departure of so many would devastate the institution because the future livelihood of the region seemed to be in doubt. It was perhaps in an effort to stem the tide that the church called attention to those Forty-Niners who had met failure or something even worse: "Many have died in California, or on the journey thither; and several have returned thence quite debilitated. A few have returned with a considerable amount of the precious metal; but it has unsettled them, and they are far from being happy."[44]

For those who stayed behind, the gold rush was not necessarily an unmitigated disaster. Some actually benefited from the exodus. Because so many had abandoned the lead mines for California, lead production fell, the price of lead ore soared to three times its previous level, and enterprising men with skill and knowledge were in a good position to cash in. Edward Weatherby, a Northumberland miner who emigrated to Shullsburg in 1846, eyed nearby lead mines that had been abandoned due to flooding and the gold rush exodus. He quickly leased them out, reopened them with specialized draining and pumping tech-

niques that he apparently had learned in England, and made a killing with the
high lead prices. Weatherby then discovered some of the richest lead deposits in
the county, and the resultant economic spurt helped to revive the town's
growth.[45]

Although the gold rush was temporary, the mining industry of the Upper
Mississippi River Valley never fully recovered. Ore supplies were declining there,
and agriculture was replacing mining as the dominant part of the economy.
Accordingly, the gold rush marks the time when the bulk of British immigrants
to Wisconsin, Illinois, and Iowa changed from being miners to being farmers,
although many would continue to do both when it suited them.

Whether they left from the Upper Mississippi region, the copper and iron
regions of Lake Superior, the coalfields of Pennsylvania, or some other part of
the United States, British immigrants who trekked to California were a varied
lot and did not necessarily have mining experience. British farmers in America
were not immune to gold fever. Nor were their wives. James and Mary Fisher were
tenant farmers who left Monmouthshire in 1849 and rented a farm near Cincinnati until they heard about the gold discoveries and headed west with four
young men. Their chosen route was supposed to make their trip easier, but instead it nearly killed them. Sailing down the Mississippi to New Orleans, they
proceeded to Panama, by which time their party had increased to eighty persons.
After crossing Panama, they boarded a Spanish vessel that they knew had been
condemned as unsafe and that sprung a leak after twenty-one days at sea. They
limped into a Mexican port, where they were stranded for three weeks without
one member of the party being able to speak Spanish. Finally, after six long
months of grueling hardship, the party reached San Francisco. In the end, the
Fishers ran a boardinghouse, which paid off handsomely, rather than mined.
With their savings they returned to England in 1854, only to emigrate again three
years later, this time accompanied by two brothers, to take up farming in Wisconsin.[46] Participating in the gold rush in order to raise capital for land purchases
or, in the case of immigrants such as John Sardeson, a Lincolnshire miller, to
purchase a mill, was common at mid-century.[47]

The saga of William Monies provides an idea of what some British Forty-
Niners went through and the strength of their characters. Monies was a Scot who
seems to have been chasing adventure as much as profit in his many moves in
the United States. A young baker from Ayrshire, he emigrated in 1849 to fulfill
"his ambition and inherent love for a wider sphere of action." He settled in
Carbondale, Pennsylvania, where he earned $6 per week for an established baker.
Within only six months he had his own bakery, but then he heard about
California's gold and, with his "natural love for adventure," organized an expe-

dition. By the time they set out, the original band of eighteen men had dwindled to only five for lack of courage. Yet with his "indomitable pluck and heroism" William Monies left his wife and led his men west as the "entire population of Carbondale turned out to wish them Godspeed on their dangerous and supposedly foolhardy journey."

With twelve oxen and two wagons the party trekked for more than five months and had more than its fill of adventure and narrow escapes from death. Three hundred miles short of California they ran out of provisions and nearly starved. During his first year in California, where the gold in circulation grossly inflated prices and wages, Monies chose to work for a baker for $5 a day, after which he panned for gold. Then he invested his earnings in the construction of flumes and dams but lost everything when a flood swept away the entire project. He returned to Carbondale to see his wife once again, resumed baking, and then made another, more profitable, trip to California, working again as a baker and saving enough money to open his own baking and milling business back in Pennsylvania. Later he visited Scotland several times. During the Civil War he even raised his own company of soldiers and was elected colonel of a regiment soon known as "Monies' Tigers." The extraordinary drive and leadership abilities of Colonel Monies, and no doubt his colorful war record, got him elected mayor of Scranton in 1869.[48]

The story of the Jewell brothers illustrates how mobile and assertive Cornish miners could be. After immigrating and mining in Illinois in the 1840s, William Jewell and his four brothers went to California in 1850. They woke up one morning in the Black Hills to find themselves surrounded by Indians but managed to scare them away by convincing them that they were afflicted with smallpox. After a six-month journey, they mined near Sacramento, but because their expectations had not been met they moved further south, where they did much better and continued to do even better still, repeating this process half a dozen times. This continued mobility in the West paid off, as William Jewell often carried with him several thousand dollars in cash and speculated in livestock in California. In 1854 he returned to Illinois with his savings and eventually became extremely successful in real estate and money lending. He also introduced new breeds of cattle and sheep to Jo Daviess County. But Jewell never lost his wanderlust. He visited England four times (once to find a wife), returned to California via Nicaragua, and frequently traveled to Nebraska and Iowa, where he had purchased large farms that he rented out. To Cornish miners like Jewell, the opportunities that America offered must have seemed virtually unlimited.[49]

Many of the Cornish who had originally come to the lead mines of southwestern Wisconsin found Michigan's copper mines almost as attractive as

California's goldfields. Flattering reports of mining in the Lake Superior region pulled so many of Platteville's miners to Michigan in 1846 that the town's mining and business activities suffered a severe slump in much the same way as during the California gold rush a few years later, although not to that extent.[50] Again, the Cornish were willing to move repeatedly and temporarily take up the most lucrative work they could find, often leaving family behind in the Upper Mississippi lead region for months or even years. Examples abound. Many made several trips to Michigan, to lead mines in Missouri and elsewhere, or to the far west. But most returned to take up farming when they had the cash they needed.[51] There were incentives, however, for Cornish miners to remain in the Lake Superior mining region. They were mine captains, shift bosses, and leading engineers, and they taught other miners how to dig for ore. Even into the twentieth century they were in charge of the underground work there.[52]

Coal Miners

In many ways British coal miners and hard-rock miners in America shared the same story. In fact, their stories converge: Coal miners routinely moved between America's coalfields and the mineral mines of Michigan and Wisconsin in search of the highest wages, and Cornish tin and copper miners spent time in American coal mines. Such occupational flexibility entailed geographic mobility. As with hard-rock miners from Cornwall, Yorkshire, and other places, immigrant coal miners did not seem to hesitate to move once they had arrived in America. No doubt most made at least one additional move to more promising places, which at mid-century usually included California. Many of the numerous Scottish coal miners who came to Pittston in Luzerne County, Pennsylvania, to mine, for example, had come via the California goldfields.[53] The mobility of James Jones, an immigrant miner from Gloucestershire in 1845, was not that extraordinary. Emigrating ahead of the rest of this family at only age fourteen, Jones mined coal near Pittsburgh until the rest of the family followed. Then he mined in several parts of Illinois before returning to Pittsburgh; after that he mined coal in Pottsville and other parts of Pennsylvania, Maryland, Virginia, Kentucky, and California (where he discovered several silver mines) before returning to Illinois.[54]

As Jones's story also illustrates, British coal miners who moved to the coalfields of Pennsylvania, Illinois, and other states during this time were similar to hard-rock miners in that they, too, relied on networks or chains of information that had been established by earlier British immigrants. As early as the summer of 1830, twenty Welsh families arrived in Carbondale, Pennsylvania. They were among the seventy Welsh miners recruited by the Delaware and

Hudson Railroad to bring advanced mining methods to the area and who established a Welsh community that attracted many others from their country. The numbers of Welsh and other British immigrants in the region increased so dramatically over the next fifteen years that by the mid-1840s British coal miners were routinely leaving Britain and coming to American coalfields to live among relatives, former countrymen, and old acquaintances.[55] Being able to go to familiar people and communities encouraged emigration by rendering it a more immediate option that had less anxiety attached to it. In effect, the existing British communities in the United States lowered the threshold of emigration.

Like the British immigrants who mined lead and copper in America, those who mined coal quickly rose to prominent positions. Priscilla Long has observed that "in the pre–Civil War days, every mine boss in the anthracite region was English, Welsh, or Scottish."[56] The British proved to be the essential element of coal mine exploration and development in much of the United States. A classic example is James Whittaker, an experienced miner who left Lancashire in 1850 at age twenty-three and after a few years of work in Pennsylvania came to Tazewell County, Illinois. His experience and instinct told him that coal was underneath the soil of Tazewell County, and although others scoffed at him he searched for the deposits he knew to be there. When he found one of the richest coal mines in the state Whittaker became a wealthy man.[57]

About the same time Whittaker found his mine, William Goalby arrived in Illinois and opened a mine near Belleville. He also sank the first shafts of many other mines in various parts of the state. After a five-year adventure in Nevada, Goalby returned to Illinois to open still more mines and become one of the wealthiest coal dealers in the state.[58] Other English immigrants made similar contributions to the coal industry in Illinois. Joseph Collier, a Somersetshire miner, had performed some of the "finest and most scientific work" in English and Welsh mines before emigrating around 1848, and William Howe, another miner from Somerset, had gained much expertise in South Wales.[59]

In the adjacent state of Indiana, British immigrants also proved to be catalysts for the emerging coal industry. Among them were Richard Freeman, the "father of the coal industry in Knox County," and his brother Job, who was credited with making Linton in Greene County known as "the Pittsburgh of the West." The sons of a Staffordshire miner, the Freemans emigrated in 1850, started out as miners themselves, opened coal mines in Indiana, became mine owners and operators, and by the turn of the century were among the state's leading coal magnates.[60] The importance of British coal miners to Pennsylvania's development was even more profound and can be seen in the fact that such places as Jermyn Borough were named after prominent British coal discoverers and operators.[61]

British immigrants did not necessarily have to be miners to contribute to America's coal-mining industry, however. Machinist and inventor Andrew Nicol, who migrated from Ayrshire to Pennsylvania in 1851 without prearranging his employment, was hired as a mine superintendent on the day of his arrival in Carbondale. After inventing several devices and machines for increasing production and extracting water and waste, Nichol was appointed by the governor of Pennsylvania to be the mine inspector of the eastern part of the state.[62]

Finally, a small percentage of English and Scottish immigrants were quarrymen, as were larger proportions of the Welsh (chapter 6). Most quarrymen were taking advantage of opportunities in America rather than escaping hardship in Britain. In 1850, for example, an English immigrant in Connecticut was sent back to England by the company that employed him to recruit 150 quarrymen, some of whom were given free passages, to work for that company.[63] Some of these and other quarrymen who came to New York state did very well in the trade and, like the lead and coal miners, rose to high positions and became owners of their own quarries. Also like miners, quarrymen showed a keen interest in securing farmland.[64]

One obvious and powerful incentive for British miners and quarrymen to switch to farming was the inherent danger of working in mines, which took a frightening toll. After only six months in the United States, Aaron Heaton was crushed in a cave-in while tunneling in the mines of Somerset County, Pennsylvania. William Woolcock, a Cornishman who arrived in 1845, managed to work for twenty years in Schuylkill County before a mine explosion took his life.[65]

British immigrants took such risks for granted for they were hardly immune from them in Britain, where many mines went to dangerous depths. What they did not likely anticipate, however, were the type of dangers unique to the rougher and sometimes lawless American mining towns. Joseph Graham, who left Glasgow in 1851 to mine coal in Madison County, Illinois, lasted only four years before he was shot to death by another miner.[66] Not that all British newcomers to the American mines were mild-mannered pacifists. In Mineral Point, the Welsh introduced a form of duelling that involved throwing stones until one combatant was knocked unconscious or killed.[67] It may have been a less deadly way to settle disputes than using pistols or bowie knives, but the image that comes to mind is still a grotesque one that counterbalances the sanitized depictions of the immigrants that prevail in many sources.

The land appears rich and fruitful and I am happy to say that I feel quite at home. I would not for a considerable sum return to Wales again.
—Richard and Margaret Pugh to the Rev. E. Jones, Nov. 15, 1846

The Welsh

The American coal industry owes a lot to the modest numbers of Welsh immigrants who settled in the United States during the nineteenth century. More than any other group, they unlocked America's vast coal reserves with the advanced skills and methods that they had acquired in the mother country. The Welsh were also important for the development of related industries, especially iron. In both the coal and iron industries the Welsh prospered and rose to become mine bosses, operators, and owners. But like the hard-rock miners discussed in the previous chapter, Welsh industrial workers were also greatly interested in American land. Many had been born on farms and had entered industry to make ends meet but always intended to return to the land, in America if not Wales. In America they could combine farming with mining or iron-making if that suited them. Both were often convenient ways in which to earn money to purchase land. For many Welsh migrants, mining and farming were complementary forms of work.

The parts of the Old Northwest that the Welsh most favored in 1850 were counties in Ohio and Wisconsin and a few in Illinois and Indiana (fig. 5). There,

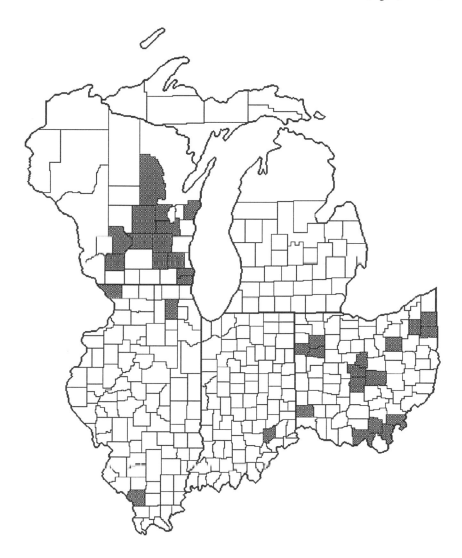

Figure 5. Welsh natives above Old Northwest average of 5 percent, 1850. (Gregory S. Rose, "Indiana's Ethnicity in the Context of Ethnicity in the Old Northwest in 1850")

opportunities in both farming and mining or iron production were richest and immigrants could do both if they wanted. The high concentrations of Welsh immigrants in Jackson and Gallia counties in southeastern Ohio came primarily from Cardiganshire, beginning in the 1830s. Their great numbers and success were based on chain migration and the fact that by the 1850s they could pursue both agricultural and industrial work—generally, charcoal iron production, for which the region was particularly well suited—and could move "freely between the two."[1]

In this region of good water routes, fertile land, and rich iron ore deposits, the Welsh found that farming and iron production could go hand in hand because the markets for iron, farm produce, and labor were efficiently integrated. As devout Calvinist Methodists, they were very much guided by their faith. Part of the reason that many had left Wales for America was because of the perceived ungodliness with which rampant commercialism and industrialism were threatening their values in Britain. In America, religion was so central to their lives that it even determined the nature and operation of their iron industry, primarily in the form of adopting low-risk, conservative business strategies that rejected borrowing money and debt and were aimed at building a moral economy that would be pleasing to God. Their skills and strategies worked, for the Welsh came to own more wealth than any other group in the area. But gradually they left iron work for farming or some other occupation because of the dangers and unpleasant working conditions inherent in the industry. Generally, the Welsh in southeastern Ohio were highly successful not only in raising living standards but also for preserving their culture in what became known as "little Cardiganshire."[2]

The Welsh tended to settle in ethnic communities—more so than the English or Scots although not as much as most other European immigrants.[3] They were also more determined than the English or Scots to preserve their old culture, especially their language and religious heritage. Because the religious dimension was especially important to Welsh migrants, it is not surprising that Welsh migration grew as the evangelical movement expanded in the nineteenth century. America offered opportunities to establish nonconformist churches, most commonly for Welsh Congregationalists and Calvinist Methodists. These religious incentives were for some perhaps as important as the more worldly ones of buying American farmland or working in American mines, industries, or crafts. Once in America, the Welsh immediately started religious institutions, including prayer meetings, Bible societies, and Sunday schools. They began church services in crude log shanties until a proper sanctuary could be built and thereby experienced a religious continuity that the English and Scots did not always have.[4] Although most could speak English, many chose to hold their services in Welsh and attempt to preserve the language beyond the first generation. The shift to English was inexorable, however. In fact, some showed a striking willingness to become Americanized, even to the extent of neglecting to teach the Welsh language to their American-born children.[5] Generally, they were more willing than the English to become American citizens because they were less likely to retain feelings of loyalty to the British crown.

Some fundamental knowledge about Welsh migration to the United States is still elusive.[6] The problem, due in large part to the notorious lack of adequate American and British statistics on the Welsh, has led to inconsistent interpretations of Welsh migration, especially on the extent to which the Welsh were agricultural or industrial in nature.[7] For example, whereas Maldwyn Jones asserted that "until the Civil War the exodus from Wales was overwhelmingly one of agriculturalists from the rural counties of the west and north," Alan Conway concluded that "from mid-century on, [the Welsh movement] was predominantly but not exclusively an industrial emigration, primarily from the iron and steel and coal mining regions of south Wales."[8] Even the size of the mid-century Welsh emigrant population, not to mention their demographic characteristics, remains a mystery.

Some potential to solve these questions lies in the passenger lists. In 1851 an estimated 3,250 Welsh arrived in the five major American ports.[9] Because the total Welsh population in 1851 was only about a million, these numbers are not quite as "negligible" as Brinley Thomas assumed, although it was surely not a mass movement on the Irish or German scale.[10] One of the reasons the Welsh never emigrated in the massive numbers that the Irish and Germans did was because growing industrial work in South Wales and England drew off prospective emigrants.[11] Although most of the Welsh traveled in family groups that included children, a large portion (more than a third) were adult males and females traveling alone. Adult males who traveled alone outnumbered those traveling with family members by well over two to one. In general, then, the Welsh movement was mostly a family or folk migration. Adult males were predominantly single individuals, a characteristic of labor migrations that has been observed for other immigrant groups of the late nineteenth century. Such characteristics are related to the migrants' occupations.[12]

During the 1840s, the occupational profile of Welsh immigrants changed dramatically. Nearly 40 percent were farmers in 1841, a proportion that had dropped to only 10 percent by 1851. Thus mid-century Welsh migration to America was certainly not an agricultural movement (table 5). Few were as reluctant to emigrate as Welsh farmers even though English farmers were emigrating in unprecedented numbers at the same time, mainly because of the repeal of the Corn Laws,

Table 5. Occupations of Welsh Population and Welsh Immigrant Males 20+ (1851)

Occupation	Ship Lists Number	Ship Lists Percent	1851 Census	Index of Representation[b]
Agriculture				
Farmers[a]	14	10.6	16.2%	65
Farm laborers	0	0.0	17.8	0
	14	10.6	34.0	31
Laborers (unskilled)	25	18.9	8.0	236
Servants, etc.	8	6.1	6.4	95
Preindustrial, crafts				
Building trades	5	3.8	6.4	59
Mining:				
Coalminers	(19)	14.4		
Miners[c]	(27)	20.5		
Quarrymen	(14)	10.6	2.2	(482)
Total Miners	60	45.5	15.5	294
Foods (bakers, etc.)	3	2.3	3.7	62
Metals (smiths, etc.)	6	4.6	3.2	144
Clothing workers	5	3.8	5.7	67
Miscellaneous	1	0.7	2.7	0
	80	60.7	37.2	163
Industrial				
Iron and engineering	3	2.3	4.7	49
Textiles/miscellaneous	1	0.7	2.8	0
	4	3.0	7.5	40
Tertiary (professions, commercial, clerical)	1	0.7	6.9	10
Totals	132[d]	100.0	100.0	

$N = 312,058$

Source: Census figures are for Wales and Monmouthshire. *Census of Great Britain* (1851), 2, div. 11, pp. 826–52.

a. Includes the working relatives of farmers who were described as farmers.

b. Computed by dividing immigrant percentage into census percentage and multiplying by 100.

c. Miners not otherwise designated.

d. Including males aged 15+ years, 146 employed males (an estimated 1,460) are in the 1851 sample. The data for males aged 20+ years are used because the 1851 census data are also for males aged 20+ years.

falling grain prices, and the inability of some to adjust to the new situation. Part of the difference is explained by the fact that the Welsh were more pastoral than the English and thus less affected by repeal, even though many Welsh farmers were poor and had much to gain by going to America. Those who did were relatively few in number—hardly the "constant stream" that David Williams describes.[13] Laborers, miners in particular, rather than farmers showed a widespread interest in emigration in 1851 and are therefore of special interest in this chapter.

The Migration of Welsh Miners

In 1851 alone, an estimated six hundred Welsh adult miners migrated to the United States. About a quarter were actually stone quarrymen, and nearly a third were described specifically as coal miners or "colliers."[14] The rest, described as "miners," were largely coal miners too, as suggested by the fact that they overwhelmingly chose Pennsylvania as their destination—more specifically, the Philadelphia region, Minersville, and other places in the Schuylkill and Susquehanna valleys.[15] This was the land of anthracite—America's equivalent to the South Wales coalfields—where Welsh colliers had been establishing communities since the 1830s.[16] Few went to the Lake Superior region, which was being reported in British newspapers as offering extensive employment in its copper, lead, and iron mines.[17] Nor were any recorded as going to find California's gold, although possibly some miners of unknown destinations were seeking quick fortunes in the West. Welsh migration to America in 1851 was dominated by a significant number of coal miners, and by comparing coal-mining conditions in South Wales and America, it becomes clear why they left in such proportions and why they chose the United States.

In spite of phenomenal mid-century growth and prosperity for the British coal industry generally, all was not well in the collieries of South Wales.[18] The root of the problem was the overdependence of the Welsh iron industry on rail production, which became painfully clear when the railway building boom collapsed in 1847. Welsh iron production fell sharply, and that lowered the demand and price for Welsh coal.[19] Coalmasters attempted to protect profits by regularly lowering wages, and miners responded with frequent strikes. Moreover, steam-coal prices fell even further between 1850 and 1852, which depressed wages by another 5 percent and made employment irregular and unstable.[20] Between 1850 and 1853, while most English and Scottish colliers were prospering, many Welsh colliers were suffering lower earnings. An "atmosphere of antagonism" prevailed as they clashed with coalmasters in attempts at self-protection.[21] Not until 1854 did the Crimean War create new demands for coal and iron, which revitalized the industries of South Wales much as the war also caused Britain's grain prices to rebound.[22]

Thus Welsh emigrant coal miners were leaving behind worsening conditions in the South Wales coalfields. That such conditions were directly responsible for increased emigration is clearly evident in the 1851 census; the net decline in the population of Llangendeirne, near Carmarthen (fig. 6), between 1841 and 1851 was attributed specifically to stoppages in the collieries and the subsequent emigration of its miners to the United States.[23] In addition, one newspaper reported

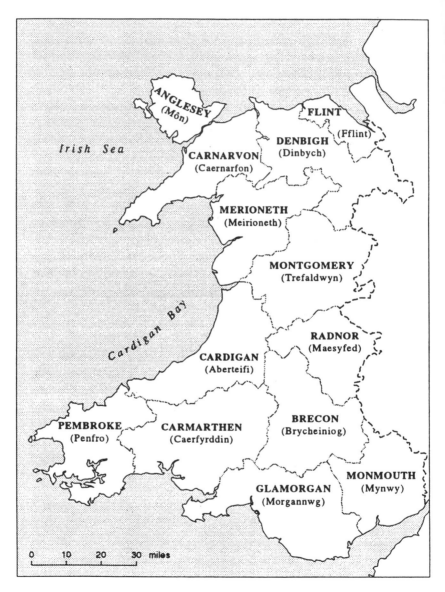

Figure 6. Counties of Wales. (Anne Kelly Knowles, *Calvinists Incorporated*, 3)

in May 1851 that a "large number" of workmen "connected with the . . . mining districts of Rhymny, Blaenavon, and Blaina" were leaving for the United States.[24] These, too, were no doubt responding to deteriorating conditions in Wales, because strikes, declining wages, and unsteady working hours prevailed there at the time. It would be surprising if many prosperous Welsh miners were among the emigrants, given the grim conditions of the Pennsylvania collieries to which most of the miners were apparently going.

Throughout the late 1840s and early 1850s, Pennsylvania's coal industry was faring badly. Local newspapers talked of the "great depression" in the coal trade and the same kinds of conflicts over wages and conditions that were plaguing the Welsh industry.[25] Americans had much to complain about. They blamed cheap British iron imports for the low prices and wages within the coal and iron industries, and coal prices fell dramatically again in 1851 as certain mining and carrying companies attempted to dominate the Schuylkill markets.[26] Work was uncertain as many undercapitalized mines were closed and many mine operators insisted on paying workers with goods instead of money, which caused much discontent and some strikes.[27] The miners' living standards were deteriorating: Housing was miserably inadequate, and drunkenness and violence were increasingly serious social problems.[28] Even the weather added to the depression as storms and floods shut down a number of collieries in 1850 and 1851.[29]

It appears, then, that Welsh emigrants were leaving one depressed mining industry for another. Such a move may seem desperate. With careful planning through letters to and from other Welsh miners already in America, however, newcomers could prearrange employment and housing and thereby overcome the main obstacles presented by a generally depressed industry. Such a network was established in Carbondale, Pennsylvania, as early as 1830, when twenty Welsh families arrived to mine coal.[30]

Welsh miners commonly used such a network of information that stretched across the Atlantic from Welsh mines and communities to American mines and Welsh farming communities in Pennsylvania, Illinois, Wisconsin, and other states. During this time a traveler in Wales observed that every one of the many miners whom he had met had a "father, brother, son, uncle, nephew, cousin, or friend in America and had been cogitating about going himself."[31] When the Welsh provided details of their migration in letters or family histories, they usually mentioned that they first went to friends and family members already in America for their first accommodation and job opportunities. Typical was Walter Treasure, a coal miner "ambitious to do more for himself and acquire a competency." In 1852 he left Wales to join his two sisters, who had already moved to Pottsville. He worked in the mines there for a few years and then moved on to other places to build his own mining business.[32] Opportunities for Welsh miners were available in Pennsylvania, they were just harder to find and generally less attractive during depressed times.

Just how attractive Pennsylvania's mines still were to the Welsh is hard to estimate. Most important for the migrants were the higher American wages, and yet the Welsh and other British miners in America often complained bitterly about the high costs of living, long hours, and irregular workdays.[33] Apparently, these disappointed miners did not get accurate information about the reality of American mining conditions. Likewise, data on comparative wages for colliers is fragmentary and uncertain, in part because in both countries miners were paid on a piece-rate basis. The data that do exist, however, support the idea that the bulk of emigrant Welsh miners suffered depressed conditions in Wales and likely lacked steady employment. Those who were fully employed would have had no immediate economic incentive to migrate to American mines. C. K. Yearley has estimated that by mid-century the average skilled miner in Schuylkill County earned roughly $20 per month, and rising charges for kerosene, rents, and powder cut these earnings considerably.[34] At the same time, regularly employed miners in Swansea were earning up to 20 shillings per week (£4 per month), equivalent to about $20 per month, roughly the same as the Schuylkill County average.[35]

If migrant Welsh miners lacked steady employment, they at least had the advantage of being mobile. Nearly two-thirds traveled alone even though, as some of the highest-paid manual workers in Britain, they were among the most able to afford multiple passage tickets. Furthermore, a comparatively high proportion were older men who no doubt had substantial savings from younger, more remunerative days.[36] Single men, because of their mobility, first dominated the movement into the Welsh coalfields; although many married and raised families, a large proportion of the miners in mid-century Wales were still single.[37] These single, mobile miners formed a "migrating tide of colliers in pursuit of higher wages."[38] Their lack of deep Welsh roots, with their mobility and relatively high wages, made migration to America less painful and complicated than for the more encumbered groups. Single men were the most able and perhaps most likely to move in search of higher wages. They could take greater risks, knowing that a return to Wales was always possible should the American dream prove elusive. Welsh colliers departing for America, then, were neither desperately poor victims of change nor strangers to migration. They were autonomous individuals who saw the problems in the industries of South Wales as a signal to pick up and seek new opportunities abroad.

For a sizable majority of Welsh migrant miners, new opportunities abroad ultimately meant buying American farmland. Although it is impossible to know what percentage of them intended to farm in America, it was surely significant, especially in light of the fact that many were originally farmers or farm laborers who had turned to mining in South Wales only as a means to get to America and buy land. In the words of Alan Conway, South Wales was but a "knight's move" for some whose ultimate goal was to own an American farm.[39]

When troubles in Welsh collieries intensified at mid-century, many chose that time to emigrate. In addition, some miners apparently without agricultural backgrounds aspired to farm their own land in America, and many first worked in American mines and quarries to earn the necessary capital more quickly.[40] That was only logical, because their decision to emigrate had already been made. Those who would find American farming less rewarding than expected knew they could always return to the mines or quarries, whether in the United States or Wales.[41] Thus for those intending ultimately to farm in America the worsening conditions of working in Welsh mines or quarries were not so much the cause of emigration as the occasion for it.

The appeal of American farming for some Welsh miners was almost magical, especially when transmitted through personal letters from friends and family already in America. Soon after Thomas Roberts left Carnarvonshire in 1844 and came to Columbia County, Wisconsin, to combine farming with his ministry in the Calvinist Methodist Church, he wrote to friends in Wales and vividly described the fine quality and easy availability of local farmland. Roberts's letters were excitedly read in Welsh mines and "created quite a furor" that resulted in the emigration of "a great many" miners and their families directly to Wisconsin, where they went to farming.[42] Further east in Waukesha County, encouraging letters were also flowing from a Welsh community back to Wales and stirring many more to migrate. In 1842 Cardiganshire was swept by "Prairieville propaganda" consisting of glowing immigrant letters that were published in Welsh newspapers and magazines, all of which prompted more people to come to America to farm. Some newcomers trusted their predecessors so much as to have them select farms for them before they arrived.[43]

Most Welsh miners in search of land first worked as miners in America because doing so was the most effective way to earn capital. Of those who came to mine in Pennsylvania and other coal-producing states and appear in the county histories, more than half became farmers eventually. Miners such as Lewis Herbert, who left Wales for Indiana in 1857, benefited from the occupational mobility that their skills and experience afforded. After only two years of mining in America, Herbert rose to mine superintendent and eight years later bought the farm he had always dreamed about, although continuing to deal in coal on the side.[44] Such openings clearly help explain the keen interest in emigration to the United States during this period.

Welsh immigrants who stayed in mining often capitalized on their experience and intimate knowledge of the industry, for the Welsh were the most able to move up the ranks of foreman, superintendent or operator, and mine owner. Contemporary observers and later historians were quick to notice the occupational mobility of the Welsh, and examples abound.[45] Although the great majority would first work as miners and then move up to positions of increasing power and responsibility, it was also possible to use migration as a step toward immediate promotion. Twenty-nine-year-old John Reese, for example, moved from being a miner to a mine superintendent after he left Monmouthshire for Schuylkill County in 1845.[46]

Because the American mining industry was, in comparison with Britain's, still in its infancy, Welsh immigrants were sometimes required to locate America's ores and open mines for development. John Lewis settled in Trumbull County, Ohio, where he recognized a kind of blackband ore that he had mined in his native Monmouthshire before emigrating in 1854. The discovery led to his rapid rise within a mill that was established by a Staffordshire immigrant and that used the blackstone ore.[47] Understandably, the Welsh (as well as the English and Scottish) immigrants and their sons benefited from such reputations over much of America's mining history.

Not all Welsh immigrants, however, pleased their American bosses. One mine owner complained that they were "a little tricky, [apt] to lie . . . as it suited their purposes" and described them as "bearing malice."[48] The sheer audacity on the part of some to organize and, if need be, strike to defend their rights and compensation made many American employers wary of them. Welsh miners also loved their beer, and according to some observers they "drank like water" to get "as drunk as tinkers" and "swear and curse worse than the demons of the bottomless pit."[49] The habit contributed to their reputation for being a formidable presence in the growing American labor force.

The Welsh had a particularly strong impact upon labor and industry in Scranton, Pennsylvania, where they found both a landscape and mode of work that were very familiar. It was there, in a region that combined anthracite and iron to produce rails, that the United States challenged British industry and, with the help of Welsh immigrants, eventually won. The Welsh were instrumental in making Scranton the anthracite capital of the world and came to enjoy a near monopoly of the position of innovation and authority. They were slow to strike for better conditions. When they did, they had the support of Scripture-quoting ministers and frenzied wives quite prepared to attack strike-breakers. The "Welsh Strike" of 1871 showed the extraordinary solidarity of the community, although after five months the strikers were forced to submit to the economic forces of low prices and industrial depression.[50]

Welsh Quarrymen

Welsh quarrymen were also significantly overrepresented as migrants at mid-century, and their story was more than a simple one of escaping distress, although that also happened (table 5). At some time between 1841 and 1851, according to the census notes, the closure of limestone quarries near Tenby in Pembrokeshire caused so much emigration to America that local populations declined.[51] Others, however, emigrated without fear of unemployment. In June 1851 it was reported that "large numbers" of the "best and most experienced" workers in the slate quarries of North Wales were preparing to leave for the United States. Many had already left, not because of a lack of work, as in the case of the Tenby quarrymen, but because of the "heavy amount of local taxation and smallness of remuneration of labour."[52] High taxation may have been more imaginary than real, but not so the relatively low wages. These men were said to be aware that American quarries would offer three times their old wages. Further, there were encouraging examples of quarrymen who had emigrated deeply in debt but had returned to Wales with their high American earnings and were about to "discharge every claim that could be brought against them."[53]

The quarrymen seem to have been temporary migrants. Whether they had emigrated for only one season of work, as in the fashion of the "birds of passage," is unclear if not doubtful. Clearly, the majority were pursuing a greater reward for their work rather than work itself, because they were leaving steady work in order to treble their wages in America. They had the added advantage of mobility and were by far the youngest and most single of all Welsh migrants. More than half were under twenty-five, and for every quarryman who emigrated with family members, more than six went out alone.[54] These were people who were seizing opportunities. Because some likely had farming experience and intended to acquire a farm in America, it is not the case that they constituted a "distressed" migration.

Of six Welsh quarrymen found in the county histories, all became farmers eventually if not immediately. Some, such as John Owens, who left Carnarvonshire's slate quarries for Wisconsin in 1845 and apparently went directly into farming, probably had farming experience.[55] Like the emigrant coal miners, most seem first to have worked in American mines or quarries for several years and then turned to farming after saving enough money. William Owens, another

Carnarvonshire slate quarryman, came to Iowa County, Wisconsin, in 1847. First he mined lead, and then he combined farming with his ministry in the Methodist Episcopal Church in Dodgeville. Others worked as farm laborers, stonemasons, and at other occupations before entering American farm life.[56] Once again, the picture that emerges is one of determined and flexible people exercising options in order to seize opportunities. In both Wales and America, many migrants alternated mining or quarrying with farming when it suited their plans.

Welsh Laborers

Less can be said about Welsh laborers, who were also overrepresented as migrants at mid-century. Their relatively large numbers suggest that some were actually agricultural laborers.[57] Unfortunately, it is impossible to determine what proportion had agricultural experiences and intentions. But if American agriculture appealed to miners and quarrymen, then it no doubt appealed as well to agricultural laborers, who could accumulate the necessary capital more quickly by emigrating and hiring themselves out as workers in America.

Many laborers were bound for Pennsylvania's anthracite region (table B12, Appendix B). These may have been surface laborers from Welsh collieries who intended to work as laborers or even hewers in American mines. Yet more than half of the Welsh emigrant laborers who provided a more precise origin on passenger lists came from North Wales, where they more likely had experience in quarrying or farming.[58] In either case, they would benefit from relatively high American wages. Welsh-American wage differentials were greater for unskilled laborers than for miners in 1851, and employment in America was easier to come by for laborers than for most skilled workers.[59] Welsh laborers could also expect more immediate social gains in America by eventually learning and practicing a trade, or perhaps farming. They stood to gain much by trying their luck in America.

Welsh Ironworkers

Welsh ironworkers were comparatively rare migrants in 1851 (table 5). That is curious, because the collapse of the South Wales iron rail industry in the late 1840s and its depressing effect on collieries seem to have been a major cause for the high proportions of emigrant miners in 1851.

According to Welsh newspapers and the 1851 census notes, many ironworkers migrated to the United States because of the collapse of the railway building boom in 1847, but only in the late 1840s, not in the early 1850s. By 1848 "gloom and heaviness" prevailed as the Pontypool Iron Works slashed wages by fully 25 percent, apparently without resistance.[60] Some puddlers resisted wage cuts at Merthyr and Blaenavon, but they had little leverage. In late January 1848, workers in Merthyr were "daily being thrown out of work from the ironworks"; by July, five of Blaenavon's furnaces were shut down and five thousand men were cut from the payrolls.[61] Dowlais's ironworks were nearly completely shut down in late February, when fifteen of its furnaces were stopped. Those companies that did remain open paid lower wages.[62]

There is no doubt that in the late 1840s many of these distressed ironworkers emigrated to the United States. In 1848 the *Carmarthen Journal* reported "vast numbers" leaving Merthyr, Blaenavon, and Pontypool for America, and the *Monmouthshire Merlin* announced that in Pontypool "emigration appears to be the order of the day," particularly among the "operative classes." Echoing the newspapers, the 1851 census noted that emigration of ironworkers to the United States, induced by "the dullness in the iron trade," was so extensive that it had caused local populations in the Blaenavon area to decline from their 1841 levels.[63] The same explanation is given for the population decline of various parishes around Neath (near Cardiff), as well as that of parishes around Carmarthen.[64]

For two apparent reasons, the emigration of ironworkers fell off by 1851. The shock of the low demand for rails had already made most of its impact, and by late 1849 America had less to offer because its own iron industry was in the throes of a depression caused by the same collapse in railway building.[65] Not until 1852 did a second railway boom revive prosperity and fuller employment, which lasted until the Panic of 1857.[66] By 1851 the worst of the depression was over, and most emigrant ironworkers had already left.[67] Meanwhile, collieries were still adjusting to the lower demand for coal, and miners were leaving in far greater numbers.[68]

Welsh migration to the United States was substantial and primarily industrial by 1851, when coal miners dominated—if not as early as 1848, when ironworkers left in large numbers. Severe dislocations within South Wales's iron and coal industries were prompting many miners to turn to American mines for higher wages and steadier work, and depressed conditions in Pennsylvania kept their numbers from being even greater. Quarrymen and laborers figured prominently in the movement as well. That supports Alan Conway's version of Welsh emigration. Although some migrants were from agricultural backgrounds and responding ultimately to agricultural incentives, they considered themselves as industrial workers, especially miners. That was their most immediate background and their immediate future in America.

Yet these distinctions can be overdrawn. The distinction between industrial and agricultural people was not always clear and constant in the nineteenth century, and it can be artificial to insist on clear distinctions in modern historical accounts. For the mid-century Welsh, industrial workers were the main participants, but many had been farmers first and were moved ultimately by land incentives.

Welsh immigrants had advantages not only in skills and mobility but also in their ethnicity. They generally knew English and were spared much of the culture shock that hit other groups.[69] Of perhaps the greatest importance were the ties between the Welsh in America and those still in Wales. That network allowed people to find opportunities in America's troubled industries and also persuaded many Welsh industrial workers to choose America over a closer new home in England or Scotland.[70] Welsh communities in America could be less strange than industrial communities elsewhere in Britain and, for many immigrants, joining them was like coming home. They offered not only prearranged work and accommodation but also a society and environment that were less unfamiliar.[71]

"Merry England" has contributed in many ways to the growth and development of our country, in none, however, have her contributions been more valuable and considerable than in the domain of the learned professions. The Pulpit, the Bench, the Bar, the domain of medical Science, all branches of college instruction are deeply indebted to the Mother Country for brain, character and scholarship.
—County history, Hillsdale County, Michigan

7

The Elite: Merchants, Professionals, and Gentlemen

The view that British immigrants were generally of a high "quality" and composed of more professional and educated people than other groups was expressed by many American observers around the turn of the century.[1] Some of this talk was no doubt a xenophobic reaction against the "new immigrants" who were flooding in from southern and eastern Europe and Asia at the time. Such attributions, however, were not entirely fabricated. At mid-century, British tertiary workers (those in clerical, commercial, and professional occupations) participated in the migration to America in proportions roughly equal to those indicated for them in the general labor force by the 1851 census. An estimated four hundred clerks, seven hundred merchants, and four hundred professionals emigrated directly from Britain to the United States in 1851 alone. Perhaps ten to twenty thousand Britons from these backgrounds entered America during the mid-century period—a number unmatched by any other nationality.[2]

Such numbers are all the more impressive in light of the reality that the American demand for these workers was low at mid-century, a discouraging fact that was widely reported in Britain. Clerks were singled out in the emigrant press and newspapers for dire warnings about the low demand for their skills in both the United States and the colonies, and it seems doubtful that these literate people, if they had emigrated as thoughtfully as other British people did, were oblivious to such warnings. The writer of a popular emigrant guide cautioned readers that "clerks and shopmen, unless experienced bookkeepers, will not I believe, generally succeed," and a correspondent for *The Times*, who had just traveled throughout the United States, reported even more discouragingly that "a great many young men in the capacity of clerks [are] arriving. This is no place for them."[3] One English clerk in America complained as early as 1843 that "every one in America wishes to be clerks so that the country is over run with them." The problem seems to have persisted throughout the period. As Montreal's emigration agent said of clerks in 1860, "In spite of reiterated warnings . . . they throw themselves, inconsiderately, into a field already overstocked . . . they become idle and dissipated, till at length, compelled to succumb, they apply for assistance from their relatives at home to enable them to return."[4]

One might suspect that the emigrant clerks were acting out of desperation, but that was not necessarily the case. In the 1850s Britain's demand for clerks greatly exceeded the supply because of the burgeoning clerical work being created by the rise in foreign trade, the proliferation of the bureaucracy, and the growing economy. It was only in later decades that the demand was filled when the rise of literacy and numeracy and the introduction of women into the clerical workforce eventually produced a glut, resulting in tougher competition, lower wages, and lack of job security. As Gregory Anderson has concluded, "In the prosperous middle decades of the nineteenth century the socio-economic position of clerks was relatively secure . . . but by the 1870s their confidence and security were being seriously eroded."[5] It is not surprising that more clerks emigrated to the United States in the late 1880s.[6]

At mid-century, prospective emigrants in commerce and some of the professions faced the same limited opportunities that clerks did. It was well known that in Australia, professional men "who held responsible situations in England" were reduced to agricultural laborers, while gentlemen's sons were "driven to become bullock drivers."[7] In America, despite its greater economic development, the employment situation was nearly as bleak, at least according to the British vice-consul in New York, who in May 1851 answered questions from a parliamentary committee on whether the number of "unsuited immigrants" arriving from Britain was "considerable": "Yes, it is considerable; there are a great number who come out to seek mercantile employment, a great number of medical men, a great number of governesses and music mistresses, and other people who depend on their head more than on their hands; for people who depend on their arms there is no difficulty in obtaining employment; but for people who depend on their head there is very great difficulty indeed."[8]

Nevertheless, British clerks, merchants, and professionals were not deterred by such gloomy prospects, and large numbers successfully defied the official advice, beat the odds, and risked a competence in Britain for something better in the United States. James Vickredge, one of the few clerks whose letters have survived, emigrated in 1850 from a good job and salary because his position did not satisfy his social ambitions. As he explained, "I was successful as a clerk and had good positions and good salary but it did not satisfy my ambitions." Vickredge's boss raised his salary to keep him in his employment, but a year later he gave it up to join relatives in America.[9] Likewise, George Anderton left his occupation as a saddler in Lincolnshire because he did not like the work. After succeeding as a shipping clerk for the North Midland Railroad, he again decided to find something he wanted to do and so emigrated in 1853 to Illinois, where he became a merchant and then business manager for a large pork-packer. His ambition and clerking experience in England had prepared him well.[10]

The same was true of D. L. Edwards, from Aberystwyth, Wales, who was apprenticed in the "mercantile business" for three years and then worked as a clerk in London for five years before emigrating to New York City in 1847. Nine years later he moved to Milwaukee, where he became head clerk for a large firm and then in 1862 bought his own drygoods store that served the farming community of Genesee Depot. He was known as one whose experience as a British clerk enabled him to "buy judiciously." With a proper education and experience and the ability and willingness to adapt, British immigrants could win the stiff competition for clerkships in America.[11]

The incentive of land ownership certainly spurred some on. Yorkshireman John Schofield is a good example. Bound out as a farm laborer to a distant relative until the age of nineteen, Schofield became a weaver and then in his early twenties opened his own general store, which made him "very successful." "Although he was doing well," however, "[he] wanted to do better and decided to try his fortunes in the United States." With what must have been carefully laid, long-term plans, Schofield abandoned his successful mercantile career in 1848, migrated to Illinois, worked as a farm laborer for someone who had migrated from England before him, and then rented and later purchased eighty acres of land. By the late 1880s he owned a highly improved farm of 240 acres as well as a 160-acre farm in Kansas.[12]

These migrants were apparently adventurous types who were willing and able to defy the discouraging reports from America. Their demographic characteristics support that interpretation. The clerks were the most individual of all emigrants, even more than miners. They emigrated almost exclusively as unaccompanied individuals; for every clerk emigrating with a family member, nine emigrated alone. They were also characteristically young. More than half were under twenty-five, and another quarter were in their late twenties (table B12, Appendix B). It is not pure speculation, therefore, to say that the clerks emigrated in an adventurous spirit and gambled several months' wages on the chance to see the celebrated American continent and pursue greater rewards and achievements.

They were especially well suited to migrate in this fashion. As single, young men they were mobile, and as clerks they risked little because clerical labor was still in demand in Britain. They could always return, as indeed many reportedly did in 1860. What lured some to the New World was the hope that in the undeveloped American economy their literacy might open doors to other occupations if clerical work were unavailable or undesirable.[13]

In contrast to clerks were merchants and professionals. If clerks can be characterized as young, single men "seeking their fortunes," merchants and professionals were mature persons, well established in their careers and possessing the experience and incomes to make a calculated, well-planned migration and thereby overcome the dismal job market that was being reported at the time. Merchants were on average older than other immigrants and distinctly familial in nature (table B12, Appendix B). Only weavers, woodworkers, and farmers were more likely to travel in family groups, and both merchants and professionals were among the most likely to have dependent children. Altogether, they were of distinct maturity.

Such maturity among persons in commerce and the professions is not surprising, because more time was normally required to become a doctor, member of the clergy, lawyer, or merchant than to be a weaver or clerk, for example. Some money was necessary for even elementary training, and some time was normally required to become established in a profession. Because this was before the era of extensive mandatory training for "paper qualifications," the concentration of these migrants in their thirties and forties indicates that many were past the beginning stages of their careers and had acquired considerable experience.[14] Inexperienced teenagers are particularly rare in the professional group, and the presence of older men described as agents, brokers, and drapers, as well as doctors, lawyers, officers, writers, and surveyors, suggests that these were trained and experienced persons. Although these emigrants were not a "migratory elite" in the sense that they were carrying valuable paper qualifications, they do seem, as a group, to have been distinctly middle class in their education, background, and perhaps financial situation. In that sense, they might be considered an elite.[15]

This interpretation is supported by the fact that merchants, professionals, and clerks were the only ones who showed a common ability to purchase the more expensive steamship tickets and cabin accommodations. The extra expense for the added comfort and speed was considerable at mid-century. Cabin rates were roughly double the cost of steerage rates, and steamship tickets were still a luxury, although not quite to the same extent as cabin accommodation. Only a few clerks took a cabin, but more than 10 per cent of them still managed to arrive by steamship—a higher percentage than for any industrial group (table B13, Appendix B).

Emigrants in commerce were still more apt to spend more on their travel. Nearly 13 percent were berthed in cabins, and more than a third arrived by steamship at a time when the vast majority of the passengers landing in New York arrived on sailing ships. Such figures are even more impressive for those described specifically as merchants: Roughly 15 percent had cabin accommodation, and more than half had taken a steamship. As a group, these people were clearly of a higher economic class than the best-paid industrial workers and most of the farmers. They may have had more wealth than emigrants in the professions. Although members of the professional class were as likely to have paid cabin fares, they were less likely than those in commerce to purchase steamship tickets (table B13, Appendix B).[16] Altogether, they stand out for being able to afford the luxury of more expensive fares through the savings accumulated after years in commercial or professional work.

Accounts of the lives of a number of emigrant professionals afford a clearer picture of this "migratory elite." Of six doctors, all had considerable training and experience before their migration, although most were young. Dr. J. Steward was liberally educated in his native Scotland and was a successful physician in Edinburgh before emigrating in 1850 at age twenty-six to Ann Arbor, Michigan, where he became a "physician of note." Steward had no apparent problem in finding his niche, nor did George Richardson of Warwickshire, a young medical student who emigrated with his teacher, a Dr. Richings, and then, after finishing his studies at Rush Medical College in Chicago, became one of the most prominent physicians in Randolph County, Illinois.[17] Immigrants with these levels of training and experience were welcome additions to a medical profession that was in shambles in mid-century America and had "degenerated into little more than a trade." At a time when many if not most American doctors were semiliterate quacks, Britons with meaningful medical qualifications could make valuable contributions.[18]

Like other British immigrants, those in the medical profession included quite a few who seemed willing, even eager, to make changes in their occupation, including a desire to take up farming. William Addenbrooke had studied medicine at Birmingham Hospital and practiced medicine aboard packet boats and in seaport towns in England and America until 1852, when he bought a 120-acre farm in Wisconsin and became a grain dealer and finally a beekeeper. He even invented a method of wintering hives in packed chaff. Donald Robertson was another young physician who earned his medical diploma at the Edinburgh medical college in 1840 and, after traveling around the world, emigrated to Michigan in 1849. After two years of medical practice, he bought a 250-acre farm, erected a sawmill, and abandoned his practice altogether. Nearly identical is the story of Henry S. Cox, who studied medicine at Bath before emigrating to Michigan in 1848. He, too, bought a sawmill but after two years went to Ann Arbor "to freshen up his professional knowledge" and subsequently became a prominent physician and surgeon who served as a lieutenant in field hospitals during the Civil War.[19]

Immigrants such as these were from an elite or privileged background, at least when contrasted with those from agricultural and industrial backgrounds. A good example is David Davis from Wales, who was well educated before entering Bartholomew Medical College in London but left medicine because of his "aversion to the dissecting room." After securing a position in the Government Printing Office through his uncle, a member of Parliament, Davis took a three-month vacation in 1854 to visit a relative in New York, where "such inducements were offered him to remain in America" that he became an immigrant and prospered in publishing and merchandising in Milwaukee. Yet in 1863 he again took up medicine, attended Rush Medical College, became an M.D., and finally entered politics, where as a member of the Wisconsin Assembly he ironically wrote the bill that legalized dissection in his state.[20]

The few lawyers who emigrated from Britain at mid-century were also generally well educated and prosperous but wanted more in America. William J. Petherick, a forty-six-year-old London attorney who in 1849 emigrated to Wisconsin, bought a farm and forty acres of real estate in Madison and proceeded to practice law in state and federal courts. He was known as a "man of broad culture" who successfully combined land ownership with a thriving law practice. Of even greater affluence was Matthew Henry Robertson, who enjoyed an outstanding liberal arts education and whose father owned a large estate near

Malmsbury. After studying law in Malmsbury, he decided to join his brother, who had already moved to New York. There, Robertson combined his study and practice of law until he was appointed to a post in state government.[21]

Such men were members of a distinct and sizable migratory elite; as such, they could overcome the reported surplus of American lawyers and rise to prominence. The professional environment they were entering was much more open than that they left because unlike Britain, the United States had few restrictions and no requirements for university education to practice law. The American legal profession had what was, in effect, an "open-door policy of professional recruitment," and competent British lawyers, who shared not only the same language but also fundamental legal doctrines and procedures as Americans, could walk through that door with relative ease.[22]

Teachers also arrived from Britain during the mid-century (an estimated sixty males in 1851), and the indications are that they had substantial qualifications, sometimes well-to-do backgrounds, but generally did not long remain in the teaching profession in America. Thomas Wainman, for example, whose father was well educated, was educated at Leeds and Cambridge, where he was also a teacher. In 1847 he came to New York to join his brother, who had emigrated four years earlier. The brother had become a close friend of the infamous Gilded Age politician Roscoe Conkling and rose to a lofty position in the New York Customshouse. Thomas, after teaching in Utica for a short time, entered the hotel and shoe business, perhaps frustrated by the low pay that American teachers endured. But farming was the most attractive alternative for teachers, as it was for other occupations. John and Mary Yarde, for example, who were "highly educated and well-to-do" principals of an academy in Devonshire, emigrated to Indiana in 1852 to take up farming. They started out with only fifty acres of unimproved land.[23]

Like the Yardes, there were other well-educated Britons coming to America, including some who at least claimed an Oxford University education but had undetermined prior occupations. Some of them also successfully switched to farming or some other form of employment.[24] Those who remained in professional life as Americans had entered a democratic culture where the professions themselves had been democratized and rid of the rigid class distinctions in which they were still embedded in Britain. The freedom and opportunity to rise in American professional life was itself a powerful attraction for these immigrants and a way to succeed in what was generally a tight labor market. The ratio of successes to failures will never be known precisely, but it was likely high enough to constitute a sizable migration of generally well-off, comparatively well-educated, men and women whose talents would be missed in Britain and welcomed in America.

Gentlemen

In addition to the immigrants in commerce and the professions came an interesting if ill-defined group of wealthy people described on the passenger lists and the official British statistics as "gentlemen" and "ladies." Many brought along children and servants, and they sailed almost exclusively in the cabins of the best ships available. They, along with the most successful merchants and professionals, constituted a sizable flow of elite members of Britain's society to the United States, and some of the gentlemen had the added prestige that came with family wealth and blue blood. Their exact backgrounds and occupations—if indeed they had them—are difficult to determine. So are their true numbers because the ships captains and port authorities seem to have used the inherently vague terms of "gentleman" and "lady" irregularly. The British Parliamentary Papers lumped gentlemen with "Professional Men, Merchants, &c" and reported that a little more than a thousand of this general group emigrated to the United States in 1857, although only a couple of hundred in both 1854 and 1855. According to the 1851 U.S. passenger lists, an estimated two hundred gentlemen arrived in 1851 through the five major ports.[25] More came via Canada, and their numbers increased in the 1860s and 1870s when American railway companies advertised their lands aggressively. The numbers of English gentlemen were high enough to attract the attention of many observers, who were often astonished to see these refined, upper-middle to upper-class individuals, wholly out of place on the wild American frontier. Most were interested in agriculture—or, more accurately, the social accoutrements and pseudo-aristocratic life-style supposed to come with owning a large estate. They were determined to have a good time.

The British men and women of gentle birth and background were most conspicuous when groups of them bought large estates and formed communities dedicated to maintaining their refined English sensibilities and pursuing an upper-class life-style and prestige that apparently eluded them in Britain. For them, migration to America was a way to climb the upper reaches of the social ladder or perhaps maintain their position on the higher rungs.

One of the first of these settlements was begun on the trans-Mississippi frontier in 1856 in Fairmont, Martin County, Minnesota. Larger numbers of the English elite came in the years after the Civil War, when railway companies began their promotions in earnest. They were a mix of urban, middle-class people and those who were considered members of the landed gentry. That they had no real background in agriculture or experience with real work would become apparent. Most were former army or navy officers, recent college graduates, or rich people's young sons who had inherited a great deal of money instead of their family's land. Many seemed as interested in hunting game as in growing crops.

The elite status of this group was made obvious when they bought their lands with cash and hired others to do the physical work—and then decided to avoid the harsh Minnesota blizzards by spending the winter seasons in England. Each year more of these immigrants arrived, such that by 1870 their numbers approached one hundred.[26]

Insofar as their agricultural intentions were concerned, the English elite in Fairmont, Minnesota, hoped to breed fine livestock, including Thoroughbred race horses for use in their own exhibitions, private races, and hunting parties. They fully believed that they could get rich quickly without getting their hands dirty or without adopting American farming methods. They did, however, plant a thousand acres of beans in 1873.

The settlement, of course, was doomed to failure, but at least the immigrants had a good time at it. The scenes they created were highly improbable, even outrageous in the eyes of their more common neighbors. To see them decked out in scarlet riding coats and distinctive headgear and attended by a pack of hounds as they raced out for a fox hunt and to see or attend their parties and fancy balls—liberally supplied with fine alcohol—was a new experience in Minnesota. Such activity and expenditure were hardly conducive to successful agriculture. But the unlikely immigrants also had the bad luck of having to endure unusually harsh frosts and thick swarms of locusts that struck the whole region in the early 1870s and devastated the crops they did manage to sow.

Soon it became obvious to all but the most stubborn or hopeful that success in Minnesota agriculture would require a major shift in life-style, one that included real physical labor. Some held out for a time by cutting expenses, reducing the number of leisure trips to England, and living less grandly. But most left during the 1870s. Some were still solvent enough to go into banking in Fairmont, although they also failed in that endeavor, in part for being too generous in lending money to other Englishmen who had left their estates to build the town's opulent Occidental Hotel. Most, however, drifted back to Britain or to American or Canadian cities where they took up professional work or continued to spend their money freely in a more entertaining urban setting.

Although the English settlement did fade away, it still is not accurate to judge the whole episode as a total failure and complete waste of time and money. The lavish spending on their fine homes and estates and their ventures into banking and hotels, as well as brewing real English beer, energized the local economy and raised the living standard of the more common folk of the community. The wealthy English newcomers also built Fairmont's first library and first church—Episcopal. But that was not all. They gave financial aid to other settlers in Martin County who had been wiped out by the same locusts that had plagued them. The act endeared the English to local farmers, who retained fond memories of them long after they had disappeared.[27] They had made tangible, positive contributions to the area. And then there is the more intangible value of witnessing extraordinary, sometimes laughable, scenes of spoiled, fun-loving, good-natured, and generous English gentlemen and women, who had more time and money than they deserved or needed, attempting to live like lords on American soil.

Such colonization attempts by upper-class English gentlefolk were made, with many variations, in various other states in the mid- to late-nineteenth century, including Tennessee and Virginia.[28] Iowa had several, including one established in 1868 in Decorah in the northeastern part of the state by a former government official from the East Indies. Le Mars, in northwestern Iowa, was started by former crewmen from Cambridge University who bought up huge tracts of land and then through advertisements in English newspapers recruited young gentlemen to join them. Although some did come to Le Mars, they seemed more dedicated to drinking and carousing than farming, and the colony soon ended.

Several colonies also came and went in Kansas. One, Runnymede in Harper County in the southern part of the state, was also dedicated to training young gentlemen in large-scale American agriculture and then helping them acquire large estates. Similar settlements were established in Crawford County in the southeastern part of the state, another near Manhattan in east central Kansas, and yet another in nearby Wakefield. Once again, most of the men seemed uninterested in actual work. They did, however, spend much of their time in sport and recreation. The sight of young, well-dressed English immigrants having an afternoon game of cricket must have struck local farmers as being odd.

One elite colony of particular importance was the one George Grant, a silk merchant, established in Victoria, Ellis County, in central Kansas in 1872. Grant bought sixty thousand acres from the Kansas Pacific Railroad and hired an architect from London to lay out the new town. The project attracted a number of gentlemen of considerable means. Some brought along French servants, chefs, overseers, and stablemen. A number of smaller English farmers came to Victoria, too, and purchased government land and got to work. But the elite dominated the scene, and they were out to live well. Because there were no foxes in the area, they took to antelope hunting, but they still did it in style—in full costume, the women riding side-saddle, and buglers making sounds that had never been heard in Kansas. After the hunt, they celebrated with fancy balls that featured fine music, elegant food, and ample supplies of the best liquor that could be imported from Denver.

The gentle immigrants of Victoria suffered the same droughts and locusts that inflicted the whole region, and, burdened with the unrealistic expectations that the frontier could not fulfil, they, too, drifted off to the towns, other farms, or back to Britain. One, Walter Maxwell, son of a Yorkshire aristocrat, sold his estate for a mere quarter of what he paid for it and then settled in Scotland, where he belonged. Another, Henry Edward Smithes, son of a rich London wine merchant, did manage to develop a large stock farm and employed German immigrants to work it and build a dam that created a large lake on the estate. But after a series of bad investments, bad weather, some unspecified lawsuits, and bad luck, Smithes moved to Colorado to start over once again.[29] Victoria's founder, George Grant, refused to abandon the project, but after he died in 1878 the community quietly dissolved.

Among the English elite in Victoria were several women whose vivid accounts of their experience on the frontier give us a glimpse at what life was really like for them. Annie Gilkeson, the daughter of prosperous English manufacturer, was raised to be a "thoroughbred gentlewoman." After her father became an alcoholic and suffered financial decline, she and her two older brothers decided to emigrate to the United States in 1856 to seek their fortunes and reestablish a life of gentility. They joined the Victoria settlement in 1871. Annie recalled that "farming seemed to them an ideal mode of occupation, involving little labor, and no knowledge of the subject whatsoever, the modus operandi being simply to scratch the ground, drop in the seed, and allow the climate to do the rest." The farm did not prosper, of course, but they were joined by other well-born English immigrants and intermarried with them. They also increased their estates and enjoyed buffalo hunts and parties as well as social interaction with other English immigrants. On the one hand, the experience for Annie Gilkeson was a mixture of pleasure and warm social activity in a tight community; on the other, she sometimes experienced sheer terror, especially when nearly killed during a winter outing and when swarms of locusts devastated their limited crops. Other women recalled Victoria as "a bit of old England transplanted in full bloom to the raw prairies of the middle west" and an "oasis of gentility" in barren central Kansas.[30]

Despite this temporarily successful transplantation of English culture on the prairies, life was not as entertaining as they had hoped. Like the men, they were ill-prepared for such a life. They had naively accepted the land companies' idealized descriptions of life on the prairies without any hesitation, or introspection. So determined were they to see the American west as a haven for gentlemen and women that it would be years before they saw the reality of their situations.

I should be exceedingly glad to see you but I cannot advise you. You might not like this country, you have lived in England so long, and are so well acquainted with the manners and customs that every thing would seem strange to you there; for the manners of the American people are so different from the English. For my own part I like it here very much. Nothing would tempt me to live anywhere else. I am a Complete American. I love my country, and I think that you would.
—Rachel Trattles to sister Sarah, from Constantine, Michigan,
　　Jan. 24, 1858

Women

By considering British immigrant women as a group, a number of significant realities become apparent, and the women's essential role in British migration to America becomes clearer. They were certainly not just wives, mothers, and daughters who were dragged across the Atlantic by men; they often made that migration possible and participated fully in the decision to leave for America.

In 1851 alone, an estimated 17,250 British women fifteen and above immigrated directly to the United States.[1] Although 42 percent arrived with husbands, a remarkable 28 percent arrived as single individuals (there is no way to determine how many were joining husbands already in America). A further 11 percent arrived without husbands but with children, presumably to meet husbands although some widows and children also emigrated.[2] Most of the remainder were daughters or sisters of a head of household. Thus, most of the British women immigrants of mid-century were participating in a family migration and bore the hopes and concerns of wives and mothers. Yet between a quarter and a third traveled without family members, nearly all on cramped sailing ships that required four or more weeks to cross the Atlantic. That impressive portion of single women is considerably greater than has been determined for 1831 and 1841, when about 16 percent traveled alone.[3] By mid-century, individual British women participated actively in the migration to America.

A few preceded husbands, a reminder that many were remarkably resilient, courageous, and equal partners in their marriages rather than servants to the husbands. That was certainly true of a well-traveled woman from Cornwall, Martha Jenkins, who lived in Brazil for five years while her husband mined there. After returning to England, Jenkins sailed to New Orleans in 1848 with her children and from there came north to Mineral Point, Wisconsin, to establish a household while the husband mined in Mexico until he joined her.[4]

Still, the thought of leaving Britain forever and enduring the transatlantic voyage made unwilling and reluctant partners of more than a few women and caused strain in marriages. Charlotte Fisher's husband emigrated alone from Nottingham to Wisconsin in 1845 and returned to her in 1847, only to leave once again in 1849—this time with their only son. Because she was "loth to leave the land of her birth," Charlotte Fisher remained in Nottingham until 1857, when she finally joined her family after her son begged her to do so.[5] Immigrant letters contain accounts of still other women who refused to emigrate altogether and stymied the plans of eager husbands.[6]

Fear of emigration was not gender-specific, however, and unwilling men on occasion held back wives who were eager to leave. In 1853, for example, a Mrs. Candler from London wrote to her son, who had emigrated to Detroit four years earlier, and expressed agony over the separation and a deep desire to join him, "All I wished to live for was to come to America, and live near my family. . . . Oh! William, how I long to see you. How little did I expect when you left I should not see you again for more than four years. It was most fortunate for you that you went out." But her husband refused to consider emigration and that was the end of the matter, although he seemed willing to let his wife leave without him.[7]

Nineteenth-century immigrants tended to be disproportionately young.[8] Only 16 percent of British women who came to the United States in 1851 were forty and above; another 16 percent were between fifteen and nineteen. Nearly half (48 percent) were in their twenties.[9] In regard to both progeny and labor, these young women were contributing their most productive years to the new nation. The significance of that age structure can be more fully appreciated in light of their occupations. Fully a quarter listed an occupation other than "wife." A little more than one-tenth were described as "farmers," but because nearly all traveled with husbands and children they could more accurately be described as farmers' wives.[10] Yet the letters of Ann Whittaker, whose family left the Liverpool area in the early 1840s and settled in the isolated parts of Monroe County, Illinois, reveal someone actively engaged in farming operations. She was clearly knowledgable and justifiably proud of what they were producing on the edge of the Illinois frontier, and she wrote the letters back to Liverpool because her husband could not write: "Our house stands at the top of a hill and we have bought eighty acres of land. We have got ten acres of wheat which will be ready in August and we are getting ready for our garden and potatoes and Indian corn. We have two cows, four calves, two horses, twenty-four pigs, two dogs and I cannot tell you the number of chickens. Before you get this letter we shall have more young pigs. So you see our stock keeps increasing continually. We killed a fine fat pig for Christmas. We had some mince pies. I wished many a time we could send you some."[11]

The Whittaker family is a good example of an urban English family's successful adaptation to subsistence agriculture in rural America. Ann Whittaker and others like her played vital roles in the backbreaking task of carving out farms on what was often unimproved or marginally improved land. Failure was not unknown among immigrant farmers from Britain, particularly those who had underestimated the amount of work and capital that success in America required, but the presence of wives greatly improved chances of success.[12] The nightmarish experience of Rebecca Butterworth demonstrates how difficult it was for some to cope with cruel hardships in a strange environment. Another example of an urban family settling on the frontier in the early 1840s, this time in Arkansas, the Butterworths were beaten by a combination of sickness, a difficult birth, and other misfortunes as well as the strangeness of that part of the new world. In 1846 Rebecca reported the bad news to her father in Lancashire and asked for help in coming home:

> I have been long in answering your and my dear sisters letters. The reason is I was taken sick a month since today. I commenced with bilious intermittent fever which nobody thought I would get over. Thomas was with me nearly all the time. He did not expect me getting over it. . . . John is not satisfied here. What little corn we had the cattle as jumped the fence and eaten it so that it will not make even cattle feed. . . . We have not bread to last above a week and no meat, very little coffee, about ½ lb of sugar. John can milk one

cow which makes us a little butter but the other wont let him. . . . I will write again soon and if you can help us along without hurting yourself we should be glad to get home.[13]

British women had influence on American farms and made decisions that required farming knowledge and good business sense. They played full and varied roles in the development of the frontier. Jane Chadwick, a dressmaker and milliner by trade, became the "administratrix" of a 560-acre estate in Illinois some years after she emigrated from Manchester in 1850. She ran the estate with "full powers to manage" it as she "saw fit." Friends later remembered her "administrative ability which would be highly creditable to one of the sterner sex," and she was "looked up to by everyone."[14] Mary Brooks, another English immigrant, possessed "in her own right" forty-five acres of good farmland in Jo Daviess County, Illinois, after she emigrated with her husband in 1860 and was widowed. She was "everywhere recognized as the possessor of more than ordinary intelligence and good business ability."[15]

More evidence for the indispensability of British immigrant women lies in the birth and marriage certificates migrants signed (or failed to sign) before leaving Britain. Of thirty marriage certificates and sixteen birth certificates from the mid-century period (from which the literacy of forty-one men and thirty-six women can be deduced), the ratio of literate to illiterate men was three to one; for women, the ratio was three to two. That difference is not as great as one might expect given the stark educational disadvantages females had before the Forester Act of 1870 widened opportunities for both sexes. In a half-dozen cases, a wife showed the ability to sign the document whereas a husband did not. If these women brought literacy into the family, as did Ann Whittaker, their contributions were truly significant.[16]

Altogether, British women in American agriculture were a varied and colorful group, important not only for the economic development of the frontier but also for cultural development. Although direct evidence is sparse, they must have been, like the native-born women, "civilizers" who ultimately extended domestic and middle-class values to areas that had only recently been settled by white people.[17] Philippa Kistle, a twice-widowed, educated Cornish immigrant of 1846, was known as "a lady of more than ordinary intelligence" who kept herself "well posted upon current events" and political affairs. She also financed the building of the Methodist Episcopal Church in Scales Mound, Illinois. As the owner of one of the "finest residences" in Scales Mound as well as large farms in Illinois, Wisconsin, Iowa, and other western properties, Phillipa Kistle was a formidable woman.[18] She and others like her no doubt appreciated the fact that women generally enjoyed a higher status and more independence in America than in Britain.[19]

But the costs could be high. Hard work, roughness, and isolation made life difficult. Cornish immigrants James and Mary Bennett were among the first settlers in Mineral Point in the late 1830s, and Mary begged her husband to take her away from that "hardly discovered wilderness," where "Indians and wild animals were numerous," and back to civilization in England.[20] The strain took a heavy toll on these women, who could not have anticipated just how alien the American mining frontier was. As John Rowe observed, "In Cornwall it was the miner who was old before he was thirty-five; on the early American mining frontier it was his wife."[21]

More numerous than farmers were laborers, who composed 17 percent of the women with occupations. Laborers were a varied lot, and one can only speculate on the form of work in which they had experience or that they sought. Unlike males, skilled female workers significantly outnumbered female laborers from Britain; one-fourth had occupations and a great variety of work experience.[22] Among them were cabinetmakers, cutlers, printers, bookbinders, painters, saddlers, shoemakers, and miners.[23] More numerous were hatters—most of whom had arrived without family members—weavers, and others involved with the cotton industry.

Weavers are noteworthy because they were few in number, considering the vast size of the textile industry of Britain and America.[24] In part, that was because low-paid Irish workers and transient New Englanders already supplied nearly all the unskilled labor required to operate the power looms and other machines. On the other side of the Atlantic, Britain was enjoying a "cotton boom" that drew in women and held down the numbers coming to America. The working-class consciousness and militancy of some British female weavers also made them less attractive to employers, especially as Irish labor became plentiful. One manager at a mill in Holyoke, Massachusetts, complained in 1857 that those he had hired from Scotland were "not sufficiently docile" and had become "a source of expense and trouble rather than profit."[25]

A surprising number of women were described as needlewomen (and can also be called seamstresses). An estimated 810 arrived in 1851 alone, and they outnumbered by more than two to one all the other skilled women combined and formed 18 percent of employed immigrant women.[26] British newspapers took specific interest in emigrant needlewomen, but only those taking part in the Female Emigration Society, a short-lived, privately funded program under the direction of Sydney Herbert, M.P.[27] The program was a sympathetic response to a series of heart-wrenching articles that appeared in the *Morning Chronicle* in 1849 and described the deplorable conditions needlewomen suffered in London's sweatshops. The society's aim was to assist them, particularly those who were young and single, in emigrating to Australia and New Zealand. There they could likely find work as domestic servants if not at their trade. Unfortunately, many were reluctant to emigrate and did so only as a last alternative to absolute poverty. That lack of enthusiasm and their frail health made the women unsuitable immigrants, and the society soon lost public support and collapsed, although not before assisting roughly 1,200 needlewomen.[28]

Those arriving in America were very different from the women being assisted to Australia, although their mode of work was similar. Needlewomen bound for Australia were young, single Londoners, whereas nearly a fifth of those going to the United States were thirty-five and above and not solely dependent on individual earnings. More than a third were thirty and above; nearly half arrived with families headed by adult males. Husbands of an additional 20 percent had likely preceded them, for the women were accompanied only by their children, many of whom were fifteen or more and probably had some kind of income.[29]

Furthermore, America-bound needlewomen had different origins than those who were assisted. Only one of the thirty whose county or city of origin was recorded in 1851 had come from London. Five hailed from Lancashire, and the rest were evenly distributed over a wide variety of counties (table B10, appendix B). These were not women trapped in London's sweatshops and emigrating as a last resort. Nor were they destitute, as were those being helped by the Female Emigration Society. Rather, they were part of a family movement, and their incomes—no matter how meager—usually contributed to a family income, making the migration a less formidable financial undertaking than it otherwise would have been.[30] For some families that money made migration possible— another way in which women played a vital role in the increasing British migration to America in the mid-nineteenth century. Once in America, wives and daughters made indispensable contributions to family incomes, and "working the needle" was a common way of doing so. As Robert Hails reported to his brother in England in 1849, "I sometimes make more money, for my wife earns considerable by her needle, 5 or 6 shillings per week on average."[31] Extra income could make the difference between success and failure.

Shopkeeping and teaching were common occupations among women who had tertiary occupations in service jobs and the professions. Most, however, were described as "doctors," an estimated 110 of whom immigrated from Britain in 1851. Some might have been more accurately described as nurses or midwives, and others perhaps considered themselves to be doctors after having gained a village reputation for being good with home remedies and having practical medical sense. Yet it is also possible that many, even most, had meaningful training or experience in medicine and were able to provide services in their new country, if within the limitations of what was still a backward profession. The dedication of such women can be seen in the life of Helen McAndrew, an educated Glaswegian who emigrated with her husband to Ypsilanti, Michigan, in 1849, and had extensive experience caring for the sick. Sensing a dire need for qualified women physicians, McAndrew soon left her husband and three-year-old son in Michigan to attend medical college in New York, graduating in 1855. She then returned to Ypsilanti to practice and later became influential in persuading Michigan State University to admit women.[32]

Most British women who immigrated to the United States at mid-century were domestic servants—42 percent of those with occupations. An estimated 1,880 female servants immigrated directly to the United States in 1851 alone. They also dominated Britain's domestic female labor force, numbering more than four hundred thousand of those twenty and above in 1851. That figure dwarfs the sixty-one thousand needlewomen age twenty and above who were enumerated in the same census.[33] Therefore, although a large number of servants migrated, it constituted a lower proportion than that for needlewomen.

Domestic servants were rapidly multiplying in Britain but not because of high wages and a high demand. On the contrary, the supply of servants was growing faster than demand for them. Britain's rapidly growing urban population and the limited availability of steady, remunerative work combined to swell the ranks of girls and women who sought domestic work. Many rural families sent out daughters at an early age to work as servants. Some no doubt did so to stave off poverty. What little was earned beyond living expenses could be sent home to poor rural households that also benefited from having extra room and fewer mouths to feed.[34]

Servants entering the United States in 1851 were young (a quarter were under twenty, more than half were under twenty-five, and nearly three-fourths were under thirty), and more than half were single.[35] They were apparently capitalizing on their youth and mobility in order to take advantage of the comparatively high wages America offered. In this respect they resemble Irish immigrants—also young, single, and arriving in huge numbers throughout the late 1840s and early 1850s—as well as those from southern and eastern Europe later in the century.[36] By mid-century, poor Irish servants had come "virtually to monopolize" unskilled jobs for both males and females in American cities, particularly those for domestic servants.[37] British women who entered service in America at mid-century had to compete with numerous Irish servants who would accept extremely low wages. They may have been leaving a dismal work environment in Britain, but they were not entering a Promised Land in America. Unless they had somehow managed to prearrange their employment, servants were not in the more confident positions that many married needlewomen or farmers' wives enjoyed.

If the limited opportunities for domestic servants in America were one reason for more British women not immigrating in 1851, then another might be a well-publicized demand for female servants in Australia. By 1850 "good servants" there were said to be earning £20–25 per year—considerably more than in America.[38] Many single women also viewed the male-dominated colony as the most likely place to find husbands.[39] Perhaps most significant, the British government and some private charitable organizations assisted many hundreds of female servants in finding their way to Australia during the late 1840s and early 1850s. Hundreds of others went there on their own resources and still the demand for female domestic servants was reported as "great."[40] Newspaper reports of young, assisted servants sending £10–15 to "their friends in England" after only eighteen months' work in Australia could only have encouraged others to select that country rather than America.[41]

That Australia attracted more servants than the United States at mid-century should not overshadow the dominating presence of servants among those who immigrated from Britain to the United States. It does, however, constitute a good example of the internationally complex and interrelated characteristics of mid-nineteenth-century migration. Without the distinct advantages of domestic service in Australia—particularly assisted passages and ready employment—even more British women would have entered the United States, and even more would have been domestic servants than was actually the case.

Thus, large numbers of women came from Britain to the United States at mid-century. Although most were part of a family migration, between a quarter and a third arrived without family members and appear to have been young and in search of higher rewards for their labor. These proportions of single women had grown noticeably since 1841. Among women who listed occupations, unskilled laborers were prominent. Yet considerable numbers were also skilled in crafts, teaching, and medicine. Much more prominent were needlewomen, not the desperate individuals of London's sweatshops, as were those being assisted to Australia, but rather wives and daughters who would make essential contributions to a family income and thus ensure a successful settlement in America. Most common were young domestic servants, who entered a crowded labor market—a discouraging fact that, combined with the greater attractions of Australia, no doubt kept their numbers from being even greater.

In their diversity of occupations and family status, British women appear to have been active participants in the migration process rather than passive victims of men's decisions.[42] They were also distinct from the other immigrant women arriving in larger numbers at mid-century. In contrast to the more restricted occupational and demographic characteristics of Germans and the Irish, British women filled more varied roles, and their cultural advantages provided wider choices of places and situations in which to adjust to American life.[43]

I believe that we who have made it a profession of Christian principles are bound not to live to ourselves but to live to God and if he in his providence opens up to us A way whereby we may provide for ourselves and dependents it is our duty to embrace that way.
—William Wilson to his brother Thomas in Scotland, June 11, 1848

Becoming Americans: Religion, the Civil War, and Institutions

In December 1856 a spiritual revival blazed through a community of Primitive Methodists, most of whom were British immigrants, in Benton in southwestern Wisconsin. Other Primitive Methodist communities in the region had also had revivals during which people were "powerfully awakened under the preaching," and those who "cried aloud for mercy in the love-feast" were "made happy in a few minutes."[1] But in 1856 the spiritual fires burned especially bright. Dramatic conversions occurred for nearly seven weeks, backsliders were reclaimed, and "believers were made happy in the love of God." People came from miles around to be part of this "camp meeting" and experience how "the Spirit of the Lord was poured out in a striking and powerful manner."[2]

Although evangelical camp meetings were common in antebellum America and an essential aspect of the Second Great Awakening, those taking place among the Primitive Methodists in the mining region of the Upper Mississippi Valley were a British import. More accurately, they were an American export being reimported by British immigrants. The Primitive Methodists (called "Ranters" by their detractors) had originally been inspired by American evangelists who had led camp meetings on the frontier. The denomination itself had been formed in 1811 by Wesleyan Methodists in England who were expelled for holding the American-style camp meetings that were too emotional for church authorities.

Primitive Methodists entered the Old Northwest for the first time in 1842, when a young convert from Teesdale, Joseph Grieves, moved to Galena, Illinois. The church grew in the region through conversions of local people, who included members of the rival Episcopal Methodist Church. But additional British immigrants accounted for most of the growth. By maintaining "constant correspondence" and a "Perfect Union" with the "Parent Society" in England, Primitive Methodists in America built a convenient channel for more immigrants, including some Primitive Methodist preachers. The Upper Mississippi River Valley was an ideal place for these Englishmen, who could also turn their hand at mining and farming. Whatever their precise goals in migrating, it was the religious connection that facilitated the movement and inspired so many to come in the first place. Although there were never more than a few thousand Primitive Methodists in the United States, enough had emigrated that their numbers in England declined during the 1850s.[3]

Primitive Methodist communities illustrate how social and economic forces do not adequately explain all British migration to America in the nineteenth century. In an age when faith and church membership were central to the identity of many people, religion and emigration were bound to be related. According to the religious affiliation of 539 British immigrants between 1845 and 1855, the socioreligious network that funneled Primitive Methodists to Illinois and Wisconsin was part of a larger picture (table 6).[4]

This profile of the migrants is especially revealing in light of the religious census conducted for England and Wales in March 1851, which indicated an equal number of conformists (Anglicans, or members of the Church of England) and nonconformists.[5] Nonconformists were much more likely to migrate to the United States than conformists. The same phenomenon was true for other immigrant groups, including the Janssonists and Haugean Lutherans of Norway and Sweden and the Dutch Reformed Seceders, who in the late 1840s formed a little more than 1 percent of the Dutch population but nearly half of all Dutch migrants to the United States. Religious institutions were essential to their decision to move and governed their exact choice of destination.[6]

Table 6. Religious Denominations of British
Immigrants to the United States (1845–55)

Denominational Group	Percent
Church of England/Episcopal[a]	12.6
Presbyterian[b]	19.7
Nonconformist	
Methodist[c]	44.7
Congregational[d]	10.2
Baptist	4.6
Other[e]	8.2
	67.7
Total	100.0
N = 539	

Source: See "U.S. County Histories" in the Bibliography.
a. Most were described as Episcopal, although there was no significant difference between Episcopal and Church of England (Anglican).
b. Most of these were Scots and therefore were conformists, but the English Presbyterians among them were nonconformists.
c. Most were described as either Methodist or Methodist Episcopal, but this group also includes Methodist seceders, including Primitive Methodists (primarily miners in south-western Wisconsin), Calvinist Methodists, and Welsh Methodists.
d. Includes Congregational, Welsh Congregational, and Welsh Calvinist denominations.
e. Includes a few Catholics, Mormons, Independents, Unitarians, Quakers, Universalists, and others.

British immigrants, with the possible exception of some Welsh Calvinist Methodists, were less reliant upon church institutions than their continental counterparts because they could function and prosper in America without them. It was far easier for them to move as independent individuals or families and to integrate with American society. Religious nonconformity had predisposed many adherents to migrate to America in the first place, however. That was clearly true of the Methodists, who were especially more likely than Anglicans to migrate.[7] Methodism had a dramatic personal and behavioral impact upon believers. The conversion of sinners, often through charismatic revivals that transformed individuals, heightened the zeal of new and old members alike and instilled greater diligence, frugality, and ambition.

Miners, laborers, and poorer members of the working class were particularly receptive to Methodism and found the conversion experience and the new work habits and attitudes that often accompanied it to be a road out of poverty, which for many led ultimately to America.[8] Some orthodox Welsh Calvinists appear to have rejected emigration because they were taught to believe that leaving the land of one's birth was a violation of God's preordained plan and a faithless assertion of the fallen human will.[9] But for most nonconformists there was no theological prohibition against emigration, and coming to America for some was nothing less than the fulfillment of God's perfect plan.

There were additional reasons for nonconformists being more susceptible than conformists to the temptation of moving to the United States. In a sense, they had already broken away from Britain. They were already outsiders who felt socially and culturally detached from the British political and cultural mainstream, even though the laws barring them from political offices and the universities had been repealed by 1828.[10] With one less tether keeping them attached to the mother country, they found it easier to leave and establish new loyalties to the United States, where there was no established church. Their emigration threshold was naturally lower than most. At the same time, as illustrated by the Primitive Methodists in southwestern Wisconsin, there were far stronger social and institutional links and networks between Methodists in Britain and America than between Anglicans and Episcopalians. These important transatlantic links of communication had been forged since the days of John Wesley, and they became migratory channels that members of the established church did not have.

A good example of how nonconformity led to chain migration involves the story of John Ewbank from Yorkshire, who married a Wesleyan in 1792, converted to her faith, and suffered the consequences when the ninety-nine-year lease on his farm expired in 1805 and his landlord refused the customary renewal because of Ewbank's nonconformity. At age fifty-three Ewbank found himself without a farm and with no means to support his wife and ten children. He emigrated alone to New York, where he worked on a farm for two years and then sent for his family, who had remained in Yorkshire. In 1815 the Ewbanks moved to Dearborn County, Indiana, where they were able to purchase five and a half quarter-sections of virgin land. They were merely the "advance guard," for soon they were joined by other Methodist families from Yorkshire who had known the Ewbanks and had apparently stayed in close touch with them. These newcomers in turn attracted still others from Yorkshire, such that a colony of Yorkshire families was established in what became called York Township.[11] In this way Methodism was not just a catalyst but a means and a channel for British migration. The church was also a force in American assimilation by providing a point of contact at which the immigrants interacted and intermarried with Americans and inevitably became more like them.[12] Although some new immigrants complained in 1856 that "we are looked upon as foreigners," such barriers were already melting.[13]

Among the nonconformists were large numbers of British Mormons, who at mid-century settled almost exclusively in Utah Territory and are therefore vastly undercounted in table 6. In 1840, only three years after Mormon missionary work began in Britain, converts crossed the Atlantic to initiate the most important religious-based British migration to America since the Puritans. More than five thousand left for America between 1848 and 1851, and some sixteen thousand followed between 1853 and 1856. By 1870 the English numbered nearly thirty-eight thousand and formed 18.5 percent of Utah's population, the highest percentage of English-born people anywhere in America.[14]

It is not easy to distinguish religious motives from social and economic ones among the British Mormons who came to America. Indeed, the distinction may be artificial because the converts believed it was God's will that they lift themselves up from poverty in Britain to prosperity in the American west, where they would help build Zion. The blending of religious with economic incentives also applied to British Mormons who were recruited to Salt Lake City to start up its industrial development. Among them were a "large number" of ironworkers and miners who left South Wales in April 1851 to establish the first ironworks in Utah, where ore was plentiful. A furnace was working by 1852, but technical and managerial problems plagued the operation. Gradually, though, British newcomers brought vital industrial skills and experience to Utah, as they did in other parts of America, and helped make the Mormon project viable.[15]

In some respects, Mormon immigrants were similar to non-Mormons. They not only made unique economic contributions but also were overwhelmingly familial—even more so than non-Mormons. And Mormon conversion and migration spread through chains of information, almost as if by "contagion," whereby early converts and migrants paved the way for neighbors and relatives. But the differences between the two groups were still stark. Mormons were more concentrated in the poorer echelons of society. More of them were urban industrial workers or general laborers from poor, low-wage areas. Nearly half the migrants used financial assistance from the Mormon Church, which came in the form of loans to be repaid with labor in Utah and helps explain their high numbers. Some converted to Mormonism primarily because the church provided an affordable and convenient means of getting to America. Most, however, made their decision to emigrate after a genuine spiritual conversion.[16]

It was above all their faith that set the Mormons apart from the other British migrants. In Britain they were viewed with contempt, as converts to a strange, new, distinctly American religion that amounted to immoral paganism. Some were mocked and harassed by their neighbors. British newspapers reported the emigration of converts and ridiculed them for the practice of polygamy. As one newspaper remarked, "They are composed, we are told, nearly exclusively of

English and Welsh converts to the Mormon religion and morality (or immorality) . . . more than half were women, mostly young buxom-looking lasses."[17] Primitive Methodists chimed in by openly condemning "the absurdities, fooleries, and wickedness of the people who embrace this strange system."[18] Occasionally converts themselves bitterly rejected their new faith after settling in America. Alfred Milnes, for example, emigrated to Utah in 1854 with his father, who had converted, but later became "much disgusted" with the church and left it to go to Michigan.[19]

The experience of Mormon migration from Britain to America is vividly illustrated in the well-documented story of Steeple Ashton, a village in Wiltshire where disruptive economic changes created fertile ground for the growth of the faith. Enclosure, agricultural mechanization, and a withering demand for workers in nearby clothing industries all combined to impoverish many people, some of whom responded warmly to the Mormon mission that came to West Wiltshire in 1844. The coming of Mormonism to this area is itself a testament to the key role of chain migration. It was one John Halliday who first emigrated from nearby Trowbridge to America, converted to Mormonism, and then was sent back to Wiltshire as a missionary. His first converts were family members and former neighbors whose social and economic status had recently declined but who had intelligence, determination, and some education.[20]

The converts did not have a happy time in Wiltshire. Angry neighbors hurled insults at them and pelted them with stones and rotten eggs. When in 1849 a rock crashed through the window of Robert Berrett's home and nearly struck his infant child, Berrett decided it was time to join the Mormons in Utah. He and his family and some neighbors borrowed money from the church and tapped the well-established network of people and information to facilitate the long migration. At least one member of the party later left Utah and the church and settled on a farm in Iowa.[21]

Immigrant Mormons did not live typically American lives. They lived and farmed communally and thus were never driven by the individualistic spirit and cash nexus for which nineteenth-century Americans were known. Yet in another sense the whole episode was quintessentially American. British conversion to Mormonism and migration to Utah was an ultimate experience in assimilation to American culture, one that began even before participants had set foot in the new world. Mormonism was a unique religion whose dispensation could only have occurred in America; the faith was based on an available promised land and freedom for religious expression.[22] In a sense, British Mormons were Americans even before they left Britain, so profound was religion and the assimilation that came with it.

Temperance

For most British immigrants, religion was a foundation for living moral lives, and for many Methodists and other nonconformists doing so involved temperance. Britain and America shared a transatlantic temperance movement linked by philanthropists from both countries and strengthened by frequent communications and visits. Originating in the American evangelical movement, rooted in New England's Scottish Presbyterian immigrant culture, the temperance movement spread to England with the help of American sea captains and other reform-minded persons, some of whom were armed with Lyman Beecher's *Six Sermons on Intemperance* and similar reformist literature.[23] Thus British immigrants who had dedicated themselves to temperance had yet another cultural similarity with their new homeland. The temperance movement, like American religious denominations, was familiar to them and a force that hastened assimilation.

Not that all or even most British immigrants supported temperance. British workers in New England mills and in coal-mining towns in Pennsylvania were notoriously fond of beer and too often became drunk and unruly. But there was a difference between heavy beer drinking and the guzzling of whiskey that Americans were known for doing.[24] When compared with German and Irish immigrants, the British generally were much more likely to become temperance activists. The British Temperance Emigration Society had been organized to promote migration within the context of abstinence, and although the organization was short-lived it did succeed in getting nearly a thousand people to America—all of whom at least had taken the pledge not to drink.

Certainly, the movement gained strength from many other British immigrants, especially but not necessarily Methodists or Baptists. Twenty-one-year-old Robert Scott from Fifeshire, educated at Edinburgh and dissatisfied with his lot as a journeyman shoemaker, came to America with his wife in 1852 and became a successful shoemaker in Jo Daviess County, Illinois. He then established a successful meat market. But he made his deepest impression in the community as one of the area's strongest advocates of temperance. As a trustee of the Methodist Episcopal Church, Scott supported the local Women's Christian Temperance Union, and his two daughters, Mary and Kate, became the "leading spirits" of the organization. Mary was also the associate editor of the organization's column in the local newspaper in Elizabeth, Illinois. Robert enjoyed the game of checkers, and in 1873 he won the championship of a tournament whose entrants came from Wisconsin, Illinois, and Iowa.[25]

Other local leaders of temperance included Stephen Galt, a Scottish tailor from Aberdeen who came to Wisconsin in 1850 and took no pains to hide the fact that he had abstained from alcohol for nearly thirty years. Indeed, he "looked upon the use of toxicating liquors with abhorrence."[26] Likewise, most knew Henry Bowman, an immigrant farmer from Staffordshire who sailed with Mazzini and Garibaldi when they visited America in 1850 and became a prominent merchant in Genesee in Waukesha County, Wisconsin, as one of the town's "staunchest temperance men."[27]

Other British immigrants joined the temperance movement after their arrival and became prominent leaders. Benjamin Hopkins, who emigrated in 1847 from Staffordshire through the Potter's Emigration Society, had a long history of drinking problems and failed business attempts in England. His inability to earn money farming in Wisconsin—only 6 cents a day after expenses—deepened his dependence on alcohol. After hitting the whiskey jug he affectionately called "Black Bet" particularly hard one night, he pulled himself together, picked up the jug, and addressed it in true Dickensian fashion: "Black Bet, thou hast deceived me, and been leading me on to ruin, and now I will banish thee from the face of the earth, and will never again touch, taste, or handle the accursed poison so long as I live, so help me God." After smashing Black Bet on the cellar floor and watching her contents seep into the ground, Hopkins sobered up and dedicated his life to getting others to do the same. As the founder of the area's Good Templars Lodge and leader of the Baptist Church, he found many opportunities to do so.[28]

Although the culmination of the temperance movement, in the form of the Volstead Act and Prohibition in 1919, would prove to cause more trouble than it was worth, the movement did serve a constructive purpose in many parts of the country during the era of westward expansion. Churches, especially those dedicated to temperance, were "calming influences on the frontier" when they exhorted moral behavior and enforced social order.[29] Temperance leaders, including those of British origin, were justified in seeing themselves as civilizers of what was still a comparatively wild, untamed land whose rough inhabitants desperately needed the restraining and liberating force of temperance.

The truth behind such potentially self-aggrandizing and pietistic perspectives lay in the lawlessness, violence, and public disorder that stemmed from alcohol abuse and addiction in rough mining towns. It was true that whiskey was too cheap for the public good and that both young and old widely abused it, as Alexis de Tocqueville and other European travelers graphically recorded. But what many temperance leaders failed to see was their lack of tolerance as well as the fact that a pint of beer or a dram or two of whiskey never did much harm for many people.

Ultimately, the temperance movement was part of a larger "complex of Anglo-American philanthropic activity" that also included penal reform, Christian missions, and the abolition of slavery.[30] Like religion, anti-slavery sentiments moved the soul, and for many British immigrants abolition had the same assimilatory power that could predate the actual migration. The British were not slow to show either their hatred for slavery or their willingness to risk life and limb for its extinction.

Living in a Flawed America: The Curse of Slavery

British immigrants and the friends and relatives with whom they corresponded were keen observers of some of America's important social and political issues. During the antebellum period they usually focused on one issue with passion— slavery—while some also expressed concern over the treatment of Native Americans. With some exceptions, the English held the enlightened view that by permitting slavery and oppressing Native Americans the United States was violating its principles and ideals. Although British immigrants in the colonial period were hardly known for their sympathy toward Native Americans, by mid-century many did hold sympathetic if idealized notions and recognized their treatment for what it was. As for slavery, all but a few saw the institution as not "peculiar" but evil. Sometimes they wrote about Indians and slaves simultaneously. One Northamptonshire immigrant in Utica, New York, made observations in 1852 that still sound enlightened and balanced: "America is a fine country and . . . it is generally a land of profit; but while half of its States are Slave holding States and between three and four Millions of poor Africans are in Bondage and groaning under oppression, and besides this the Noble Indians, the original occupiers and owners of this land are by artifice and cruelty driven to far distant Mountains for Refuge, I consider it an awfull profanation of the Name to call it a Land of Liberty, yet in a variety of ways a part of it is so."[31]

If British immigrants in America did generally have more sympathy for Native Americans than did native-born whites, one important reason was that they had been born and raised an ocean away from the American frontier. In a sense, the newcomers could afford to be more sympathetic now that Native American "removal" was in full swing. They did not see that their land purchases and settlement were part of the economic force pushing people off their own lands. But British attitudes seem authentic, heart-felt, and widely held. During the 1830s the English artist George Winter was in Indiana observing the displacement of the Potawatomis and Miamis from their ancestral lands, an event that culminated in the infamous "Trail of Death" that forced the survivors across the Mississippi River. Winter's empathetic paintings, sketches, and journal entries on these and other Indians have survived as an important record of these people and tragic events.[32] At the same time, Samuel Fowler Smith, an English shoe-maker, traveled through the same area and witnessed the same events. His observations were likely shared by few native-born Hoosiers. He was clearly angered by the "greedy horde of land speculators" and the "rascalities" inflicted upon the Native Americans.[33]

Those British immigrants who came into close and extended contact with Native Americans, while maintaining a respect and even admiration for them, also gradually adopted attitudes more consistent with those that prevailed among most white Americans. Native Americans, it was thought, were not developing and using the land in the way that God intended, and their inferior culture was doomed to extinction. That was the view of Matthew Dinsdale, who came to southwestern Wisconsin from Yorkshire to serve as an itinerant Methodist preacher. During his long and frequent journeys he met many Native American hunters "with painted faces . . . which had not a disagreeable appearance," and he "grew familiar" with many of the Menominees and others at the Brothertown and Oneida missions in the region of Lake Winnebago. But, showing a common lack of understanding of Native Americans' cultural use of land and a bias toward the acquisitive nature of European culture, Dinsdale remarked, "Would they only cultivate it there is enough to make every one of them wealthy." He also interpreted their decreasing numbers and increasing poverty in a way that most native-born whites would have agreed with, although ultimately with more sympathy:

> It appears to me that the Indian race is doomed to . . . extirpation. This I think is a judgment from God in consequence of their thriftless idle habits and the debasing and demoralizing influence of their violence. The Almighty designed the Earth to be cultivated, the Indians as a general thing will not do this, consequently they are removed by Heaven, that another race may occupy. In this God is righteous as it cannot matter what race of mankind inhabits the Earth so long as the Divine purposes are accomplished. But the Indian tribes ought to have, and must have, if we do our duty, our sympathies & prayers, and Christian labors.[34]

As immigrants such as Dinsdale heard the familiar stories of violence between whites and Native Americans, their attitudes hardened, a process that was an unfortunate but real part of their assimilation into American life. E. Chapman's letters reveal a growing animosity toward Native Americans that was intensified by his reading of American newspapers. Writing to his friends back in Northamptonshire, Chapman noted that "the Indians are a fine race of men but very bad hands to fall into." He then related the newspaper story that had shaped his opinion on them: "A large party of these Indians . . . approach[ed] the White Settlement . . .

from whence they took a Mrs. Smith and her Daughter. The Mother they put to Death and after their brutal conduct to the Daughter put her to Death. They were pursued but the dreadful work was done their scalps taken of[f]. . . . This is almost their universal practice to scalp all that come in their way."[35]

The interest British immigrants showed in Native Americans was overshadowed by their concern for slavery. Virtually all had an opinion on the topic, and all but a small fraction of these held a visceral hatred for it. For some Britons, slavery was the reason, if not the excuse, for not joining family members in America. John Wood of Sykehouse, Yorkshire, wrote to his brother in Illinois in 1852 to explain why he would never come to America: "For my own part I never think of coming to America. I deem it a cursed land. The curse of slavery is on it. You may call it a free country but the Blacks are not free, but are bought and sold as Cattle."[36]

In Wisconsin, the Kimberleys received a similar letter from relatives still in Lincolnshire: "I have often thought I should like to know something about Slavery where you are. I have read Uncle Tom's Cabin . . . and could not of supposed that America, which stands so high in the estimation of other Nations could be so guilty of such acts of cruelty. She certainly has many boasts & privileges, but slavery is a deep stain. Oh that she might free herself of it."[37]

Such thinking was rooted in the evangelical movement, especially the Methodist secession movements that had attacked slavery in the British Empire as early as the late eighteenth century. It was partly due to these pressures that Britain abolished slavery at home in 1807 and in the empire in 1833.[38] Because Methodists were overrepresented as British immigrants to America, some of that fervor was carried to the United States during the antebellum period. Then, in 1839, the British and Foreign Anti-Slavery Society was established, dedicated to abolishing the slave trade throughout the world. The optimistic, Quaker-dominated society had the United States as its foremost target for reform and gave significant support to America's own anti-slavery movement by building contacts with it and providing propaganda and personnel.[39]

So great was the impact of British people and agitation in the United States that America's abolition movement, for Frederick Douglass, "was largely derived from England." "Surely in this sense," he continued, "it ought to be no disgrace to be an Englishman."[40] Abhorrence for slavery did not necessarily translate into sympathy for slaves, however. Concerns for the economic future of whites in the West and whether there would be competition with unfree labor and slaveowners were often the real sources of anti-slavery passions. More likely, British people, including immigrants to America, held idealized perceptions of American slaves and demonized slaveholders. Douglass's 1847 lecture tour in Britain was highly popular, and the press reprinted his speeches extensively. Although only a minority of the newspapers were in support of the Union during the war, many of them, as well as journals and travel books of the period, contained frequent and sometimes vicious attacks on slavery and had a significant impact upon British public opinion.

But it was Harriet Beecher Stowe's phenomenally successful *Uncle Tom's Cabin* (1852) that did the most to shape British attitudes toward slavery and helped make immigration to the United States during the antebellum period a contributing force in American abolitionism. During its first year of publication, the book sold seven times more copies in Britain than in the United States.[41] When she read it, Queen Victoria wept. So did many of her subjects. More Britons than Americans bought and read the book for another reason: It was glaring proof that the United States, for all of its pompous and conceited boasting of being the land of liberty and equality, with superior institutions and an enlightened people, was as fatally flawed as any other nation. Britons tired of such smug self-satisfaction and thus found *Uncle Tom's Cabin* a remedy for American national vanity. British enthusiasts for America—especially those contemplating migration—were newly inspired to see slavery as the single institution marring that nation's achievements and threatening its future.[42]

For a number of reasons, revulsion toward slavery was most widespread among Britain's working classes and their leaders. They were the most likely members of British society to migrate to America or have family members living there. Many saw their own struggle for complete freedom and equality in Britain as part of a larger international movement that included Emancipation. Both realities were true for Robert Applegarth. Before he became secretary of the Amalgamated Society of Carpenters and Joiners of England, he migrated to America in 1854 but returned because his wife was too ill to join him. Traveling down the Mississippi River, he became so outraged by the spectacle of a slave auction that he took a slave-dealer's receipt, which he presented to the National Liberal Club in London. He later became a champion for American abolitionism in Britain. Like so many others, *Uncle Tom's Cabin* moved him deeply. He had met Frederick Douglass and helped raise the moral issue of slavery and Emancipation in the consciousness of English workers. England's industrial workers quite naturally rallied to the cause of Lincoln and the North, at least until the cotton famine of 1863–65 struck the industrial North, threw thousands out of work, and caused many cotton towns to petition the British government either to recognize the Confederacy or mediate for peace and a restoration of cotton supplies.[43]

The universality of the American Civil War was articulated in England most effectively by John Bright, a Quaker and liberal member of Parliament for

Manchester and later Lancashire and along with Richard Cobden an arch-foe of the Corn Laws. Although Bright and Lincoln never met, the two developed a friendship through correspondence and professed similar ideals about liberty. Bright naturally sympathized with the cause of the North. For him, it was part of a larger struggle in which England was also engaged: extending the franchise and moving from aristocratic to democratic government. Intellectuals and nonintellectuals alike shared these sentiments at a variety of levels and meanings. As Asa Briggs said, "Partisanship on the American issue veiled a hidden English civil war, and the triumph of the North was 'the force that made English Liberalism powerful enough to enfranchise the workmen, depose official Christianity in Ireland, and deal a first blow at the land-lords.'"[44]

It was natural then that most British immigrants carried with them a deep instinctual revulsion for the Peculiar Institution and that so many would risk their lives to stamp it out. Their hatred of slavery had been well established before they migrated, and it grew once they stepped on America's shores.

Of course, some did not condemn slavery and even supported it on biblical grounds or migrated to southern states and came into contact with it there. Thomas Wozencraft and Nathan Haley adopted pro-slavery views in the Deep South because of a perceived pressure to get along with their new neighbors.[45] But only a minuscule proportion of British immigrants settled in southern states, primarily because slavery made doing so repugnant to all but a few. Some who attempted settlement in slave states soon moved north. Shortly after he arrived from Leicestershire in 1852, William Jackson, a former shepherd, decided to pursue work in Louisiana. When he witnessed a slave auction, however, the event so sickened him that he left for a free state. Similarly, Titus Crawshaw rejected a job in Delaware after his migration in 1853 because that was a slave state. Thomas Edwards, who left Bristol in 1843, went to Illinois and then Kansas in 1856. On his arrival, "border ruffians" barred his entry into the territory because he opposed slavery, and he returned to Illinois.[46] To these and the majority of other British immigrants, slavery was an anomaly, a contradiction to what America stood for, and a source of shame and embarrassment.

As the American "house" became ever more divided, British immigrants' hatred toward slavery took on deeper meaning. The newcomers could hardly have missed the rising tension. It was the time of the Compromise of 1850, with its fugitive slave law; the Kansas-Nebraska Act, which allowed popular sovereignty to determine whether these territories were to be free or slave; the Dred Scott decision, which made it appear that slavery might spread to northern states; and increasing activity, in which some British immigrants participated, in abolitionism and the Underground Railroad. When the fugitive slave law enabled southerners to arrest and kidnap a runaway slave named Joshua Glover in Racine, Wisconsin, in 1854, local citizens, including many recent British immigrants to the area, were appalled and newly inspired to join abolitionist causes.[47]

Many became active abolitionists. Winnifred Roberts and her husband came to Racine from northern Wales in 1846 and eventually accumulated more than a thousand acres of land, but they were best known for becoming "staunch" abolitionists and some of the "first movers in the good work of liberating the slaves," who "spent much time and money to further that end."[48] Scottish immigrant Peter Kinnear was one of the earliest and most prominent abolitionists in Albany County, New York. He attributed his commitment to the fact that he took "from his native land a strong love of freedom" and was "a firm believer in American institutions before placing his feet upon American soil."[49] The family of Henrietta Ramsden, natives of Yorkshire, were well known for their contributions to abolitionism. They provided their home in Salem, Ohio, as a resort for Wendell Phillips, William Lloyd Garrison, and other leaders of the cause.[50]

These supporters of black freedom and equality sometimes put themselves at risk, as did Samuel Angel, an eccentric Englishman who joined the English colony in Floyd County, Indiana. In spite of bitter race prejudice that festered there, Angel welcomed a refugee slave family to live with him in his own house. When he donated his land for the site of the Methodist Church in New Albany, he did so under the condition that a seat in the church be reserved "in perpetuo" for his black friends.[51]

With their loathing for slavery and awareness that it violated the ideals of liberty and equality that had drawn them to America, British immigrants were among the earliest and most enthusiastic volunteers for service in the Union army. They were eager to serve their new country. English immigrant E. J. Bentley was the second man in Platteville, Wisconsin, to enlist.[52] Ella Lonn has indicated that more than fifty-four thousand English-born men served in the Union army. That was a much higher proportion than the Irish immigrants who served, disproportionately high when factoring in the percentage of immigrants eligible to serve.[53]

Surviving evidence makes the participation of some British immigrants in the Civil War other than heroic. Few would have bragged later that they joined the army for the pay or for the reduced passage fares offered to some migrants who would enlist. But J. P. Geraghty, a surveyor from Lincolnshire who landed in New York "without a shilling in his pocket," seemed more concerned with finding employment than with serving a cause. After finding only "precarious employment," he eventually joined the federal army, and his letters back to Market Rasen made their way into local newspapers. His vivid descriptions of the horrors of war must have made good reading, especially because he served with black soldiers. "We had some nigger soldiers engaged in the storming," he remarked. "They fought like tigers."[54] Henry Morton Stanley came to New Orleans in 1859, volunteered for the Confederate army at sixteen, was captured at Shiloh, and then joined the Union army. His chief loyalties seem to have been devoted to his own life of adventure, which continued after the war when as a reporter the *New York Herald* sent him to find Dr. David Livingstone in the heart of the "Dark Continent."[55]

One of the features that distinguished the British from other immigrants who served in the Civil War was their lack of need to form ethnic regiments. Although German and Irish regiments multiplied there was but one Scottish regiment—the 65th Illinois Infantry—and even then "its ethnic identity was diluted from its inception." As with American society in general, the British were more able and likely to blend in with typical American regiments, whose members did not consider them to be foreigners.[56]

Another distinguishing feature of the British was that many felt stronger pressure than other immigrants to prove their patriotism. It was a time, after all, of strained relations between Britain and America. Lingering hostilities from the War of 1812 and the more recent conflict over the western border between the United States and British North America—when James K. Polk's bellicose "54-40 or Fight" slogan became popular—put considerable pressure on the newly arrived Britons to demonstrate loyalty to their new government. Such pressure grew as Britain considered recognizing the independence of the Confederacy during the early years of the war and then declared its neutrality.[57] The American government still insisted upon special oaths of loyalty for British immigrants, who were to swear their intention to become citizens and "renounce forever all allegiance and fidelity" to Queen Victoria. Such shrill and strident nationalism, which disgusted most European observers, could be abrasive and threatening. English immigrants in America who spoke fondly of their place of birth were often confronted with hostile accusations of disloyalty. When Cornish miners displayed their own flag during Fourth of July celebrations in southwestern Wisconsin, they were met with ugly threats and forced to remove it.[58] Some English farmers in the Old Northwest painted great American flags on their barns so as to leave no doubt about their patriotism.[59] Thus, when the war came, immigrants from Britain lined up to serve. There was no better way to demonstrate loyalty.

Many recalled their precise motivations for enlisting. "To preserve the Union," to show "loyalty to his adopted county," "to defend the honor of his adopted country," and "love of adventure and patriotism" were the common explanations.[60] Titus Crawshaw enlisted because, as he wrote to his father in England, "I thought the Capitol of Washington was in danger of falling into the hands of the rebels . . . I was not forced to go, but I thought it my duty to do so."[61]

Such loyalty and patriotism quickened the assimilation process and enhanced a sense of belonging to an American community. But in the border states it could also bear a heavy cost, as it did for Ebenezer and Margaret Allison, who left Scotland in 1856 and settled in Missouri three years later while war was brewing. When they professed a loyalty to the Union and Ebenezer joined the Union's military service, their pro-southern neighbors harassed the whole family, stole their livestock, and put their lives in "constant danger."[62] Their commitment in the face of personal risk, so soon after arrival, demonstrated their patriotism and how rapid and complete assimilation could be.

Truly remarkable were those British immigrants who volunteered to fight within a short time of their arrival. One can only wonder why Dawson Smith, for example, left his wife and children in Yorkshire in 1864, sailed for America, and "at once allied himself with the cause of the American Union . . . and immediately went to the front."[63] Still other cases of individuals from England, Scotland, and Wales enlisting shortly after immigration show that such an early willingness to serve was common. Archibald Thompson, son of a physician in Edinburgh and himself a successful veterinarian, had served in the Crimean War. After emigrating to Ohio in 1859, he enlisted in the spring of 1861, served throughout the war, participated in thirty-seven battles, was wounded three times, and rose to the rank of captain.[64] Others with combat experience in the British army served as officers in the Union army. Among them was Col. Thomas Stevens, a member of the Queen's Life Guards and one of the English army's finest swordsmen, who immigrated in 1840 and organized the Second Wisconsin Cavalry and served heroically as its leader.[65] Even old-timers felt the call. John Foreman from Kent enlisted as a private at age sixty-three and was killed at the battle of Resaca in Georgia toward the end of the war at sixty-six.[66] British immigrants served in other important ways as well—as military carpenters, blacksmiths, buglers, surgeons, mechanics, drummer boys, and other essential occupations.[67] Scottish immigrant mechanic Alexander Wood, who had been captured by Confederate soldiers, attributed his survival to the fact that he was an "excellent mechanic" and was put to use by his captors.[68]

Like other soldiers in the Civil War, British immigrants were soon shocked by the scale of the horror that unfolded, and they witnessed and endured some of the worst carnage imaginable. County histories record scores of those who died, were wounded and dismembered, or suffered in places such as Andersonville Prison. Henry Nobes, a native of London who enlisted in the Seventy-second Indiana Infantry, emerged from that nightmarish place a skeletal eighty-three pounds and carried the physical and mental scars for the rest of his life. Still, he was more fortunate than Edwin Hall, also from England, who died there, or John Pacey, who was wounded, taken prisoner, had a limb amputated, and then slowly wasted away in Virginia's Libby Prison.[69]

The Civil War not only killed and maimed the immigrants but also tore their families apart in various ways. William Matthews was refused permission to enlist from his father, a stonemason from London, so he ran off and joined the army anyway, as did two of his brothers. Even more poignant is the story of Jonas Rhodes, an English immigrant whose four sons all went off to fight, one to join the Confederate army after marrying the daughter of a slaveholder. One died in battle, his body never found, and two others died shortly after their return from the front. James Hayes, an English immigrant of 1856, lost two sons to the war, after which he returned to England, no doubt cursing the day he left for America.[70]

In later years, British veterans of the Civil War recalled with justifiable pride their participation in the struggle to preserve a nation they had only recently come to call their own. They fought and died in virtually every major campaign and battle, including those that have become legendary: Shiloh, Gettysburg, Sherman's March, the Siege of Atlanta, Antietam, Chickamauga, and the final episode near Appomattox Courthouse.[71] Those who enlisted for the adventure were not disappointed. James Miller, who left Lanarkshire in 1853, was a master mechanic and marine engine builder with his own foundry and machine shop in Illinois. He had "become strongly attached to the institutions of his adopted country," raised his own company called the Mechanics Fusileers, and became its captain. He also saw action as a chief engineer for the navy's Mississippi Squadron.[72]

The American Civil War provided British immigrants with the opportunity of proving their loyalty, patriotism, and commitment to the Union. For others, it was also a way to prove their manhood and satisfy a need for adventure. But it was also an occasion to fight for black freedom. At least two English immigrants became officers of "coloured regiments." Ebenezer Denny came with his parents from Yorkshire in 1855, enlisted in 1862, and finished his service as first lieutenant of the Fiftieth (Colored) Regiment from Illinois. John Cartwright, who emigrated in 1849, rose to the rank of captain of the Twenty-seventh (Colored) Infantry but was killed while leading a charge in the battle of Petersburg.[73] William Stockdale and his family never forgot why the war was ultimately worth fighting. Having immigrated during the conflict, he immediately enlisted, lost an eye and a leg in battle, and received reassurance from his father, still in Manchester: "You fought in a good cause. . . . You were one that were the means of giving the blacks freedom."[74]

After the carnage ceased, British immigrants who had witnessed it or seen their fathers, sons, and brothers march off to participate found themselves changed. For many, the war was a catalyst for assimilation and hastened and intensified the process of Americanization. That was the experience of the Cornish and other British immigrants in the Upper Mississippi River Valley. In Linden, Wisconsin, the Civil War marked the time when British immigrants there began to hold annual Fourth of July celebrations that were sometimes so grandly planned that festivities spilled over into the next day. Marching bands, parades, patriotic recitations of the Declaration of Independence, and an abundance of food marked the event, as did a series of baseball games with nearby competing teams, which were taken very seriously indeed. The Cornish took to this all-American game with unusual gusto, and from the 1870s through the rest of the century teams composed of Cornish immigrants and their children were a force to be reckoned with throughout the region. Yet they remembered the Civil War as the turning point in their identity as Americans.[75]

In their religion, abhorrence for slavery, and quick and profound response to the Civil War crisis, British immigrants demonstrated that they had far more in common with Americans than differences. Some of the differences that did exist were softened or eliminated by their assimilatory experience with Native Americans, slavery, and the Civil War. Life in the West hardened their attitudes toward Native Americans and fostered the common idea that the superior white Americans had a "manifest destiny" to rule and develop the West, although it did not necessarily eliminate their sense of justice or sympathy. Slavery and the war galvanized their sense of being American and set aside lingering doubts about loyalty to their new country. They were now more than ever what Charlotte Erickson has termed "invisible immigrants."

Assimilation: Institutions and Pastimes

Although assimilation was more immediate and less jarring for British immigrants than for any other group, many still chose to maintain a part of their old culture or at least keep abreast of the latest news from the old country by reading publications that catered to them. The Welsh immigrant press relied on those who spoke Welsh. During the 1840s these publications were tied to the major Welsh religious denominations—the Calvinist Methodists and Congregationalists—and featured sermons and church news. The successful *Y Drych* (Mirror) began in 1851 and at its peak had twelve thousand subscribers. Gradually, however, Welsh periodicals converted to English, as did their readers.

The English and Scots also had their own newspapers and periodicals. Among the most important were *Albion* (1822–76) and the *Scottish-American Journal* (1857–1919). These periodicals and others like them featured the latest news, often culled from British newspapers, that would appeal to the expatriates. When compared with the presses for every other immigrant group in America, however, the British immigrant press was limited in circulation and duration—an obvious reflection of the relative ease and quick pace of assimilation for British immigrants.[76]

More important for the British were the variety of lodges, immigrant societies, and various cultural organizations that sprang up in the nineteenth century. Lodges were familiar social institutions for the English and many Scots. Freemasons were transplanted to America during the eighteenth century and eased the transition of many so inclined to join. As English immigrants continued to enter the country, the Odd Fellows and similar organizations followed. In Scranton, Pennsylvania, English miners established the Sons of St. George in 1870, and other lodges and friendly societies flourished, at least for a while. By World War I, 292 lodges in the United States had more than thirty thousand English and Scottish immigrants as members, and women's auxiliaries were also popular.[77]

The earliest St. George's, St. Andrew's, and St. David's Societies grew out of a need to help destitute English, Scottish, and Welsh immigrants stranded in American ports begin their move into the American mainstream. Soon, however, their charitable purpose gave way to desires to celebrate and commemorate British culture. Highlights of the societies' year became the banquets at which participants toasted first the Queen and then the American president.

Rather than unity, the societies promoted greater definition and separation among the English, Scots, and Welsh, something that might have been expected given the three national subgroups' attitudes about the queen and the resentment some Scots and Welsh harbored toward England's cultural and political domination of Great Britain. Yet in America differences were buried. The Scottish-Americans in particular were disinclined to see the distinction between Highlanders and Lowlanders that prevailed in Scotland. Scottish culture in the various Caledonia Clubs that sprang up in the United States was fostered without regard to the precise origins of the immigrants. They also held traditional Scottish sporting events, concerts, and festivals that celebrated the poetry of Scotland's national icon, Robert Burns. Clubs devoted to the promotion of Bobby Burns were first established in New York in 1847, and throughout the rest of the century they held public recitations of his work and erected statues of him in towns throughout America.[78]

Promoting their culture was important for the Welsh in America, although doing so took a unique twist. Because Welsh middle and upper classes had become Anglicized, native culture had become the preserve of the working class. Thus it was common to hear Welsh songs sung deep in American mines. Above-ground, the Welsh took choral singing seriously and composed and performed sophisticated music that culminated in the well-known *eisteddfod* competitions first held in New York in 1841 and then regularly throughout the rest of the century. Prizes for these performance contests were attractive enough to bring contestants all the way from Wales itself, and by the latter part of the century Welsh Americans were returning to Wales to compete. Some commented that Welsh Americans were "more Welsh" and more patriotic toward their land of birth than the Welsh people themselves.[79]

The English, except for most Cornish, showed less interest in preserving a distinct culture in America because they noticed fewer differences with Anglo-American culture. They did not sense that their culture was under threat in America, as did some Welsh and most European immigrants generally. Still, English farmers in Wisconsin sometimes met to sing old songs. More generally, the English continued to revere the queen and the royal family, notwithstanding the oath to renounce her that becoming an American citizen required. Expatriation tended to magnify the sense of loyalty on the part of many immigrants, especially as nostalgia cast memories of the Old Country in a soft glow. Upon Victoria's marriage to Prince Albert, the British in New York celebrated with ardent enthusiasm for two full days, something they might not have done had they remained in Britain. Likewise, Victoria's Diamond and Golden Jubilees of 1887 and 1897 were celebrated by English immigrants in America visibly and passionately—too much so in the eyes of many Irish, Welsh, and native-born Americans.[80]

British immigrants also retained their Old World culture on traditional holidays such as Christmas and Boxing Day. English-style feasts, celebrations, and methods of decoration for the Christmas season were distinct and more festive than the staid, Puritan-influenced American celebrations. The English brought their "Yuletide" traditions to America and were usually intent on keeping them alive. The celebrations of English immigrants on the Wisconsin frontier in the early 1840s nearly ended in disaster when terrified American neighbors mistook the midnight caroling for an Indian attack. For Scottish immigrants, Hogmanay (New Year's Eve) was the most important holiday of the season and was celebrated by consigning the old year to "Auld Lang Syne," singing, and revelry.[81]

The immigrants found the adaptation to American sports an easy one. Sports could be experiences in assimilation as well as cultural preservation. Nearly all major sports that Americans enjoyed during the nineteenth century either originated in England or had been brought to America by British immigrants.[82] Although many Americans thought of sport as a waste of time, English textile mill workers and coal miners introduced cricket, soccer, and other games and played them frequently. Baseball, the "All-American sport," came directly from the old game of rounders that British immigrants played well before 1839, the year Abner Doubleday supposedly invented baseball. There were also links between cricket and baseball because of the similarities between the two and the transferability of many of the skills. That linkage was most obvious in the fact that Harry Wright, an immigrant from Sheffield who had been a professional bowler for the St. George's Cricket Club of New York, organized America's first professional baseball team, the Cincinnati Red Stockings.[83]

The Scots did their part by organizing Highland Games, first held in New York in 1836. They also introduced curling and golf, the first club being St. Andrew's Golf Club in New York in 1887. Other British sports such as lawn tennis, polo, English-style horse racing, and yachting and rowing were primarily pursuits of America's elite. They also indicate the wide and profound cultural affinity between Britons and Americans. That the immigrants were at once both Britons and Americans is neatly illustrated by the career of James Fisher. Twenty years after his immigration in 1847 he was simultaneously the treasurer of the St. George's Society and captain of the Capital City baseball club in Madison, Wisconsin.[84]

Although some immigrant institutions tended to sharpen the distinction between the English, Scots, and Welsh in the United States, there was a growing force that ultimately pulled the three subgroups together to form a more unified British American community toward the end of the century. That force was the growing presence and political power of Irish immigrants. Irish resentment toward the British was naturally carried over to America, where it grew and frequently led to conflict and violence. The Irish often protested when Britons in America celebrated the queen's birthday or when they expressed pride in England. This was understandable enough given their differing experiences under British absentee landlords and domination by the British government. When the Fenian "army" attempted to invade Ontario in 1866, and after the ugly Orange Riots ripped New York in 1870 and 1871, British immigrants rallied and began to think of themselves more as Britons rather than as English, Scots, or Welsh.[85] Conflict arose in the mines and other places where the British and Irish worked together. That workers from England and Wales dominated most skilled jobs and managerial positions embittered Irish workers, who often found it difficult to work under a British mine boss or factory foreman.

These Old World animosities and sectarian antagonisms produced a situation that drew the British American community together. But their political response was comparatively feeble. There were some attempts at naturalization drives to get British immigrants in polling booths. The Democratic Party was the natural political home of most immigrant groups, including Irish Catholics, whereas Whigs and Republicans appealed to native whites, many of whom harbored strident sentiments against foreigners. It is revealing that the British were the only immigrants to show strong support for Whigs and Republicans, as though they were already Americans.[86] Thus, as immigrants from England, Scotland, and Wales became more British in their response to Irish immigrants they began to take citizenship more seriously. In the process, they became more American as well. They could feel at home because they were not so much foreigners as "cousins" joining others from their countries who had preceded them to America and had done more than any other nationality to shape it.

Conclusion

Ah, Old England with all thy faults I love the[e] still.
—E. Chapman, Utica, New York, to J. C. Gotch,
  Kettering, Northamptonshire, May 1, 1850

British immigrants were indeed a motley set of people who defy generalization and categorization. What is clear, however, is that the difficulty and distress that accompanied Britain's economic growth and industrial change do not account for the great surge of British migration to America at the middle of the nineteenth century.

To be sure, there was some distress-related emigration. The repeal of the Corn Laws in 1846 caused a drop in grain prices, which precipitated the emigration of many small tenant farmers who were unwilling or unable to increase their production or somehow compensate for the loss of protective tariffs. Many feared ruin and appeared to be leaving Britain out of desperation. These very real problems were short-lived, however, as prices rebounded and stabilized in 1854. Furthermore, many of these farmers had contemplated emigration for some time and saw the late 1840s and early 1850s as the best time to make their move. In other words, the temporary crisis among some British farmers was more the occasion than the cause for their migration. Farm laborers were more poorly situated, but their drive and resourcefulness took them to America, where they generally prospered as farmers. The unprecedented opportunities during the 1840s and 1850s to get to America cheaply and purchase prime farmland, especially in the Old Northwest but also in other states, at truly bargain prices were attractions strong enough to entice Britons from every conceivable occupational background. Therefore, we cannot ultimately assign the unprecedented magnitude of agricultural migration from Britain to the United States to distress and hardship alone.

The dire social and economic consequences associated with industrialization and urbanization also spurred the migration of skilled and industrial workers to America. During the worst years of the "hungry forties," unemployed textile workers and Welsh iron workers emigrated, as did some rural craftsmen who felt the pinch of rural depopulation. But they never dominated the movement. Furthermore, the recovery and rapid expansion of the British economy during the mid-Victorian boom absorbed potential emigrants as textile mills, iron foundries, and coal mines hummed and groaned with dynamic activity.

Welsh coal miners left in significant numbers at mid-century because of wage cuts and managerial problems, but, as with the farmers, the economic stimulus from the Crimean War in 1854 mollified this temporary bleak situation. Furthermore, many migrant Welsh miners were originally farmers who intended all along to return to the land in America. Similarly, many tin and lead miners left Cornwall and Yorkshire as mines in those regions approached exhaustion. These people were exceptionally mobile and independent, however, and did not make desperate moves. They certainly did not see themselves as desperate. They knew they could participate in a flourishing tradition of British mining in America, where earnings were high (fantastically high in the goldfields of California); where nascent lead, iron, and coal mines awaited the application of British skills and know-how; and where they could both mine and farm their own land near friends and relatives who had been neighbors in Britain.

The lure of American agriculture was a powerful reason for the migration of people from virtually all backgrounds, which is explained in part by the fact that many nonagricultural workers had originally come from agricultural backgrounds or had at least some close affinity with the land. By the middle of the century more than any other time, people who had been on the land as children or young adults but had moved into crafts, professional work, or labor in the towns used migration to the United States to become landowners. It was a propitious time for Britons to become American farmers, and to a great extent that fact defines the period as far as British migration to the United States is concerned.

In addition, the remarkable occupational and geographic mobility and adaptability of the British causes us to appreciate the tenacity and resilience of these men and women. They were mobile and willing to make long, arduous journeys, often many journeys, to fulfill their desires and ambitions. All kinds of people made repeated moves, both within America and between Britain and America. Even many of the laborers, who included both agricultural and general laborers and were usually the poorest migrants, were active players in the Atlantic economy.

Although many migrants had suffered meager wages and grim living conditions, they were generally not forced out of Britain or leaving as a last resort. Rather, they were discontented with the status quo and determined to have a say in their future. A lively sense of adventure characterized many, including those at the upper end of the socioeconomic spectrum—clerical workers, merchants, and professionals. Generally not facing hardship or declining opportunity in Britain, these wealthier migrants were willing to risk time and money to try life in America. For them especially, return to Britain was feasible.

Steamships, of course, enhanced the immigrants' mobility. Eli Beckley's experience was not unique. After his initial migration to Illinois in 1854 he made ten return trips to England, some of them to import Clydesdale and Englishshire horses.[1] The mid-century immigrants would make return visits for almost any imaginable reason: to preach a funeral sermon, for health reasons (which surely included homesickness), to find suitable brides, to see family, or to fight in the Crimean War.[2] Clearly, many could undo their migration if they chose, and many did. An estimated 40 percent of the English and Welsh who emigrated between the 1870s and World War I returned, likely the highest percentage of all nationalities.[3] They flowed back and forth across the Atlantic almost as easily as the information that had facilitated their migration in the first place.

Neither poverty nor the disruptive effects of industrialization and socioeconomic change explain why a large wave of British migration to the United States occurred at mid-century. What does explain it is the combination of an expanding American nation (especially the growing availability of good farmland), an increasing ability to afford migration, and the network or "chains" of contact and flows of information between Britain and America—all within the context of the Atlantic economy. There was no extensively used safety valve for victims of industrial change. Few were fleeing hunger or immediate hardship, although more feared that a future in Britain might bring such hardship. Instead, the migrants were selective among people who usually had some resources and could have survived adequately in Britain but knew they could do much better in the United States and secure a better future. Their families and neighborhoods often had a tradition of migration that had created overseas contacts and allowed them to follow someone who had already gone to America. Their threshold of emigration was comparatively low. It required less inducement to mobilize them. That was especially true for nonconformists who had remained outside Britain's dominant culture. They already felt a special kinship with the United States that was born out of shared political and religious ideals and societal connections. For them, the move was a natural and highly practical step.

This positive interpretation should in no way minimize or obscure the hardship, poverty, and degradation that were all too real among Britain's poor during these years of industrialization and socioeconomic change. Far too many were at least temporary losers in the struggle to cope with the march of industrialization and urbanization or eke out a living as laborers. Many lacked adequate employment and lived lives that seemed hopeless—as any reading of the historical record will make painfully clear. But they were not the ones who migrated to the United States in significant numbers. Those who did were people with energy and tenacity, ambitious to expand their horizons and fulfill their capabilities and hoping to become rich or at least be independent and secure. They were not complacent or willing to settle for the cards dealt to them in Britain. They were moulders of their own destinies, determined to make or break their futures and take some risks if necessary. They were Britain's loss and America's gain.

The flow of Britons to the United States during the antebellum period was an essential part of the long migratory and symbiotic relationship that the United States and Britain shared over the centuries. The migration involved not only people but also capital, ideas, literature, and political and religious beliefs—the very essence of culture. Immigrants of the colonial period arrived in four discernible waves, each of which established a particular folkway that formed the basis of American society and persisted long enough to influence American culture in profound ways.[4] On the eve of the Revolution, British immigration surged again as a wide variety of enterprising people, most of whom were poor but few of whom were desperate or totally impoverished, followed well-established migratory channels to seize a better future. They were augmenting America's thriving British culture, even while the Colonies were on the verge of political independence.[5]

At mid-century, British immigrants were no longer establishing folkways. Rather, they were joining a society already more familiar to them than not by virtue of its deep roots in British culture and the long, almost continuous, flow of British people to America that had started early in the seventeenth century. The symbiosis between Britain and America had reached a new phase by mid-century, when the two economies were more developed, interconnected, and interactive than ever before. The impact of the repeal of the Corn Laws provided one example. The elimination of tariff protection for British farmers not only squeezed some out of British agriculture but also made America more appealing now that her farmers could tap the British market. That spurred agricultural expansion in America, which in turn created enticing new openings for all types of British immigrants who wished to own and farm land. The American frontier was very much also a British frontier where people could start over and rise above their former station in life.

The mid-century period was also auspicious for those who did not farm. America still needed skills and technology that only Britain could provide. More generally, the American economy was growing such that most skilled and professional British immigrants could readily find work at good wages, as could general laborers. Opportunities in mining and building were especially rich. Altogether, the antebellum period proved most advantageous for British migration to the United States.

Throughout their complete migratory sequence—from the initial thought of leaving to full assimilation into American life—British migrants had the advantage of sharing the language and culture of the host country. They could immediately engage in the culture of the United States and participate in institutions that were familiar to them. That can be seen in the fact that the British, unlike all other immigrant groups, never formed ethnic military regiments, ethnic neighborhoods, or a distinctly "British vote" in American politics. Their "largely symbolic ethnicity" did not get in the way of immediate participation in American institutions and culture.[6] They did, however, join lodges and fraternal and immigrant societies. They also read a lot about the old homeland because they enjoyed doing so.

As British immigrants merged themselves and their culture into American life, few would completely shed their Britishness or love for their native land. More would have echoed Matthew Dinsdale after he settled in Wisconsin. Even as he began his rise in social and economic status, his heart was in his old village in Yorkshire: "My thoughts are often at Askrigg. I should much like to see it once again, it will ever be dear to me, more so than any other place on the earth."[7]

Appendix A: Sources

Several types of sources were extensively used for this project, and their nature and how they were selected are as follows.

U.S. County Histories

During the last quarter of the nineteenth century and the first decade or so of the twentieth, a large number of county histories were published to satisfy a widespread interest in local history that grew in part out of America's Centennial celebrations. Most counties, especially in midwestern states, had at least one lengthy volume on their history published. These tell much about settlers and those who played important roles in the county's early development—including many British immigrants.

The nature and quality of these volumes vary. In most, the standards of writing and scholarship are high. Some have been called "mug books" because they consist largely of short "biographical sketches" of "leading and prominent" persons in the county. Evidently, persons who agreed to purchase a copy could have their personal history included in it.[1]

British migrants who appear in the county histories are largely those who desired and could afford to have their stories told. Those who failed in America and returned to Britain are not represented, although there are glimpses of relatives who failed and returned. Despite the inherent biases of county histories, they still contain much valuable information that can be applied to the migrants as a whole. The biographical sketches are particularly rich in the migrants' background: the county or village from which they came, their past occupations, why they left, and how they settled in America. None of that information would have been biased by the future success of the immigrant.

An attempt was made to include representative proportions of urban and rural counties in New York, Pennsylvania, and the states of the Old Northwest. This study examines the county history biographies of 1,372 people who migrated between 1845 and 1855, as well as many others from earlier and later years. Although that cannot be considered a true scientific sample, the accounts do provide intimate views of a significant number of British migrants.[2]

Census Notes, Newspapers, and Letters

Notes in the published British Census of 1851 often provide valuable explanations for a significant rise or fall in population in a given village or parish. The notes are likely accurate, for one of the qualifications for being a census enumerator in 1851 was to be "well acquainted with the District in which he will be required to act" and to "obtain a thorough and minute knowledge of the District which he has undertaken to enumerate."[3]

In addition to the census notes, we have the many British newspapers that were published during the period and many letters that immigrants in America wrote to families in Britain, some of which have been published and others still in archives in Britain and the United States. Immigrant letters have a power and intimacy that still make compelling reading. Historians agree that the information in them was more influential to other potential emigrants than the information found in the many guidebooks and pamphlets that were published to tap the emigrant market, some of which are cited in this book.[4] Diaries, journals, trade publications, and various other manuscripts were consulted as well.

Passenger Lists

Because immigration to the United States from the time of the American Revolution to the end of the Napoleonic Wars was so slight—on average probably no more than three to four thousand per year—there seemed to be no reason for American officials to regulate and take account of this minor inward flow of people. But after the Peace of 1815 and the poor European harvest of 1816, immigration increased dramatically and reached more than twenty-two thousand in 1817. With these greater numbers came increased problems with poor hygiene, ship epidemics, and other atrocious conditions resulting from immigrants traveling in the overcrowded and unsanitary steerage compartments of cargo ships. The U.S. Congress responded to these new problems in 1819 with a regulatory act that not only attempted to improve ship conditions but also required that, beginning January 1, 1820, all captains arriving from any foreign port must deliver to the collector of customs a sworn list of the names of all passengers along with their sex, age, occupation, nationality, and country of destination. The name of the vessel, its place of registry, port of embarkation, tonnage, date of arrival, and later its mode of power (whether sail or steam), together with the captain's name, are also indicated at the top of each list. In 1855 the act was amended to require captains also to designate whether each passenger traveled by cabin, second cabin, or steerage, although many captains had previously made such distinctions anyway. Some lists also provide valuable details on the migrants' precise origins and destinations.

These passenger lists (also referred to as "ship lists") are the single most important source for determining the basic characteristics of British immigrants to the United States.[5] They do, however, have inherent deficiencies. Although many were obviously filled out with great care and calligraphic neatness, some are illegible either because of poor penmanship or physical damage. Others appear untrustworthy, as though the captain was not taking the clerical side of his job seriously. In particular, some lists have "labourers" or "labourers and farmers" scribbled at the top of the occupational column, with dittos or hasty slashes running down the rest of the list. Obviously, such lists cannot be relied upon, because there is no way to determine who was a laborer and who was a farmer. Those lists that describe every passenger simply as a "labourer" through a liberal use of dittos are also suspect because it is statistically improbable if not impossible that all emigrants aboard the ship were laborers, with no experience in farming or some sort of craft. Other lists lump the English, Welsh, Scots, and Irish together under the vague heading "British and Irish." These, too, are deceptive and thus cannot be relied upon. Finally, even with the aid of a computer there is the forbidding task of listing and coding the voluminous data on hundreds of thousands of emigrants.

These problems can be overcome, however, by using reliable sampling methods that eliminate bad lists and reduce the overabundant data without introducing biases.[6] I selected the lists of 1851 for detailed study because that was a year of the British census and a comparison of the occupational structure of the emigrants with that of the home population will reveal the kinds of workers who are overrepresented or underrepresented on the lists—those who were most or least prone to emigrate. Also, in 1851 both prosperity and emigration rose, and that apparent paradox has inherent interest. Finally, 1851 was the year when the United States was taking fully 80 percent of all British emigrants (table 1), and so the omission of persons going elsewhere is not as serious as it would be for other years. Some 1851 lists provided details on the migrants' origins and/or destinations. Of these lists, some fell into the sample and others did not, but all of this information was retained. The 1851 sample lists and the nonsample lists with this extra data are identified in table A1. Lists from selected months from 1847 and 1854 were also examined for occupational comparisons (tables A2–A3).

Occupational Classifications

In examining the passenger lists and census information about the migrants' occupations, it is helpful to group them into six occupational categories.[7]

Agriculture: All types of people working on the land are included here: farmers, agricultural laborers, gardeners, shepherds, and graziers.

Labor: The passenger lists and other sources describe many migrants as "labourers." Presumably, they were unskilled, although some could well have worked in British factories or coal mines at some unskilled task. Perhaps many had worked on farms, although the lists provide no evidence for that.

Service ("preindustrial tertiary workers"): Domestic servants comprise the bulk of this group. Seamen, soldiers, grooms, fishermen, and workers on roads and waterways are also included.

Crafts ("preindustrial skilled workers"): The most prominent people in this group are miners, building trades workers, food processors, blacksmiths, woodworkers, saddlers, wheelwrights, tailors, and boot and shoemakers. Generally, nineteenth-century industri-

Table A1. Ships Arriving in American Ports Whose British Immigrants Were Analyzed for This Study (1851)

Port	Reel Number[a]	Ship Number
Boston (277)	37	*55, 179
	38	277, 478
	39	578, 705, 844
Philadelphia (425)	184	*26, 50, 85
	185	*126, 144, *152, *153, 176, *196, *198, 202, *219
Baltimore (255)		*53, *68, 76
New Orleans (259)	33	*18, 55, *101, *120, 130
	34	222, *251, *262, *268, 296, *309, 345
New York (237)	95	*6, *17, 28, *30, 49, 107, 144
	96	174, 210, 232, 263, 288, 301
	97	*328, 331, *335, *339, *344, 357, *358, 376, 419, *423, 446
	98	459, 480, 532, *542, 548, *561, *565, 569
	99	590, 643, *662, 678
	100	*727, 729, 761, *795, 824
	101	*854, 871, *874, 896, *909, 927
	102	978, *995, 1024, *1039, 1044, 1070
	103	1121, *1137, 1155, *1164, *1166, *1187, 1191, 1205
	104	1247, *1281, 1282, 1304, *1328
	105	1339, 1354, *1370, 1401, *1416, 1418, *1442, 1445
	106	1479, 1510, 1552, *1575, 1587
	107	1616, 1646, *1662, 1664, 1680, 1702
	108	1728, 1751, *1752, *1784, 1800, *1812

Note: Ships marked by an asterisk are not part of the one-in-ten sample but include details on the migrants' origins and destinations. The following sample ships, not marked with an asterisk, also include details about the migrants' origins and destinations: Boston, 277; Philadelphia, 144, 202; Baltimore, 76; New Orleans, 130, 222, 345, 296; New York, 1304, 1339, 1510, 419, 446, 480, 532, 590, 643, 824, 1070, 1304, 1339, 1418, 1479, 1510, 1646, 1800.

a. National Archives microfilm series 277, 425, 255, 259, 237.

Table A2. Comparative Occupational Structure of British Immigrants to the United States (Males 20+) and the General Population, 1851, with Indexes of Representation for 1831, 1841, and 1885–88

	1851			Index of Representation[a]		
	Lists	Census	Index of Representation[a]	1831	1841	1885–88
Agriculture	23.0%	27.3%	84	76	68	61
Laborers	25.7	6.9	373	59	154	360
Servants, etc.	3.8	9.3	41	34	26	25
Crafts						
Building	8.3	7.4	112		101	199
Mining	6.8	5.2	131		115	125
Food	3.1	4.2	74		86	50
Metal	3.1	2.8	111		83	55
Clothing	5.2	6.4	81		81	34
Woodworking	1.7	2.2	77		76	25
Miscellaneous	1.2	2.0	60		113	73
Mechanics	1.7					375
	31.1	30.2	103		104	113
Industry						
Textiles	2.9	8.9	33		205	37
Iron/steel and engineering	5.0	4.8	104		104	31
Miscellaneous	1.4	2.0	70		155	47
	9.3	15.7	59		165	46
Commerce/professions	7.2	10.7	67		94	98
Totals	100.1	100.1				
$N = 2,224$[b]						

Source: For exact ship-list sources for the 1851 sample data, see table A1. Indexes for 1831, 1841, and the late 1880s were calculated from data in Erickson, "Emigration from the British Isles to the U.S.A. in 1831," 186; "Emigration from the British Isles to the U.S.A. in 1841, Part II," 25, 28, 29; and "Who Were the English and Scots Emigrants?" 363.

a. The index of representation is calculated by dividing the ship-list percentage into the census percentage and multiplying by 100. Thus an index value of 100 means that the ship-list percentage and census percentage for that group were equal. (The 1831 and 1841 data are for the English and Welsh only, and the 1831 index is incomplete because of imprecision in the 1831 census occupational headings.)

b. This number is for males 20+ because the census figures are also for males of that age. Including males 15+, there were 2,496 employed males in the sample. Not included in these figures are twenty described as "gentlemen" (chapter 7).

Table A3. Occupational Structure of Employed British Immigrant Males 20+ to the United States, Arriving at the Port of New York for Selected Months (1847 and 1854)

	1847				1854			
	April	May	Sept.	Average	April	May	Sept.	Average
Agriculture	38.1%	57.0%	19.6%	44.8%	17.6%	19.8%	4.9%	13.9%
Labor	1.2	15.3	5.4	10.2	15.7	41.8	17.7	26.9
Service	6.0	1.3	4.3	2.9	1.9	1.1	3.1	2.0
Crafts	25.0	0.0	40.2	14.1	47.2	24.2	37.8	34.6
Industry	20.2	26.4	18.5	23.4	11.1	9.3	34.1	18.7
Commerce/professions	9.5	0.0	12.0	4.6	6.5	3.8	2.4	3.9
	100.0	100.0	100.0	100.0	100.0	100.0	100.0	100.0
N	84	235	92	411	108	182	164	454

Source: National Archives microfilm series 237. Reel and ship numbers: April 1847 (reel 66), 141, 151, 178; May 1847 (reels 66, 67), 287, 243, 273; Sept. 1847 (reel 69), 667, 694, 727, 755; April 1854 (reels 137, 138), 259, 299, 318, 347, 390; May 1854 (reels 138–40), 422, 481, 512, 565, 612; Sept. 1854 (reels 145, 147), 1178, 1224, 1253, 1292.

alization neither threatened them with technological unemployment nor drastically altered the nature of their work. They might, however, have been victims of cyclical unemployment. Some craftsmen may also have suffered the rise of industrial areas, some of which drained local populations from the countryside and limited or extinguished the livelihood of skilled workers who had relied on a thriving and expanding rural economy. In America they could expect to resume their traditional form of work with few, if any, occupational adjustments.

Industry: All of these people were skilled workers in industries that were changing because of new technology. They worked in the staple industries, minus mining, plus such secondary branches of metal manufacturing as cutlery and tool making. Some miscellaneous occupations—printers, publishers, machinists, chemical workers, and earthenware and glass manufacturers—also fall into this category. This group is especially interesting to observe in the 1850s because during this time some workers were gaining from new technology while others were losing a great deal. Just as new machinery and techniques created new kinds of employment, so, too, did they bring destruction to some of the traditional types of work—the continuing rise of power loom weaving over handloom weaving being a prime example.

Commerce and the professions ("modern tertiary workers"): Like preindustrial tertiary workers, modern tertiary workers were nonproducers. But here the similarity ends. People in this class include service workers in the new railway industry and those with commercial, clerical, and professional occupations. Thus, merchants, army and navy officers (i.e., professional men), medical workers, and all types of clerks fall under this heading. It is the broadest classification, a partial compromise necessitated by the census categories.

Appendix B: Details of British Immigrants to the United States, 1851

Table B1. Size of Town of Origin of British Immigrants, by Occupational Group (1851)

Occupational Group	Population Over 20,000	Population Under 20,000	Number
Agriculture	64%	36%	61
Labor	56	44	78
Service	70	30	50
Crafts	69	31	137
Industry	93	7	30
Commercial/professional	85	15	20
None	70	30	270
Totals	69	31	646

Source: Appendix A, table A1.

Table B2. Nature of Male-Headed Migrating Units of British Immigrants, by Occupational Group (1851)

Migrating Unit	Agriculture	Labor	Services	Crafts	Industry	Commercial/ Professional	Total
Individuals traveling alone[a]	59.9%	70.4%	75.6%	69.0%	62.7%	70.0%	67.1%
Married couples without children	12.9	11.5	15.9	12.1	14.8	10.0	12.3
Married couples with children	22.5	16.5	8.5	16.9	20.6	16.3	18.0
Males without wives but with children	4.7	1.7	0.0	2.0	1.9	3.8	2.6
	100.0	100.0	100.0	100.0	100.0	100.0	100.0
Number of units	488	601	82	688	209	160	2,228
Units headed by males with dependents aged 0–14 years	25.8%	20.1%	11.0%	19.5%	23.0%	18.1%	21.0%

Source: Appendix A, table A1.
a. That is, traveling without a wife or children. Some traveled with a sibling or perhaps some other companion of unknown relationship. Cases here were not separated because they are not concerned with the questions about the immediate family and the ability to pay multiple passage fares. (Siblings, for example, likely had their own incomes and did not rely on elder brothers.)

Table B3. Nature of British Immigrant Families, by Occupational Group (1851)

Migrating Unit	Occupational Group						
	Agriculture	Labor	Services	Crafts	Industry	Commercial/ Professional	Tot:
Families extended in some way[a]	18.2%	12.1%	5.9%	13.4%	15.0%	7.8%	12..
Life cycle of family							
Married/widowed without children	35.0	36.7	25.5	38.2	40.2	36.4	31
Married/widowed with one infant	10.6	9.0	5.9	8.3	11.8	11.4	9.
Married/widowed with children 0–14 years	32.2	44.7	54.9	39.6	30.3	40.9	41
Married/widowed with some children 0–14 years and fewer 15+ years	7.2	5.9	3.9	5.1	5.3	6.8	5.
Married/widowed with some children 0–14 years and more 15+ years	7.2	2.1	7.8	3.2	2.6	2.3	5
Married/widowed with all children 15+ years or without children and wife 45+ years	7.8	1.6	2.0	5.5	9.2	2.3	6.
	100.0	100.0	100.0	100.0	100.0	100.0	100.
Average family size	4.2	3.8	3.6	3.7	3.6	3.7	3.
Number of families	180	188	51	217	76	44	929

Source: Appendix A, table A1.

a. For the demographic rules and explanations for extension, see Lasslet, ed., *Household and Family in Times Past,* 28ff.

Table B4. City of Destination of British Immigrants, by Selected Occupational Groups and Occupations (1851)

City	Preindustrial Bu	Mi	Fo	Me	Cl	Wo	Industrial Te	I/E	Selected Occupations Mi*	We
Fall River, Mass.							1	1		1
Boston, Mass.					3		2			
Providence, R.I.						1				
Woonsocket, R.I.					1		1			1
New Haven, Conn.	1						1	1		
Albany, N.Y.					1	1				
Bellmont, N.Y.							1			1
Brooklyn, N.Y.	1		2							
Buffalo, N.Y.	2									
E. Bloomfield, N.Y.								1		
Morristown, N.Y.							1			1
Otego, N.Y.				1						
Rochester, N.Y.				1	1			1		
Troy, N.Y.							1			
Utica, N.Y.					1	1				
Carbondale, Pa.		1							1	
Chester, Pa.							1			
Minersville, Pa.		15			2			2	9	
Philadelphia, Pa.	6	12	1	4	10	1	10	4	10	5
Pitstonferry, Pa.	1	1							1	
Pittsburgh, Pa.	1	12		1				3	3	
Pottsville, Pa.		5							2	
St. Clair, Pa.		1								
Tamaqua, Pa.		2							2	
Cincinnati, Ohio	2		1	1	6	1		1		
Cleveland, Ohio	1				2					
Columbus, Ohio		1								
Detroit, Mich.		1								
St. Louis, Mo.	2			1	1			1		
Baltimore, Md.	1	1			3			4		
Mt. Savage, Md.		4								
Columbia, S.C.							1			1
New Orleans, La.	2	2	1		3			1		
Totals	20	58	5	9	34	5	20	20	28	10

Key: Bu = building; Mi = mining; Fo = food; Me = metals; Cl = clothing; Wo = wood; Te = textiles; I/E = iron/engineering; Mi* = miners not otherwise designated; We = weavers.
Source: Appendix A, table A1.

Table B5. U.S. Destinations of British Industrial
Immigrants, by Occupational Group or Selected
Occupation (1851)

Destination	Textiles	Iron/Engineers	Weavers
New England			
Vermont	1.1%	0.0%	2.3%
Massachusetts	9.9	1.2	11.4
Rhode Island	3.3	1.2	6.8
Connecticut	5.5	1.2	4.5
	19.8	3.6	25.0
Mid-Atlantic			
New York	26.4	44.0	18.2
Pennsylvania	24.2	20.2	25.0
	50.6	64.2	43.2
Old Northwest			
Ohio	5.5	1.2	9.1
Indiana	2.2	1.2	4.5
Michigan	0.0	2.4	0.0
Wisconsin	3.3	1.2	2.3
	11.0	6.0	15.9
West North Central			
Iowa	4.4	0.0	0.0
Missouri	2.2	2.4	4.5
	6.6	2.4	4.5
South Atlantic			
Maryland	2.2	4.8	2.3
Virginia	0.0	3.6	0.0
South Carolina	1.1	0.0	2.3
	3.3	8.4	4.6
West South Central			
Louisiana	1.1	1.2	0.0
Mountain			
Utah	7.7	14.3	6.8
Totals	100.0	100.0	100.0
N	91	84	44

Source: Appendix A, table A1.

Table B6. County and Region-Type Origins of English Preindustrial Immigrants, by Occupational Group (1851)

County/Region-type	Building	Mining	Food	Metal	Clothing	Wood	Misc.	Mechanic
Low-wage agricultural: Southwest								
Dorset	8.6%	0.0%	0.0%	0.9%	0.0%	0.0%	0.0%	0.0%
Wiltshire	0.0	0.0	0.0	0.0	1.6	0.0	0.0	0.0
Somerset	0.0	18.2	0.0	8.3	0.0	0.0	0.0	0.0
Shropshire	8.6	0.0	0.0	0.0	0.0	26.7	0.0	0.0
	17.2	18.2	0.0	8.3	1.6	26.7	0.0	0.0
Low-wage agriculture: Southeast								
Hampshire	2.9	0.0	0.0	0.0	0.0	0.0	11.1	0.0
Berkshire	2.9	0.0	0.0	0.0	1.6	0.0	0.0	0.0
Buckinghamshire	2.9	0.0	5.6	0.0	0.0	6.7	0.0	0.0
Hertfordshire	2.9	0.0	0.0	0.0	4.8	13.3	0.0	0.0
Northamptonshire	2.9	0.0	11.1	0.0	4.8	0.0	0.0	0.0
Cambridgeshire	0.0	0.0	0.0	8.3	0.0	0.0	0.0	0.0
Norfolk	5.7	0.0	5.6	0.0	3.2	0.0	0.0	0.0
Essex	0.0	0.0	5.6	0.0	1.6	0.0	0.0	0.0
	20.2	0.0	27.9	8.3	16.0	20.0	11.1	0.0
Total low-wage agricultural	37.4	18.2	27.9	16.6	17.6	46.7	11.1	0.0
High-wage agriculture								
Lincolnshire	8.6	0.0	22.2	8.3	3.2	13.3	0.0	14.3
Sussex	0.0	0.0	5.6	0.0	0.0	0.0	0.0	0.0
Kent	2.9	0.0	0.0	8.3	1.6	0.0	0.0	0.0
Cumberland	0.0	0.0	0.0	0.0	4.8	0.0	0.0	0.0
	11.5	0.0	27.8	16.6	9.6	13.3	0.0	14.3
Low-wage industrial								
Cornwall	2.9	18.2	0.0	0.0	3.2	0.0	11.1	0.0
Worcestershire	0.0	0.0	5.6	0.0	4.8	0.0	0.0	0.0
Leicestershire	2.9	0.0	0.0	0.0	0.0	0.0	0.0	0.0
Staffordshire	2.9	9.1	5.6	8.3	9.7	0.0	0.0	0.0
Warwickshire	0.0	0.0	11.1	0.0	0.0	0.0	0.0	28.6
Gloucestershire	0.0	0.0	5.6	0.0	0.0	0.0	0.0	0.0
	8.7	27.3	27.9	8.3	17.7	0.0	11.1	28.6
High-wage industrial								
London	5.7	0.0	11.1	8.3	8.1	13.3	22.2	0.0
Cheshire	0.0	0.0	0.0	0.0	3.2	0.0	0.0	0.0
Lancashire	22.9	18.2	0.0	8.3	22.6	20.0	33.3	57.1
Durham	0.0	18.2	5.6	16.7	4.8	0.0	0.0	0.0
Nottinghamshire	8.6	0.0	0.0	0.0	3.2	0.0	0.0	0.0
Derbyshire	0.0	0.0	0.0	0.0	1.6	0.0	0.0	0.0
	37.2	36.4	16.7	33.3	43.5	33.3	55.5	57.1
Total industrial	45.9	63.7	44.6	41.6	61.2	33.3	66.6	85.7
Yorkshire								
North Riding	0.0	9.1	0.0	25.0	4.8	6.7	11.1	0.0
West Riding	0.0	0.0	0.0	0.0	3.2	0.0	0.0	0.0
Not defined	2.9	9.1	0.0	0.0	3.2	0.0	11.1	0.0
	2.9	18.2	0.0	25.0	11.2	6.7	22.2	0.0
Southeast Scotland	2.9	0.0	0.0	0.0	0.0	0.0	0.0	0.0
Grand total	100.0	100.0	100.0	100.0	100.0	100.0	100.0	100.0
N = 169	35	11	18	12	62	15	9	7

Source: Appendix A, table A1.

Table B7. Size of Town of Origin of British Preindustrial Craft Immigrants, by Occupational Group (1851)

	Occupational Group						
Population	Building	Mining	Food	Metal	Clothing	Wood	Mechan⸲
Over 20,000	67%	73%	42%	54%	84%	67%	100%
Under 20,000	33	27	58	46	16	33	0
N	21	15	12	13	44	12	5

Source: Appendix A, table A1.

Note: These data probably contain an inherent bias toward the larger cities. Just as people from small towns no⸲ tend to identify with the nearest larger city, particularly when asked where they are from, so, too, many emigran⸲ from smaller villages likely gave a nearby city as their origin when asked by a ship's captain who might not ha⸲ recognized small villages or towns as readily as large provincial cities. Thus, for example, people from Greenwic⸲ might tend to declare themselves as Londoners. Furthermore, emigrants from large cities of origin were probab⸲ more likely to give their city of origin than those from more obscure towns or villages, who naturally tended ⸲ describe their origins in more general terms of county of origin. Assuming that this bias is evenly distributed ov⸲ the occupational spectrum, the comparisons between the different occupational groups are still valid.

Table B8. Nature of Migrating Units of British Preindustrial Immigrants, by Occupationa⸲ Group (1851)

	Occupational Group						
Migrating Unit	Building	Mining	Food	Metal	Clothing	Wood	Mech⸲
Individuals traveling alone	66.1%	81.0%	70.4%	74.3%	63.4%	53.7%	7⸲
Married couple without children	13.4	3.5	14.1	14.3	11.0	22.0	⸲
Married couple with children	18.3	13.4	12.7	11.4	14.0	22.0	14⸲
Man without wife but with children	2.2	2.1	2.8	0.0	1.7	2.4	⸲
Women[a] with children	0.0	0.0	0.0	0.0	9.9	0.0	⸲
	100.0	100.0	100.0	100.0	100.0	100.0	10⸲
Number of units	186	142	71	70	172	41	4⸲
Units headed by male with dependent children 0–14 years	21.5%	14.9%	15.5%	12.9%	25.2%	20.0%	20⸲

Source: Appendix A, table A1.

a. Females are included because of the considerable numbers in the clothing trades traveling with their childre⸲ without husbands (who were likely already in America).

Table B9. Age of British Preindustrial Immigrants, by Occupational Group (1851)

Age (Years)	Occupational Group						
	Building	Mining	Food	Metal	Clothing	Wood	Mechanic
15–19	7.8%	8.7%	15.9%	5.3%	11.0%	13.0%	14.6%
20–24	31.2	31.8	36.4	42.7	28.6	26.1	33.3
	39.0	40.5	52.3	48.0	39.6	39.1	47.1
25–29	27.3	20.8	10.2	30.7	24.7	28.3	25.0
30–34	16.1	16.2	18.2	17.3	16.7	21.7	16.7
35–39	8.8	9.2	8.0	0.0	8.4	4.3	4.2
40–44	3.9	6.9	4.5	1.3	5.3	0.0	4.2
45–49	2.4	1.7	2.3	2.7	1.3	2.2	2.1
50–54	1.5	1.2	4.5	0.0	1.8	0.0	0.0
55–59	0.0	2.3	0.0	0.0	0.9	2.2	0.0
60–64	1.0	0.0	0.0	0.0	1.3	2.2	0.0
65+	0.0	1.2	0.0	0.0	0.0	0.0	0.0
Total	100.0	100.0	100.0	100.0	100.0	100.0	100.0
N	205	173	88	75	227	46	48

Source: Appendix A, table A1.
Note: Females are included because of their strong presence in the clothing trades.

Table B10. County of Origin of British Immigrants, by Selected Occupations (1851)

County	Weavers	Miners[a]	Quarriers	Needlewomen
England				
Wiltshire				1
Somerset		1		
Hertfordshire				2
Lincolnshire				1
Kent				1
Cumberland				1
Cornwall		2		
Worcestershire				1
Staffordshire		1		5
Gloucestershire	1			
London	1			1
Cheshire	1			2
Lancashire	3	1		5
Durham		2		1
Yorkshire[a]	5		1	2
Yorkshire, North		1		1
	11	8	1	24
Wales				
Carmarthen		7		2
Pembroke		1		
North Wales			6	
	0	8	6	2
Scotland				
Northeast				1
Southwest		1		1
Southeast				1
Highlands/Isles				1
	0	1	0	4
Total	11	17	7	30

Source: Appendix A, table A1.
a. Not otherwise designated.

Table B11. British Immigrant Males 20+ in Clerical,
Commercial, and Professional Work (1851)

Occupation	Number	Percent of Immigrants	Percent of British Labor Force
Railway drivers	4	0.2	0.2
Clerks	37	1.7	
Shop assistants	2	0.1	
Salesmen	1		
	40	1.8	2.1
Shopkeepers	5	0.2	
Merchants	43	1.9	
Publicans	3	0.1	
Agents	4	0.2	
Ironmongers	3	0.1	
Drapers	5	0.2	
Brokers	7	0.3	
Booksellers/others	4	0.2	
	74	3.3	5.9
Doctors	11	0.5	
Clergymen	6	0.3	
Lawyers	2	0.1	
Teachers	6	0.3	
Army officers	2	0.1	
Writers	3	0.3	
Musicians	7	0.3	
Surveyors/others	5	0.2	
	42	1.9	2.5
Totals	160	7.2	10.7

Source: Appendix A, table A1.

Table B12. Age and Traveling Status of British Immigrant Males 15+ in Clerical, Commercial, and Professional Occupations (1851)

	Clerical	Commercial	Professional	Merchants
Age (years)				
15–19	11.1%	8.6%	6.7%	6.5%
20–24	40.0	21.0	11.1	19.6
	51.1	29.6	17.8	26.1
25–29	26.7	18.5	22.2	15.2
30–34	11.1	16.0	24.4	21.7
35–39	4.4	14.8	13.3	17.4
40–44	4.4	8.6	11.1	10.9
45–49	0.0	7.9	2.2	4.3
50–59	0.0	4.9	6.7	4.3
60+	2.2	0.0	2.2	0.0
Total	100.0	100.0	100.0	100.0
Percent traveling				
alone	86.4	56.3	57.8	56.5
N	45	81	45	46

Source: Appendix A, table A1.

Table B13. Type of Passage and Ship of Modern Tertiary Male Immigrants 15+, by Occupational Group or Selected Occupation (1851)

	Clerical	Commercial	Professional	Merchants	Doctors
Type of passage					
Steerage	97.8%	88.9%	82.2%	87.0%	76.9%
Cabin	2.2	11.1	17.8	13.0	23.1
Type of ship					
Sailing Ship	88.9	64.2	80.0	45.7	76.9
Steamship	11.1	35.8	20.0	54.3	23.1
N	45	81	45	46	13

Source: Appendix A, table A1.

Notes

Introduction

1. The following overview of the Dinsdales is based on the Matthew Dinsdale Papers, and the biography of John Dinsdale is from *The Counties of Rock, Green, Grant, Iowa, and Lafayette, Wisconsin,* 111–12. Dinsdale described himself as a "merchant" on his marriage certificate (Askrigg, April 1853, 427/149). All certificates are located in St. Catherine's House, London, with the exception of one located in the Public Records Office. Short titles of the county histories will be used in these notes; see "U.S. County Histories" in the Bibliography for full references.

2. Erickson, *Invisible Immigrants.*

3. Thistlethwaite, *The Anglo-American Connection,* 3–11; Potter, "Atlantic Economy, 1815–60."

4. Thistlethwaite, "Migration from Europe Overseas," 22.

5. Hansen, *The Immigrant in American History,* 192.

6. For a convenient summary of the shortcomings of British statistics, see Jones, "The Background to Emigration from Great Britain," esp. 21–25. For a good overview of Welsh migration statistics, see Williams, "Some Figures Relating to Emigration," 396–415.

Chapter 1: "A Motley Set"

1. Maldwyn Jones estimated that British migrants to America numbered "72,000 in 1849 and remained around the 60,000 mark for the next three years." Jones, "The Background to Emigration from Great Britain," 28.

2. Redford, *Economic History of England,* 200; Burn, *The Age of Equipoise,* Briggs, *The Age of Improvement,* 394.

3. Hughes, *Fluctuations in Trade, Industry and Finance;* Briggs, *The Age of Improvement,* ch. 8; Best, *Mid-Victorian Britain,* 229 (first quotation); Gregg, *A Social and Economic History of Britain,* 295 (second quotation). Some historians hesitate to use the term *Great Victorian Boom.* Rostow called the phrase ambiguous and said that the only thing to be said with absolute certainty is that the previous downward trend in interest rates was finally arrested and that real wages rose during the 1860s. See *British Economy of the Nine-*

teenth Century, 20. Roy Church has scrutinized the term in more detail. He denies that the period from 1850 to 1873 saw generally rising prices because the standard calculations are based on wholesale prices rather than on retail prices of manufactured articles, which were falling during the period. Church also warns that it can be misleading to project the euphoria that surrounded the Great Exhibition upon the following two decades, at least as far as the business community is concerned. Church, *The Great Victorian Boom,* 13, 75–78. Church, Rostow, and others also believe that mid-Victorian prosperity, at least in terms of rising real wages for the masses, occurred mostly from the 1860s onward. In the final analysis, however, Church does concede that, because of the tremendous growth of the period, one may talk of a boom so long as these qualifications are kept in mind. Thus the association of the early 1850s with growing prosperity persists in the view of most historians. See also Saul, *The Myth of the Great Depression* (1962), 32.

4. This fact contradicts early historians of British migration such as C. E. Snow, who assumed that emigration and prosperity were negatively correlated to a very high degree— that depression produced emigration and prosperity absorbed it. See Snow, "Emigration from Great Britain," 2:239, 252. In fact, peaks in nineteenth-century British emigration occurred during the early 1850s and in the late 1860s and early 1870s. The absolute peak was during the 1880s, when industrialization was thriving in Britain and the two main capital goods industries—coal and steel—were seeing "enormous expansion." See Mathias, *The First Industrial Nation,* 377–78.

5. English silk workers emigrated en masse to the United States in the early 1860s because of foreign competition, as did ribbon workers of Coventry because of a declining market. See Margrave, *The Emigration of Silk Workers from England to the United States,* and Tiratsoo, "Coventry's Ribbon Trade in the Mid-Victorian Period."

6. Perloff et al., *Regions, Resources, and Economic Growth,* 113–14, 120.

7. Jeremy, *Transatlantic Industrial Revolution;* Berthoff, *British Immigrants in Industrial America.*

8. See the case of P. H. Naylor, who emigrated from Rutland in 1851 in *Morgan and Scott Counties, Illinois,* 427.

9. Gates, *The Farmer's Age,* 77–78. For details on land warrants and their sales, see Oberley, *Sixty Million Acres,* 9–37.

10. *The Counties of Rock, Green, Grant, Iowa, and Lafayette, Wisconsin,* 556. Similar expressions were made by James Dodd, who arrived from Yorkshire the previous year. Ibid., 635.

11. Bryson Collection, D/B/119C (41), Department of Archives, Merseyside County Museum.

12. Erickson, *Invisible Immigrants,* 30.

13. Immigrants Frederick Patrick and Alfred Cheney were among many who identified a concern for their children's future as the main reason for their migration to America in the 1840s. See *Ionia and Montcalm Counties, Michigan,* 202–5, and *Branch County, Michigan,* 272–73.

14. These considerations are explored by Dudley Baines in *Emigration from Europe.*

15. Thomas, *Migration and Economic Growth,* 102–7.

16. Philip Taylor reminds us that emigrants often endured bad conditions on the worst of the steamships, at least until the twentieth century. Taylor, *Distant Magnet,* 150–51.

17. From Pinchbeck, Lincolnshire, to Green County, Wis., Jan. 7, 1853, Edwin Oscar Kimberley Papers.

18. Harley, "The Shift from Sailing Ships to Steamships, 1850–1890."

19. Coleman, *Passage to America*, 22–23; Donaldson, *The Scots Overseas*, 101.

20. *Lincoln, Rutland, and Stamford Mercury*, March 30, 1849. See also Thomas Noy Diaries, March 26, 1849, Bentley Historical Library, and the many cases in chapter 5 for examples of group migration providing the necessary emotional support for emigration.

21. Jones, *Destination America*, 36–37.

22. William Smith, *An Emigrant's Narrative; Or, A Voice from the Steerage*, 17, as cited in Jones, *Destination America*, 37.

23. Walsh, "The Voyage of an Iowa Immigrant," 141. Graphic stories about the misery of sailing the Atlantic are to be found in many histories of migration. See Guillet, *The Great Migration*, ch. 8.

24. Entries for Oct. 28, Nov. 11, 1847, Joseph Hurst Diary.

25. Burnley, *Two Sides of the Atlantic*, 19.

26. Mary Harrison in *Album of Genealogy and Biography, Cook County, Illinois*, 290; diary entry for Sept. 14, 1844, Matthew Dinsdale Papers. Robert Nightingale claimed to have a "pleasant voyage" in 1851, see *Portrait and Biographical Record of Cook and Dupage Counties, Illinois*, 499.

27. For these stories see *The Counties of Rock, Green, Grant, Iowa, and Lafayette, Wisconsin*, 767; *Portrait of Jo Daviess and Carroll Counties, Illinois*, 346; *Madison County* [Illinois], 137; *Kalamazoo, Allegan, and Van Buren Counties, Michigan*, 502; *Portage and Summit Counties, Ohio*, 956; and *Winnebago and Boone Counties, Illinois*, 388.

28. *The Counties of Rock, Green, Grant, Iowa, and Lafayette, Wisconsin*, 25.

29. Both Thomas Trainer and Thomas Snow, who emigrated from England in 1853, buried their mothers at sea. See *Will County, Illinois*, 697, and *Kane County, Illinois*, 190. The rest of this paragraph is based on the stories found in *Kane County, Illinois*, 600; *McHenry County, Illinois*, 646; and *Will County, Illinois*, 378 (Chadwick's story).

30. These are the lists that ship captains submitted to the collector of customs upon arrival at the ports of New York, Philadelphia, Baltimore, Boston, and New Orleans. The nature of the lists and their method of selection are discussed in Appendix A.

31. Erickson, "Emigration from the British Isles to the U.S.A. in 1841," 352–53; Baines, *Emigration from Europe*, n2, 49, n2, 50. According to Robert P. Swierenga, the actual number of Dutch immigrants to the United States from 1835 to 1880 was nearly double the official published number. See "Under-Reporting of Dutch Immigration Statistics," 1596–99.

32. Jones, "The Background to Emigration from Great Britain," 77, 82–90; Baines, *Migration in a Mature Economy*, 75–76; Bailyn, *Voyagers to the West*, 92.

33. *Biographical History of Tippecanoe, White, Jasper, Newton, Benton, Warren, and Pulaski Counties, Indiana*, 2:810–11.

34. Thomas, *Research Memorandum on Migration Differentials*, 11.

35. Only 16 percent of the English and Welsh and 20 percent of the Scots immigrants were between twenty and twenty-four in 1841, compared to 21 percent of the English and Welsh and 25 percent of the Scots immigrants in 1851. The 1841 data are in Erickson, *Leaving England*, 141.

36. Ibid., 143; Erickson, "Emigration from the British Isles to the U.S.A. in 1841," 362. For 1851 data, see Appendix B, table B2.

37. Köllmann and Marschalk, "German Emigration to the United States," 535, 541–42; Conzen, "Germans," 405–25; Runblom and Norman, eds., *From Sweden to America,* 131–32; Semmingsen, "Norwegian Emigration in the Nineteenth Century," 150–60; Hvidt, *Flight to America,* 99. With the more abundant data available to them, these historians have been able to ascertain the timing of the shift to labor migration, which began no sooner than the mid-1860s for Germany, the 1870s for Sweden, and the 1880s for Norway and Denmark. The Dutch retained their folk characteristics until the early twentieth century. See Swierenga, "The Delayed Transition from Folk to Labor Migration," 406–24.

38. By the late 1880s males traveling with family members were outnumbered by those traveling alone by a ratio of eight to one. Erickson, *Leaving England,* 143.

39. Ibid., 101, 164. The sources for the 1851 data are provided in Appendix A, table A1.

40. These censuses also indicate that nearly 10 percent of the foreign-born population and 1.5 percent of the entire American population were English-born. At this time more than 70 percent of Utah's foreign-born residents were English and Welsh thanks to the success of the Mormon mission in Britain. See Erickson, *Leaving England,* 60–64.

41. Rose, "Indiana's Ethnicity in the Context of Ethnicity in the Old Northwest in 1850."

42. Appendix A, table A2. More detailed analysis shows few significant occupational differences among the English, Scots, and Welsh. The English and Scots were most similar. A quarter of the English and a fifth of the Scots were from agriculture, as opposed to a tenth of the Welsh. Twenty-four percent of the English were listed as labourers, as opposed to 32 percent of the Scots and 19 percent of the Welsh. The biggest difference was that although 30 percent of the English and 27 percent of the Scots had preindustrial backgrounds, 61 percent of the Welsh did. For these reasons, the Welsh deserve individual attention in chapter 6. Otherwise the three subgroups will be usually discussed collectively as the "British," although national distinctions will be made when appropriate.

Chapter 2: Emigrant Farmers

1. *Northampton Herald,* June 12, 1847.

2. Engels, *The Condition of the Working Class in England,* 278.

3. Lebergot, *The Americans,* 227.

4. Caird, *English Agriculture.* Caird was hired as an agent by the Illinois Central Railway and wrote a book extolling the qualities of the soil for new farmers. See Gates, *The Illinois Central and Its Colonization Work,* 214–15.

5. Ibid., 475–77, 504, 526–27; for the cases in Oxfordshire and Wiltshire, see 28 and 86. Caird expressed faith in improved farming methods in his earlier publication, *High Farming . . . the Best Substitute for Protection.*

6. Prothero, *English Farming,* 370–71. Since Prothero, historians have debated the timing and extent of repeal's effect on British agriculture. For a summary of the literature, see Van Vugt, "Running from Ruin."

7. Hansen, *The Atlantic Migration,* 264–65, 283.

8. Appendix A, table A2. The index of representation conveniently indicates the extent to which specific occupations were under- or overrepresented among the migrant popu-

lation. Because greater proportions of the English were farmers than were the Scots and Welsh, the migration of English farmers is of primary interest in this chapter.

9. Howkins, "Labour History and the Rural Poor," esp. 116. Rollo Arnold also believes that many of the "labourers" found on New Zealand's passenger lists were actually farm laborers. See *The Farthest Promised Land*, 346–47.

10. The nine were Francis Banks, John Burden, Joseph Cooper, George Danby, Samuel Hall, Marsh Harnden, William Sturman (the only one who took up non-agricultural work in America), John Sumpter, and William Webb. In addition to these, John Dixon was described as a "servant" on his marriage certificate, his father as a "farmer." For sources and references in the county histories, see "Birth and Marriage Certificates" in the Bibliography.

11. Among many such references, see the *Lincolnshire, Boston, and Spalding Free Press,* Aug. 27, 1850; *Constitutional and Perthshire Agricultural and General Advertiser,* Nov. 6, 1850; *Doncaster Chronicle,* March 28, 1851; and *Cardiff and Merthyr Guardian,* March 29, 1851.

12. Examples of English farmers emigrating with small amounts of capital to take up unimproved land are presented in the following chapter.

13. Although more than 70 percent of the other occupational classes traveled as individuals, fewer than 60 percent of the farmers traveled in that way. The average size of an emigrant farmer's family was 4.2 members, compared with 3.7 for most other groups. (Appendix B, tables B2–B3).

14. *Cornwall Royal Gazette,* Jan. 18, 1850.

15. *Liverpool Chronicle,* March 1, 1851; *West Briton and Cornwall Advertiser,* July 4, 1851; *North British Agriculturalist,* Nov. 14, 1850.

16. For example, see the *North Wales Chronicle,* May 7, 1850; *Doncaster Chronicle,* March 28, 1851; and the excerpts to follow in the text.

17. Semmingsen, "Norwegian Emigration in the Nineteenth Century." In the 1851 sample of British emigrants, farmers and laborers were the least likely to leave from the larger towns and cities (table B1, Appendix B).

18. *The Constitutional and Perthshire Agricultural and General Advertiser,* Nov. 6, 1850.

19. See the issues of Jan. 4, Jan. 18, Feb. 1, and April 12, 1851. For an assessment of the newspaper's politics, see Murphy, *Cambridge Newspapers and Opinion,* 102–5.

20. James Finlay Letters.

21. The public alarm over free trade is expressed in the *York Herald,* Jan. 26, 1850, supplement, p. 1, and the *Sussex Agricultural Express,* April 26, May 3, 1851.

22. For reports on Buckinghamshire and Devon, see *Devizes and Wiltshire Gazette,* May 15, 1851 (quoting *Bucks Herald*); and *Plymouth, Devonport, and Stonehouse Herald,* Jan. 12, Feb. 16, 1850. See also the *Somerset Herald,* April 27, 1850. For a report of farmers emigrating from Bideford, Devon, to the United States because of free trade, see *North Wales Chronicle,* April 26, 1851.

23. *Lincolnshire, Boston and Spalding Free Press,* July 2, 1850.

24. Quoted by the *Doncaster Chronicle,* April 18, 1851.

25. Letter to Edwin Kimberley, Nov. 12, 1850, 364, Edwin Oscar Kimberley Papers.

26. Joseph and Jane Sensicke [?] to Edwin Kimberley, March 11, 1851, Edwin Oscar Kimberley Papers.

27. Henry Squire to Edwin Kimberley, June 27, 1851, Edwin Oscar Kimberley Papers. The letters continue to 1860, with references to agricultural distress again in 1857 and 1858 after grain prices fell from the high points reached during the Crimean War.

28. According to the price data in Mitchell and Deane, *Abstract,* 488, the previous low point for wheat was in 1780 (36s. 9d.), for barley in 1788 (22s. 8d.), and for oats in 1797 (16s. 3d.).

29. Fairlie, "The Corn Laws," 90–94, 102–7. On the inelasticity of the demand for grain and how repeal caused an immediate fall in prices, see also Gayer, Rostow, and Schwartz, *Growth and Fluctuation,* 2:307, and 1:307n3; and Thompson, *English Landed Society,* 242.

30. Vamplew, "The Protection of English Cereal Producers," 391–95; Williamson, "The Impact of the Corn Laws Just prior to Repeal." Surely the farmers' laborers felt the impact of repeal as well.

31. Caird, *English Agriculture,* 86; Sykes, "Agriculture and Science"; Sturgess, "The Agricultural Revolution on the English Clays"; Thompson, "The Second Agricultural Revolution," passim. The dairy farmers of Wiltshire told Caird that free trade had affected them far less seriously than their neighboring corn-growers.

32. Farmers who were using improved drainage, fertilizers, and rotation methods were actually able to increase their yields sufficiently to make profits even at times of low prices—times when their neighbors who were not involved with "scientific farming" were being driven to despair. See Moore, "The Corn Laws and High Farming."

33. Ibid., 551, 557; Caird, *English Agriculture,* 394–95.

34. Vamplew, "The Protection of English Cereal Producers," 391–93.

35. Before selection of the sample ship lists, every 1851 list was examined, and all data on precise origins were saved so as not to waste that information (table A1, Appendix A). The lists from 1846 to 1854 were searched for more cases. Of the 114 known farmers who had their county recorded between 1849 and 1854, 28 were also in the 1851 sample. Most cases are from 1849 or 1851. No cases were found for 1846 to 1848. Of course, this data must be used with caution and can only suggest broad patterns.

36. Of these farmers, thirty-three (43 percent) were from the "severely distressed" counties listed in table 4 (fifteen were from Yorkshire and seventeen from Lincolnshire); fourteen (18 percent) were from "moderately distressed" counties; eleven (15 percent) were from "minimally distressed" counties; three (4 percent) were from "prosperous counties"; and fifteen (20 percent) were from counties not defined by Caird. The seventy-six farmers were found in the county histories listed in the Bibliography.

37. Caird, *English Agriculture,* 185–87, 196–97. Caird also pointed to the problem caused by landlords maintaining high rents during a time of falling prices.

38. *The Victoria History of the Counties of England: A History of the County of Yorkshire,* 2:461, 467; Caird, *English Agriculture,* 287ff.

39. Caird, *English Agriculture,* 265ff.

40. Ibid., 117–25.

41. *The Victoria History of the Counties of England: A History of the County of Suffolk,* 395; Caird, *English Agriculture,* 152, 145. That there was some success on clays that had been drained shows the importance of this improvement.

42. Caird, *English Agriculture,* 199–201, 467–68.

43. Ibid., 113–14, 46–51, 252–53, 229–33, 350–57, 334–38, 162–84.

44. Essex might be an exception, but those described as London farmers may have been

from Essex. The grain farmers nearest the capital were actually in Essex. Caird, *English Agriculture*, 133–42, 185–87.

45. Ibid., 434ff, 90–96, 107, 113–15.

46. Caird refers to the "many excellent farmers in the county." Ibid., 416.

47. Farmers on ill-drained clay soils also suffered during the early 1830s. Prices were low then, but not critically low, as they were twenty years later. See Clapham, *An Economic History of Modern Britain*, 2:133–35; and Fussell, "Four Centuries of Lincolnshire Farming," 13, 18.

48. Caird, *English Agriculture*, 119, 125, 185. Compensation was sometimes practiced in Warwickshire (222).

49. Ibid., 118–19.

50. Ibid., 265. These landlords were actually making wise economic judgments. Thompson, *English Landed Society*, 248–55, has pointed out that such capital investments in land resulted in low returns for landlords during the 1850s and that many landlords' incomes were saved only by their industrial interests.

51. Fairlie, "The Corn Laws," 109, touched on this idea in her explanation for the net decline in British wheat production during the years following repeal. She said that the decline was caused by the "withdrawal of precisely those low-efficiency farmers on marginal lands (perhaps mostly small farmers) who had previously been most dependent on the Corn Laws for protection." She did not mention emigration as a possible result.

52. See the case of Derbyshire farmer Thomas North, who migrated to Wisconsin in 1847 because he was nearly fifty and had not yet "attained that financial success which brings comfort and ease," in *The Counties of Rock, Green, Grant, Iowa, and Lafayette, Wisconsin*, 199.

53. Farmers composed a much lower percentage of the immigrant population in 1854 than they did in 1851 and especially in 1847, right after repeal (table A3, Appendix A). That is likely a reflection of the partial recovery underway in British agriculture by this time.

Chapter 3: Britons in American Agriculture

1. Latrobe, *The Rambler in North America*, cited in Pooley, "The Settlement of Illinois from 1820 to 1850," 163.

2. Brown, *America*, 32.

3. Sturgess, "The Agricultural Revolution on the English Clays," 120.

4. Historians of American agriculture have emphasized that immigrants generally had to conform to American methods and cropping systems in order to succeed. See Curti, *The Making of an American Community*, 80–83, 91–97, 179–97; Bogue, *From Prairie to Corn Belt*, 211, 238; Ostergren, *A Community Transplanted*, and Swierenga, "Pioneers and Profits in American Agriculture," 323–44.

5. Poucher, "An English Colony in Floyd County."

6. Although hard to establish, the widespread literacy of Britain's emigrant farmers to the United States is indicated by the fact that of eight emigrant farmers whose marriage or children's birth certificates were examined, only one was unable to sign his name. "Birth and Marriage Certificates" in the Bibliography.

7. *The Counties of Rock, Green, Grant, Iowa, and Lafayette, Wisconsin*, 559. Other examples can be found in Fisher, ed., *Grand Rapids and Kent County, Michigan*, 117–18;

History of Muskegon County, Michigan, 97; *Portrait of Jo Daviess and Carroll Counties, Illinois,* 595; and *Portrait and Biographical Album of Lake County, Illinois,* 719–20.

8. *Morgan and Scott Counties, Illinois,* 427.

9. Quaife, *Wisconsin,* 2:217, 240–41.

10. Loehr, "The Influence of English Agriculture on American Agriculture"; Danhof, *Change in Agriculture,* 52–53, 168–69.

11. Swierenga, "Ethnicity and American Agriculture," 341; Barney, *The Passage of the Republic,* 46; Danhof, *Change in Agriculture,* 262.

12. Phillips, *The Underdraining of Farmland in England during the Nineteenth Century,* 241.

13. Smith, ed., *History of the City of Buffalo and Erie Counties,* 47–48. According to Lyth's marriage certificate (York, Oct. 1843, 23/755), he could sign his name.

14. Bogue, *From Prairie to Corn Belt,* 84; Gates, *The Illinois Central and Its Colonization Work,* 165. The contributions of English farmers to drainage of lands in the Old Northwest date to at least the time when George Flower and Morris Birkbeck established in Edwards County, Illinois, in 1817, an English settlement whose members drained wet lands that the Americans had previously deemed impossible to farm. See Flower, *History of the English Settlement in Edwards County, Illinois,* 288, 350.

15. Bogue, *From Prairie to Corn Belt,* 107.

16. *Rock County, Wisconsin,* 813; see also the case of Joseph Johnson, in *Waukesha County, Wisconsin,* 989.

17. Quaife, *Wisconsin,* 2:240–41.

18. *Counties of Porter and Lake, Indiana,* 727–28.

19. Birkbeck, *Notes on a Journey in America,* 129; Gates, *The Illinois Central and Its Colonization Work,* 12–13. As late as the 1850s farmers settling on the prairies were ridiculed by others still skeptical about their fertility. Bogue, *From Prairie to Corn Belt,* 47.

20. Birch, *History of Benton County* [Indiana], 24–25.

21. *Winnebago and Boone Counties, Illinois,* 193.

22. *Waukesha County, Wisconsin,* 922; Allen's birth certificate, Beaminster, Dec. 1842, 8/9.

23. *Columbia County, Wisconsin,* 1025–26; *Macomb County, Michigan,* 745–46.

24. Danhof, *Change in Agriculture,* 75, 88ff. For examples of sharecropping by English immigrants, see Erickson, *Leaving England,* 71.

25. These histories were among those that provided details on land purchases. For sources, see "U.S. County Histories" in the Bibliography. The counties were selected with the attempt to strike a balance between older established counties and those with bountiful virgin land.

26. Oberley, *Sixty Million Acres,* 152–54. Oberley uses warrant files to reconstruct the story of English squatter Edward Peno, who left England in 1854 and quickly preempted 160 acres in Anoka County, Minnesota. Peno acquired the land after eighteen months of squatting. The story of the expansion and improvement of his farm is consistent with other stories found in county histories.

27. Erickson, *Leaving England,* 75.

28. "Recollections of Pioneer Life in Wisconsin," Stephenson C. L. Bewick Papers.

29. Diary entry for Nov. 19, 1847, Matthew Dinsdale Papers.

30. Hasbach, *A History of the English Agricultural Labourer,* see esp. 247–50, 254–58,

and ch. 2. Hasbach was by no means alone in his pessimism; see, for example, Kebbel, *The Agricultural Labourer*, 99–101. But Mark Blaug has shown that the Old Poor Law was not a demoralizing force among agricultural laborers and that it did not reduce wages. It did, however, make surplus rural labor at least minimally productive. See Blaug, "The Myth of the Old Poor Law and the Making of the New," and "The Poor Law Report Re-examined."

31. Hansen, *The Atlantic Migration*, 264–65.

32. Chambers and Mingay, *The Agricultural Revolution*, 147; Hunt, *Regional Wage Variations in Britain*.

33. Armstrong, "The Influence of Demographic Factors."

34. Lindert and Williamson, "English Workers' Living Standards during the Industrial Revolution."

35. Jones, "The Agricultural Labour Market in England, 1793–1872," 322; Collins, "Migrant Labour in British Agriculture." See also an early (1868) account on the seasonality of wages in Morton, *Hand Book on Farm Labour*, 137ff. The classic work on the migration from rural to urban areas is John Saville's *Rural Depopulation in England and Wales*.

36. Chambers and Mingay, *The Agricultural Revolution*, 187. Opinions vary, however, as to when the laborers felt the benefits of rural depopulation. Clapham, *An Economic History of Modern Britain*, 2:285, says that there was "steady improvement" from the mid-1860s onward, whereas Jones, *Development of English Agriculture*, 32–33, points to the 1850s.

37. *Plymouth Journal* quoted by the *Sussex Agricultural Express*, April 12, 1851; *Cornwall Royal Gazette*, June 20, 1851 (second quotation); see also *Lincolnshire, Boston, and Spalding Free Press*, June 10, 1851. Testimony for the Select Committee on the Passenger Acts said of the emigrants of 1850, "Generally speaking, they are agricultural labourers and small farmers; there are not many artisans." *Minutes of Evidence Taken before the Select Committee on the Passenger Acts*, 1851, 19:670.

38. *Bristol Times*, June 7, 1851; *Cornwall Royal Gazette*, Nov. 7, 1851.

39. Jones, "The Agricultural Labour Market in England," 322–29.

40. Caird, *English Agriculture*, 510; *Sussex Agricultural Express*, April 26, 1851.

41. *Cornwall Royal Gazette*, Nov. 7, 1851.

42. These census notes are found, respectively, in *Census of Great Britain* (1851), vol. 1/1, div. 5, div. 9, div. 4, and div. 5, and vol. 1/2, div. 9. Through a thorough reading of these census notes it is clear that the term *emigrate* means overseas migration rather than internal migration. The North Riding reference may reflect declining employment in the mines, which increased the supply of farm laborers and tended to lower wages and opportunities. See Hunt, *The Lead Mines of the Northern Pennines*, 194. On which counties were low-wage, see Hunt, *Regional Wage Variations in Britain*, 16–23.

43. *West of England Conservative*, quoted in the *Bristol Times*, April 6, 1850.

44. Van Vugt, "English Emigrant Guidebooks and Pamphlets," 62–63; Erickson, *Invisible Immigrants*, 22, 30, 90, 269.

45. Quoted in the *Northampton Herald*, March 22, 1851.

46. James Finlay Letters. The fears that men would leave their families by emigrating to America were probably well founded during these times of economic hardship.

47. The report on the Lincolnshire laborers is found in the *Doncaster Chronicle*, March 28, 1851.

48. *Kalamazoo, Allegan, and Van Buren Counties, Michigan,* 94, and 396–99 (for the similar case of Samson Fox).

49. Shepperson, *British Emigration to North America,* 39; Jones, "The Background to Emigration from Great Britain," 36. References to assisted British emigration to the United States are rare. See "'God Raised Us Up Good Friends'" for the example of two London house painters whom their parish assisted to Wisconsin in 1849. It required much effort and pleading before the parish also assisted their wives to Wisconsin. See also the case of George Fewins, in *Emigration from Europe, 1815–1914,* ed. Erickson, 128–29. Apparently, he, too, was assisted to the United States, but in his angry letters to his parish it is clear that there was to be no assistance for the family he left behind.

50. These reports are found in, respectively, *Cornwall Royal Gazette,* Nov. 7, 1851; *Salisbury and Wiltshire Herald,* April 5, 1851; and *Lincolnshire, Boston, and Spalding Free Press,* April 15, 1851. For examples in letters, see Erickson, *Invisible Immigrants,* 86, 88, 210, 214, 242.

51. Reynolds, ed., *Hillsdale County, Michigan,* 134–35. For a case virtually identical to Daniels's, see *Branch County, Michigan,* 482–83, for the story of David Prestige, an English emigrant farm laborer with an "ambitious nature," who arrived in Cleveland in 1852 with 50 cents to his name.

52. Clark later became one of Chicago's prominent contractors and builders. In 1867, after a thrilling and danger-filled trip to Denver, he was appointed by the governor of Illinois to superintend the construction of the Illinois buildings at the Paris Exposition. After the Fire of 1871 he reconstructed the Chicago Water Works and then built and owned the Chicago Academy of Design, reputedly the first building ever erected in Chicago for a fine arts exhibit. *Album of Genealogy and Biography, Cook County, Illinois,* 183–84.

53. *Will County, Illinois,* 399–400; marriage certificate, Pocklington, Dec. 1844, 23/145.

54. *Dane County, Wisconsin,* 302–3; marriage certificate, Worksop, May 1849, 15/841.

55. Conover, ed., *Ontario County, New York,* 76–77; 304. See 312 for the case of Mark Jopson, an 1856 immigrant from Norfolk, who after eight years of farm labor in New York state bought and sold four small farms within twenty-four years before finally settling on a 128–acre farm in Canajoharie. Other cases of farm laborers working up include those of Joseph Cooper in *Waukesha County, Wisconsin,* 934; Francis Banks and John Sumpter in *Racine and Kenosha Counties, Wisconsin,* 634, 657; and Marsh Harnden and Henry Winkley in *Rock County, Wisconsin,* 51, 840.

56. *Waukesha County, Wisconsin,* 895; marriage certificate, Launceston, Dec. 1842, 9/202.

57. *Hancock, McDonough and Henderson Counties, Illinois,* 423–24. For studies on how migrants were often more ambitious and educated than nonmigrants, see Marshall, "Some Aspects of the Social History of Nineteenth-Century Cumbria," 294, 304; and Kerr, "The Dorset Agricultural Labourer," 158–74. Roughly half of the English laborers whose certificates we have and were traced in the county histories were apparently literate (chapter 2).

58. *Peoria County, Illinois,* 419–20. For similar cases of farm laborers taking on nonagricultural work in Britain before emigrating, see that of John Froggatt, who had also worked in the brickyards before emigrating, and James Turnock, whose work as a railroad gang leader allowed him to buy land outright after his emigration. *Dane County, Wisconsin,* 302–3; *Kenosha County, Wisconsin,* 155–56.

59. For Fell's story, see *Will County, Illinois*, 437–38; for other similar cases, see those of John Corlett (527–28) and Scotsman David Ryburn (688–89). See also the cases of Thomas Pacey, an agricultural laborer who felt he could "do better," *Peoria County, Illinois*, 293; and Thomas Johnson, *Ionia and Montcalm Counties, Michigan*, 208–9.

60. Fender, *Sea Changes*, 5.

61. These examples of comparative wage figures come from *Kalamazoo, Allegan, and Van Buren Counties, Michigan*, 244; and *Oakland County, Michigan*, 751.

62. Danhof, *Change in Agriculture*, 78.

63. *Winnebago and Boone Counties, Illinois*, 337–38.

64. *Waukesha County, Wisconsin*, 906.

65. *Morgan and Scott Counties, Illinois*, 318–19.

66. *Fond du Lac County, Wisconsin*, 1018–19.

67. *Will County, Illinois*, 456; similar cases of emigrant farmers' sons from Lincolnshire are on 592.

68. *Dane County, Wisconsin*, 809–10. See also the case of Thomas Spooner, *History of Washtenaw County, Michigan*, 1089. Spooner, the son of a Lincolnshire farmer, arrived in 1850 with two sovereigns. He felt he could do better in agricultural pursuits in the New World.

69. *Branch County, Michigan*, 327–28.

70. *Will County, Illinois*, 571, 706. Other examples of farmers' sons laboring and then renting for years before buying include Edmund Snowdon in *Winnebago and Boone Counties, Illinois*, 1215–16; and William Catton in *Peoria County, Illinois*, 424.

71. *Kalamazoo, Allegan, and Van Buren Counties, Michigan*, 230; *Will County, Illinois*, 198–99. For a virtually identical case to Bedford's, see that of William Luck, another son of a Lincolnshire farmer, who worked as a lime merchant and manufacturer for five years, then rented for another five years before buying land, in *Rock County, Wisconsin*, 874–75. Other cases of farmers who engaged in nonagricultural work when it suited them include that of William Rundell, *Grant County, Wisconsin*, 921.

72. *Lake County, Illinois*, 325.

73. Chase, *The People's Farm*; Hobsbawm, *Labouring Men*; Anderson, *Family Structure in Nineteenth-Century Lancashire*.

74. *Genesee County, Michigan*, 268–69.

75. *Waukesha County, Wisconsin*, 969.

76. Poucher, "An English Colony in Floyd County," 212–13.

77. *Lake County, Illinois*, 290–91.

78. *Dodge County, Wisconsin*, 634–35. See also the case of George Rudge, who like Stoddart left a life of mercantile business to farm, only to return to his original calling, in *Trumbull and Mahoning Counties* [Ohio], 176–77.

79. *Will County, Illinois*, 646–47.

80. *The Counties of Rock, Green, Grant, Iowa, and Lafayette, Wisconsin*, 556.

81. *Dane County, Wisconsin*, 709, 818.

82. *Album of Genealogy and Biography, Cook County, Illinois*, 767. Bouch's marriage certificate (Holbeach, March 1840, 14/537) shows that he was literate and that his father was also a mariner. For a very similar case see that of Captain George White, a Scot who emigrated to New York in 1858 at age 55 to "retire" on his farm, in *Ontario County, New York*, ed. Conover, 204.

83. *Peoria County, Illinois*, 640. Cases like these abound. See, for example, those of wagonmaker Thomas Edwards in *Portrait and Biographical Album of Lake County, Illinois*, 342–43. James Urmson, a Lancashire blacksmith, ran his own blacksmith shop in Lafayette County, Wisconsin for about five years before he bought his farm. *The Counties of Rock, Green, Grant, Iowa, and Lafayette, Wisconsin*, 799.

84. *Album of Genealogy and Biography, Cook County, Illinois*, 499.

85. *The Counties of Rock, Green, Grant, Iowa, and Lafayette, Wisconsin*, 786.

86. Fisher, ed., *Grand Rapids and Kent County, Michigan*, 23.

87. These cases are found in *La Fayette County, Wisconsin*, 791, 733; *Kane County, Illinois*, 336; *Kenosha County, Wisconsin*, 333; and *Waukesha County, Wisconsin*, 939, 931.

88. Gates, *The Illinois Central and Its Colonization Work*, 225.

89. *McHenry County, Illinois*, 408.

90. Brown, *America*, 55.

91. *Lincoln, Rutland, and Stamford Mercury*, April 14, 1848, 3.

92. *LaPeer County, Michigan*, 183.

93. *Ionia and Montcalm Counties, Michigan*, 208–9; Reynolds, ed., *Hillsdale County, Michigan*, 121.

94. *Columbia County, Wisconsin*, 1062–63.

95. Samson Fox married again and became a prosperous farmer with "good and substantial buildings thereon." *Kalamazoo, Allegan, and Van Buren Counties, Michigan*, 396–99.

96. Birch, *History of Benton County* [Indiana], 24–25.

97. Robert Gorst Papers; Kittle, *History of the Township and Village of Mazomanie*.

98. *Dane County, Wisconsin*, 382–83; see also the cases of Charles Kerr (500), and of William Caldwell and Stephen Dawson in *Iowa County, Wisconsin*, 931.

99. Kittle, *History of the Township and Village of Mazomanie*, 32–39; *Primitive Methodist Magazine* 9 (1851): 181–82 (this and subsequent citations from typescripts at the University of Wisconsin, Platteville); Quaife, *Wisconsin*, 2:226–28.

100. Quaife, *Wisconsin*, 2:228–29.

101. Quoted in Birch, "The Editor and the English," 638.

102. Sheppard himself prospered in America, first as a journalist for the *New York Times* and then as a land agent in London for the Northern Pacific Railroad in the 1870s, when he helped organize more English settlements in Minnesota. See Birch, "The Editor and the English," 642n44.

Chapter 4: Immigrants from Industry and Crafts

1. Joseph Hurst Diary. Yorkshire dyer William Moore also arrived without prearranging his employment, in Boston in 1853, and it took him a month to find work in an iron foundry. See the William Moore Letter, Aug. 25, 1854.

2. John Curtis to Richard Cobden, May 8, 1844.

3. Stott, *Workers in the Metropolis*, 129–34.

4. Tweedale, *Sheffield Steel and America*, 18, 131.

5. Stott, *Workers in the Metropolis*, 100.

6. These estimates were arrived at by multiplying the sample number of adult male textile workers (65) and weavers (30) by ten; see table 3 in Van Vugt, "Prosperity and Industrial Emigration," 343. (Including females and males aged fifteen and over, eighty-seven textile workers were in the one-in-ten sample.)

7. Erickson, *Leaving England,* 201, 215.

8. On November 13, 1847, the *Leeds Mercury* reported that "the destitution and distress at present existing among the operatives of this town is truly appalling and pauperism is daily on the increase" and that many "have gone off in search of better fortunes across the Atlantic." This report is echoed in letters dated November 10, 1847: "Trade is very bad vast numbers out of employment many of the cotton factories in Lancashire being entirely shut up . . . although plenty are leaving this neighborhood for America." George and Nanny Ainley Letters. Nearly a quarter of the employed immigrants of 1847 were from industry (table A3, Appendix A), as opposed to under 10 percent for 1851 (table A2).

9. *Devizes and Wiltshire Gazette,* Dec. 16, 1947.

10. In 1850 there were still at least forty to fifty thousand cotton handloom weavers in Britain who faced the continual advance of the power loom, of which there were already about 250,000. Clapham, *An Economic History of Modern Britain,* 2:28. Joyce, *Work, Society and Politics,* 57. Although the transition to power looms occurred later in the woolen industries than in cotton, there were already in 1850 nearly thirty-three thousand worsted power looms and ten thousand woolen power looms. In the Bradford areas, worsted handloom weavers were being squeezed out by power looms, "either into the factory or to find a new job elsewhere." See Fay, *Round about Industrial Britain,* 121. Duncan Bythell observes, however, that cotton handloom weavers were not truly skilled and that their difficulties were not wholly due to displacement. See Blythell, *The Handloom Weavers,* 42–43, 65, 270–72.

11. Jones, "The Background to Emigration from Great Britain," 43, an opinion based on Bythell, *The Handloom Weavers.*

12. This seems to have been true of earlier emigrant weavers as well. See Jeremy, *Transatlantic Industrial Revolution,* 154.

13. Anderson, *Family Structure in Nineteenth-Century Lancashire,* 38.

14. Joyce, *Work, Society and Politics,* 54–57; Foster, *Class Struggle and the Industrial Revolution,* 79. For examples of weavers in Britain training their young sons to be handloom weavers in 1851, see Erickson, *Invisible Immigrants,* 301.

15. Anderson, *Family Structure in Nineteenth-Century Lancashire,* 72–75, 112–18; Anderson, "Sociological History and the Working-Class Family," esp. 326–27; Joyce, *Work, Society and Politics,* 54–57, 88.

16. Emigrant weavers of previous decades were also less familial than those of 1851. See Jeremy, *Transatlantic Industrial Revolution,* 154.

17. Ware, *The Early New England Cotton Manufacture,* 76–84, 209–10.

18. Warner, "Innovation and the Industrialization of Philadelphia," 66–67; Laurie, Hershberg, and Alter, "Immigrants and Industry," 120.

19. See tables B4 and B5, Appendix B.

20. Erickson, *Invisible Immigrants,* 139–74, 301–6, 329–59.

21. This is not to understate the adjustments of factory life. See Joyce, *Work, Society and Politics,* 54–57. Opportunities for men were especially good between 1851 and 1853, because these were years of a domestic cotton boom. See Hughes, *Fluctuations in Trade, Industry and Finance,* 77.

22. Joyce, *Work, Society and Politics,* 54–61; Foster, *Class Struggle and the Industrial Revolution,* 83–84, 224–38. Flax hacklers, who performed the highly skilled tasks of comb-

ing and separating the flax fibers before the spinning process, were still subject to technological displacement. For a case of a Scottish flax hackler emigrating in the early 1850s, see the Ronaldson letters in Erickson, *Invisible Immigrants,* 368ff.

23. These include eleven weavers and twelve miscellaneous workers, including calico printers, spinners, linen workers, cloth finishers, bleachers, and dyers.

24. *Morgan and Scott Counties, Illinois,* 482–83.

25. *Kalamazoo County, Allegan, and Van Buren Counties, Michigan,* 1087.

26. *Dane County, Wisconsin,* 286–88. Scotsman James B. White was also working successfully as a calico printer in a factory managed by his father but was "desirous" of emigrating to America, and did so in 1854. See *Allen County, Indiana,* 134–35.

27. Signor, ed., *Orleans County, New York,* 14–15.

28. Merrill, ed., *Chautauqua County, New York,* 699–700, 808–9. Other examples of textile workers using a network to immigrate to America include that of Allen Aspinall in *Racine and Kenosha Counties, Wisconsin,* 658; Benjamin Grundy in *LaSalle, County, Illinois,* 699–700; and Thomas Hyndman in *Madison County* [Illinois], 354.

29. Hardin, ed., *Herkimer County, New York,* 466.

30. See, for example, the case of Daniel Price, in *Jefferson County, Wisconsin,* 621.

31. Lamphere, *From Working Daughters to Working Mothers,* 90; Green, *Holyoke, Massachusetts,* 48; Cole, *Immigrant City,* esp. chs. 2–3; Gitelman, *Workingmen of Waltham.*

32. Caird, *English Agriculture,* 287.

33. See the frustrations that James Hardy, a linen worker from Yorkshire, had as a pioneer in Wisconsin in *Waukesha County, Wisconsin,* 969. See also the case of Titus Crawshaw, a Huddersfield-born cloth finisher in Wisconsin in Erickson, *Invisible Immigrants,* 337–38. In contrast, Thomas Anderton, a cloth bleacher with no apparent prior experience in farming, became a "first-class agriculturalist" in Michigan. See *Kalamazoo, Allegan, and Van Buren Counties, Michigan,* 1087.

34. Spencer, "Biographical Sketch of John Spencer," Wisconsin Historical Society.

35. Erickson, "Emigration from the British Isles," 189.

36. Hunter, "Influence of the Market upon Technique in the Iron Industry in Western Pennsylvania," 241–81; Paskoff, *Industrial Revolution,* 91. Pennsylvania's share in iron production was growing at this time. See Fogel, *Railways and American Economic Growth,* 159ff. English rolling mills used a more advanced technology than American mills. See Temin, *Iron and Steel in Nineteenth-Century America,* ch. 5. On technology, see Gale, *The British Iron and Steel Industry.* The few emigrant ironworkers who provided their city of destination on the 1851 lists were roughly divided between the east and west of Pennsylvania (table B4, Appendix B).

37. Temin, *Iron and Steel,* 115–19; Fogel, *Railways and American Economic Growth,* 157–60; Swank, *Introduction to a History of Ironmaking and Coal Mining in Pennsylvania,* 100–101.

38. Birch, *The Economic History of the British Iron and Steel Industry,* 121.

39. Clapham, *An Economic History of Modern Britain,* 1:425–29; Hunt, *Regional Wage Variations in Britain,* ch. 4.

40. At this time, British engineers were rising in status as a professional group and enjoying greater social respectability because of the steady, high demand for their skills. See Buchanan, "Gentleman Engineers."

41. For these cases see, respectively, Parker, *Albany County, New York,* 6–8; and Watrous,

ed., *Milwaukee County,* 294. See also the case of James Miller, a Glaswegian engine builder who emigrated in 1853 "to seek his fortune," in *Will County, Illinois,* 495.

42. See the case of Isaac Bates in *Winnebago and Boone Counties, Illinois,* 549–50.

43. *St. Clair County, Illinois,* 283–84.

44. See the stories of gunmaker William Onyuas in *Herkimer County, New York,* ed. Hardin, 80–81, and ironmaker Edmund Page in Parker, *Albany County, New York,* 197.

45. Tweedale, *Sheffield Steel and America,* 15–17, 130–32, 144–47, 160.

46. *History of Dearborn, Ohio, and Switzerland Counties, Indiana,* 696. See similar cases of William Marshall in *Kane County, Illinois,* 770–71, and that of Joseph Anderson in *Grand Rapids and Kent County, Michigan,* ed. Fisher, 23.

47. See the case of Philip Greening, a machinist who grew up on a farm in Devon, in *Fond du Lac County, Wisconsin,* 1034–35.

48. Clapham, "Work and Wages," 31.

49. Cairncross and Weber, "Fluctuations in Building in Great Britain, 1785–1849," 288–90; Habakkuk, "Fluctuations in House-Building in Britain and the United States in the Nineteenth Century," 236–67, esp. 239.

50. The counties with shrinking populations were Wiltshire and Montgomeryshire, which between 1851 and 1861 suffered another net loss, as did Cambridgeshire, Huntingdonshire, Norfolk, Rutland, Somerset, Suffolk, Anglesey, Brecknock, and Cardigan. Saville, *Rural Depopulation in England and Wales,* 21, 54–55. In her careful study of Corsley, Wiltshire, Davies found that by 1837 depopulation had already set in and that the most rapid decrease occurred between 1841 and 1851. See *Life in an English Village,* 83.

51. Ibid., 22–26; see also Horn, *Labouring Life in the Victorian Countryside,* ch. 5. Although the rural depopulation was caused primarily by internal migration, the external migration of farmers and laborers also played a part, as attested by the huge representation of farmers on ship lists in 1851 (chapter 2). Other farmers and laborers, of course, were bound for other destinations.

52. Graham, *The Rural Exodus,* 30–31.

53. Ibid., 18.

54. *McHenry County, Illinois,* 646–47. See also the case of Richard Day in *History of Schuyler County,* ed. Dyson, 808; and of Benjamin Beevers in *Lenawee County, Michigan,* comp. Bonner and Whitney, 317.

55. *Will County, Illinois,* 301. For similar cases see James Bale, in *Kalamazoo, Allegan, and Van Buren Counties, Michigan,* 674; William Johnson, in *Lapeer County, Michigan,* 209; and George Dyson in *Grant County, Wisconsin,* 903.

56. This was the case with John Allen, a Cornish stonemason who left for Rockford, Illinois, in 1849, and found work without such help upon his arrival. Within only three months he already had his own business as a contractor. See *Winnebago and Boone Counties, Illinois,* 229. Some British immigrants were able to learn their building trade in America, and after years of working at their new occupation used their earnings to take up farming farther west. See the examples of David Morris from Wales, who became a carpenter and joiner in New York, and William Sturman from England, who became a plasterer in Detroit in, respectively, *Waukesha County, Wisconsin,* 927, and *Oakland County, Michigan,* 200–201. See also the case of silk weaver Benjamin Grundy, who became a carpenter in Illinois, in *LaSalle County, Illinois,* 699–700.

57. For two cases see *Lafayette County, Wisconsin,* 716, 723.

58. *The Counties of Rock, Green, Grant, Iowa, and Lafayette, Wisconsin,* 265.

59. Horn, *Labouring Life in the Victorian Countryside,* 102.

60. Clapham, *An Economic History of Modern Britain,* 2:124–25; Horn, *Labouring Life in the Victorian Countryside,* 96.

61. Saville, *Rural Depopulation in England and Wales,* 22.

62. Blacksmithing seemed to be an easy trade for British immigrants to pick up in America, for there are many examples. See, for example, the accounts of William Smith, Henry Nayler, and Scotsman Alexander Cameron—all of whom learned blacksmithing in America and then took up farming—in, respectively, *Iowa County, Wisconsin,* 873; *The Counties of Rock, Green, Grant, Iowa, and Lafayette, Wisconsin,* 786; and *Winnebago and Boone Counties, Illinois,* 587.

63. For example, as the Smille family in Ohio wrote to their sister and brother in Scotland, "Morrison wants to know how a wheel-wright and turner could do here. There is not much of that kind of business here." David and Allison Smille to "Brother and Sister," box 7, file 78, Immigrant Letters Collection, British Library of Political and Economic Science; see also Isaac Taylor to Joseph Lumb, Dec. 20, 1848, and examples in Erickson, *Invisible Immigrants,* 103, 120, 195, 291.

64. Chambers, *The Emigrant's Manual,* 131. The works Chambers published sold well in the popular press, and his emigrant guides went through several editions.

65. Habakkuk, *American and British Technology in the Nineteenth Century,* 129–30. "On the whole," Robertson concluded, "the services of skilled workers were scarce in antebellum America, and only during severe business slumps was the artisan in danger of unemployment." See *History of the American Economy,* 213.

66. Horn, *Labouring Life in the Victorian Countryside,* ch. 5.

67. Friedlander and Roshier have observed that most internal migration between 1851 and 1901 was short-distance, see "A Study of Internal Migration in England and Wales," 166. That was also Saville's opinion, see *Rural Depopulation in England and Wales,* 40ff.

68. Samuel, "Workshop of the World," 8, 36–37. In addition to cabinetmakers and wheelwrights, emigrant woodworkers included a few coopers, sawyers, upholsterers, and french polishers.

69. Rohrbough, *The Trans-Appalachian Frontier,* 341.

70. Beakes, *Past and Present of Washtenaw County, Michigan,* 204–7; see also *History of Washtenaw County,* 727–28.

71. *Grant County, Wisconsin,* 889; *Rock County, Wisconsin,* 808; Signor, ed., *Orleans County, New York,* 103–4; Andrews, ed., *Marietta and Washington County, Ohio,* 1263; *Kane County, Illinois,* 335; *Lake County, Illinois,* 568.

72. *Rock County, Wisconsin,* 881.

73. Signor, ed., *Orleans County, New York,* 219; *Hancock, McDonagh, and Henderson Counties, Illinois,* 348.

74. Van Vugt, "An English Shoemaker in Indiana."

75. *Portrait of Jo Daviess and Carroll Counties, Illinois,* 788; *Winnebago and Boone Counties, Illinois,* 662–63. For similar cases see those of Jonathan Richardson in *Portrait and Biographical Album of Lake County, Illinois,* 211; and of James Philip in *McHenry County, Illinois,* 413–14. See also the example of Robert Smith, a poor shoemaker who entered farming in Michigan in the 1830s, in Erickson, *Invisible Immigrants,* 189–94.

76. *La Crosse, Wisconsin,* 779; *Trumbull and Mahoning Counties* [Ohio], 472.

77. *Columbia County, Wisconsin,* 465–67.

78. Ibid., 466; Foreman, "Settlement of English Potters in Wisconsin."

79. *Columbia County, Wisconsin,* 465–67; the case of Benjamin Hopkins is on 1051. See the *Staffordshire Advertiser,* April 10, 1847, March 1, 1851; *The Victoria History of the Counties of England: Staffordshire,* 2:46–57.

Chapter 5: Miners

1. Robinson, *Ancient History,* 391, 393; Ruoff, *The Century Book of Facts,* 659; Fawcett, *Lead Mining in Swaledale,* 5.

2. Allen, *British Industries and Their Organization,* 47.

3. Long, *Where the Sun Never Shines,* 7; Erickson, *American Industry and the European Immigrant,* 107.

4. The miners' index of representation was 131 in 1851, 115 in 1841, and 125 in the 1880s (table A2, Appendix A).

5. The port of entry is indicated for thirty-one British immigrant miners featured in *Portrait of Jo Daviess and Carroll Counties, Illinois.* Of those, eight (one quarter) came via Quebec. Some arrived in the early 1840s and the late 1850s and are thus not a part of the sample from 1845 to 1855. See also Van Vugt, "Prosperity and Industrial Emigration," table 5, 348.

6. *The Counties of Rock, Green, Grant, Iowa, and Lafayette, Wisconsin,* 223.

7. Of the 1850 figure, 11,130 were English, 950 were Welsh, and 1,034 were Scots; of the 1860 figure, 21,258 were English, 1,905 were Welsh, and 4,637 were Scots. It is impossible to determine how many of the English were actually Cornish, although Copeland, "The Cornish in Southwestern Wisconsin," 312, gives a reasonable estimate of seven thousand. See also Reed, "A Population Study of the Driftless Hill Land," 168.

8. Morris, *Dalesmen of the Mississippi River,* 72–74. See also the case of Harker Spensley and son, who came from Yorkshire to Dubuque and then to Mineral Point, where they established Spensley's Smelting Furnaces. *Iowa County, Wisconsin,* 873.

9. On the background to the early phase of British mining in the region, see Schafer, *The Wisconsin Lead Region.* See also Morris, *Dalesmen of the Mississippi River;* Quaife, *Wisconsin;* Jewell, *Cornish in America;* Todd, *The Cornish Miner in America;* and Rickard, *A History of American Mining.*

10. Todd, *The Cornish Miner in America,* 16–20.

11. *Census of Great Britain* (1851), vol. 1/1, div. 5, 57.

12. Baines, *Migration in a Mature Economy,* 153.

13. Rowe, *The Hard-Rock Men,* v.

14. Copeland, "The Cornish in Southwestern Wisconsin," 313. Rowe, *The Hard-Rock Men,* 52ff. The quotation was observed by Jenkin in "The Cornish Emigration." Quite a number of Cornish miners later explained that they were "not satisfied" with their situation in Cornwall, and some of these owned small farms in Cornwall. See cases in *Portrait of Jo Daviess and Carroll Counties, Illinois,* 268, 286, 676, 740–41.

15. Morris, *Dalesmen of the Mississippi River,* 2.

16. Quoted in Batty, *A View of Arkengarthdale,* 13. Yorkshire miners often left in large groups, which made the experience less wrenching and the option more attractive. See the case of George Buxton, who left Gunnerside in Swaledale with a large group of fellow miners in 1849. George W. Buxton Papers.

17. Batty, *A View of Arkengarthdale,* 14.

18. Copeland, "The Cornish in Southwestern Wisconsin," 301–4, 313.

19. Birch, "From Southwest England to Southwest Wisconsin." George W. Buxton, a lead miner and farmer from Gunnerside, Swaledale, also emigrated within the security of a group of migrants from the same dale in 1849. They, too, paved the way for other family members to join them. See George W. Buxton Papers. On the common group migration of miners, see also Morris, *Dalesmen of the Mississippi River,* 102–15; Batty, *A View of Arkengarthdale,* 13–14; and Batty, *Gunnerside Chapel and Gunnerside Folk,* 50.

20. Batty, *A View of Arkengarthdale,* 14.

21. *The Story of Mineral Point,* 49; Carter, "New Diggings on the Fever River," 58; *Primitive Methodist Magazine* 16 (1858): 568.

22. Jewell, *Cornish in America,* 24–25.

23. *The Story of Mineral Point,* 54.

24. Jewell, *Cornish in America,* 24ff.

25. Raistrick and Jennings, *A History of Lead Mining in the Pennines,* 309–12.

26. "The Cornishmen were loath to give up their mining for farming as the minerals became worked out." Birch, "From Southwest England to Southwest Wisconsin," 129. Copeland argues that "all the Cornishmen who settled in Wisconsin were miners" and "no Cornishman thought of farming in Wisconsin," statements that contradict abundant evidence in the county histories and other sources. See "The Cornish in Southwestern Wisconsin," 319. Todd, however, cites cases of Cornish miners prearranging their land purchases. *The Cornish Miner in America,* 20.

27. Wright, *The Galena Lead District,* 86–87.

28. Oberley, *Sixty Million Acres,* 79, 136. Many land warrants were granted to veterans in southwestern Wisconsin and were then sold, reducing the price of land there during the late 1840s and early 1850s.

29. Morris, *Dalesmen of the Mississippi River,* 74; Barker, "The Lead Miners of Swaledale and Arkengarthdale"; Rowe, *The Hard-Rock Men,* 7, ch. 3; *The Story of Mineral Point,* 134. In *New Diggings Is an Old Diggings,* 19, Carter says that the "miners from Cornwall . . . were attracted by stories of mining and farming conditions in Wisconsin Territory."

30. Todd, *The Cornish Miner in America,* 35.

31. Ibid., 16–18; Barker, "The Lead Miners of Swaledale and Arkengarthdale," 4.

32. *Portrait of Jo Daviess and Carroll Counties, Illinois,* 740–41.

33. The cases found in the county histories are too numerous to list, but for some see *Portrait of Jo Daviess and Carroll Counties, Illinois,* 765; *Grant County, Wisconsin,* 909; *The Counties of Rock, Green, Grant, Iowa, and Lafayette, Wisconsin,* 724; and *Iowa County, Wisconsin,* 885, 899, 900, 908, 924.

34. *Portrait of Jo Daviess and Carroll Counties, Illinois,* 195–96.

35. Ibid., 576.

36. Yet Ashworth emphasized to his wife that "I should not like any one to come to this country on account of any thing that I might say because they might not be so fortunate as myself." Ralph Ashworth Letters.

37. *Portrait of Jo Daviess and Carroll Counties, Illinois,* 298; the similar case of Josiah Kneebone appears on 385–86.

38. Tangye's story is told in *Portrait of Jo Daviess and Carroll Counties, Illinois,* 765. For Perry, see *Iowa County, Wisconsin,* 869; for similar cases see that of Osborne (868–69) and

of Thomas Rogers (899) and that of R. Nichols in *The Counties of Rock, Green, Grant, Iowa, and Lafayette, Wisconsin*, 724.

39. *Mineral Point Democrat*, April 18, 1845; Carter, "New Diggings on the Fever River," 92. Rowe, *The Hard-Rock Men*, 21, states that the Cornish miner "was usually an excellent carpenter and mason as well." See also *Iowa County, Wisconsin*, passim.

40. Richard Wearne Diary, quoted in Rosen, "Images of Wisconsin's Settlement Frontier," 128. Rosen misspells the family name as "Wearnes." For more details of the Wearne family, see Rowe, *The Hard-Rock Men*, 34–35, 50–55. The *Primitive Methodist Magazine* 10 (1852): 370–71, warned readers who were doing well in England not to risk their comfortable life by emigrating to the rough and backward regions of southwestern Wisconsin.

41. Reed, "A Population Study of the Driftless Hill Land," 163–68; *The Story of Mineral Point*, 96. Rowe estimates that six or seven out of ten returned to Wisconsin. See *The Hard-Rock Men*, 60.

42. *Iowa County, Wisconsin*, 676.

43. Ibid., 600, 676, 678; *The Counties of Rock, Green, Grant, Iowa, and Lafayette, Wisconsin*, 420, 571; *Grant County, Wisconsin*, 464.

44. *Primitive Methodist Magazine* 10 (1852): 368–69.

45. *The Counties of Rock, Green, Grant, Iowa, and Lafayette, Wisconsin*, 420, 572, 741.

46. *Fond du Lac County, Wisconsin*, 370–71.

47. For the cases of five Cornish immigrants mining in California to accumulate enough capital to farm, see *Iowa County, Wisconsin*, 880–81; For Sardeson, see *The Counties of Rock, Green, Grant, Iowa, and Lafayette, Wisconsin*, 788.

48. *Luzerne, Lackawanna and Wyoming Counties, Pennsylvania*, 392B.

49. *Portrait of Jo Daviess and Carroll Counties, Illinois*, 302–5.

50. *Grant County, Wisconsin*, 693.

51. *Portrait of Jo Daviess and Carroll Counties, Illinois*, 740–41, and 621 (for nearly identical stories); *Iowa County, Wisconsin*, 905, 908, 924; *Grant County, Wisconsin*, 909; and *Randolph, Jackson, Perry, and Monroe Counties, Illinois*, 800–801.

52. Rickard, *A History of American Mining*, 246–48; Todd, *The Cornish Miner in America*, 132, 139; Rowe, *The Hard-Rock Men*, 4.

53. *Luzerne, Lackawanna and Wyoming Counties, Pennsylvania*, 328.

54. *LaSalle County, Illinois*, 625–26.

55. *Luzerne and Lackawanna Counties, Pennsylvania*, 449. See the cases of James McMillan and Walter Treasure in *Luzerne and Lackawanna Counties, Pennsylvania*, 330B, and *Peoria County, Illinois*, 874–75.

56. Long, *Where the Sun Never Shines*, 57.

57. *Peoria County, Illinois*, 418–19.

58. *Randolph, Jackson, Perry, and Monroe Counties, Illinois*, 742–43.

59. *Peoria County, Illinois*, 793; *LaSalle County, Illinois*, 621.

60. *Knox County, Indiana*, 217, 225–26; *Greene County, Indiana*, 336–39. For a similar case in Wisconsin see Francis Craig, an 1850 emigrant from Durham, in *The Counties of Rock, Green, Grant, Iowa, and Lafayette, Wisconsin*, 743.

61. Jermyn Borough was named after British immigrant John Jermyn, who is described in *Luzerne, Lackawanna and Wyoming Counties, Pennsylvania*, 468A.

62. Ibid., facing 436; the case of superintendent Enoch Cartwright is on 330E.

63. *Will County, Illinois*, 365.

64. Among many examples, see those in *Orleans County, New York,* ed. Signor, 14–15, 154, 172, 182; and *Oneida County, New York,* 566–67.

65. *Schuylkill County, Pennsylvania,* 2:195, 145.

66. *Madison County* [Illinois], 448. For a case of a Cornish immigrant murdered in California, see Todd, *The Cornish Miner in America,* 50.

67. *The Story of Mineral Point,* 73.

Chapter 6: The Welsh

1. Knowles, *Calvinists Incorporated,* 30.

2. Ibid., 116, 130, 211, 213, 240–42.

3. In 1872 the Rev. R. D. Thomas published, in Welsh, *Hanes Cymry America* (History of the Welsh in America), which identified and described extant communities. Parts of this work have been translated by Davies and published as "The Welsh in Ohio" and "The Welsh in Wisconsin." Deeper analysis of one community is provided in Taylor, "Paddy's Run."

4. Hartmann, *Americans from Wales;* Berthoff, *British Immigrants in Industrial America,* 159.

5. *Histories of Lawrence and Gallia Counties, Ohio,* xxv; Page, "History of the Welsh Baptist Church, Town of Aurora."

6. For general surveys of Welsh migration, see Conway, "Welsh Emigration to the United States"; Conway, ed., *The Welsh in America;* Berthoff, "Welsh"; Berthoff, *British Immigrants in Industrial America;* Hartmann, *Americans from Wales;* Jones, "The Background to Emigration from Great Britain"; and Thomas, *Migration and Economic Growth.*

7. Not until 1875 and 1908 did the American and British officials, respectively, begin to differentiate between Welsh and English migrants. For a good overview of the available Welsh migration statistics see Williams, "Some Figures Relating to Emigration." See also Thomas, "Wales and the Atlantic Economy."

8. Jones, "From the Old Country to the New," 168. See also a similar statement in Jones, "The Background to Emigration from Great Britain," 80; and Conway, "Welsh Emigration to the United States," 192.

9. Van Vugt, "Welsh Emigration," table 1, 548.

10. Thomas, "Wales and the Atlantic Economy," 175. According to Williams, Welsh emigrants went "almost without exception" to the United States. See *A History of Modern Wales,* 259. In her study of a Welsh community in Ohio, Taylor has demonstrated that "small in numbers though the volume of Welsh migration ultimately was, its importance was out of all proportion to its size." Taylor, "Paddy's Run," 302.

11. Thomas, "Wales and the Atlantic Economy," 175, 191; see also Conway, "Welsh Emigration to the United States," 264.

12. Köllmann and Marschalk, "German Emigration to the United States," esp. 535, 541–42; see also Conzen, "Germans." For the Scandinavians, see Runblom and Norman, eds., *From Sweden to America;* Semmingsen, "Norwegian Emigration in the Nineteenth Century"; and Hvidt, *Flight to America,* 99.

13. Conway wrote that "the return of prosperity in the 1850's made the lot of the Welsh farmer much better," whereas Hartmann noted that during the mid-century "the disgruntled Welsh farmer, oppressed by high rentals, harassed by new toll roads that taxed his produce on the way to market, living on the borderland of starvation, looked to America as

a means of solving his dilemma." Conway, "Welsh Emigration to the United States," 204; Hartmann, *Americans from Wales,* 70; Williams, *A History of Modern Wales,* 259.

14. Including males fifteen and over, an estimated 670 migrated in the year. The 1851 census for Wales enumerated 26,191 coal miners, 7,692 iron miners, 4,937 lead miners, 1,092 copper miners, and 6,693 quarriers who were twenty and over. If all of the miners on the ship lists were indeed coal miners, their overrepresentation in comparison to the census figure for coal miners would be 416. Van Vugt, "Welsh Emigration," table 2, 549.

15. Eight miners also provided a more precise origin: seven were from Carmarthen and one from Pembroke. These were almost certainly coal miners. Van Vugt, "Welsh Emigration," 550n20.

16. Berthoff, *British Immigrants in Industrial America,* 48; Conway, "Welsh Emigration to the United States," 228. By the 1840s, Pennsylvania's coal mines were being worked "almost exclusively" by foreign, mostly British colliers, and Welsh miners were on the first strike committees in the region. Bowen, ed., *The Coal Regions of Pennsylvania,* 48; Berthoff, "Welsh," 1013.

17. See, for example, the *Royal Cornwall Gazette,* Nov. 1, 1850. One miner was bound for Wisconsin and possibly the Lake Superior region.

18. See chapter 5; see also Benson, *British Coalminers in the Nineteenth Century,* 6–8. Average wage rates rose steadily after 1850; estimates appear in Church, *The History of the British Coal Industry,* 3:561.

19. Morris and Williams, *The South Wales Coal Industry,* 218, 250–62. See also the wage charts in Dalziel, *The Collier's Strike in South Wales,* 8.

20. Morris and Williams, *The South Wales Coal Industry,* 253. In mid-April 1851, the colliers of Gellywion went on strike because of a "serious reduction in the wages" that was soon to take place. *Carmarthen Journal,* Aug. 15, 1851.

21. *Swansea and Glamorgan Herald,* Feb. 5, 1851; see also John, *The Industrial Development of South Wales,* 94, and Lewis, *The Rhondda Valleys,* 181.

22. The *Liverpool Chronicle* on July 15, 1854, reported of the South Wales coal and iron trades: "Since the war commenced coals cannot be raised fast enough . . . and . . . in the iron trade the demand is very great, and new furnaces are continually being put into blast. . . . None of the men are out on strike."

23. *Census of Great Britain* (1851), vol. 1/2, div. 11, 29.

24. *Bristol Times and Bath Advocate,* May 17, 1851.

25. See the *Miners' Journal* (published in Pottsville), April 20, May 18, June 22, 1850, Jan. 11, 1851. Yearley argues that the coal industry in the Schuylkill Valley during the late 1840s and 1850s was suffering a "prolonged series of crises." See "Enterprise and Anthracite," 161–62.

26. *Miners' Journal,* May 11, Oct. 19, 1850, Feb. 1, May 18, June 28, Sept. 20, 1851; see also the *Daily American* (published in Harrisburg), April 21, May 2, 1851; *Pennsylvania Telegraph* (also from Harrisburg), Oct. 2, 1850; and Yearley, "Enterprise and Anthracite," 161ff.

27. Yearley, "Enterprise and Anthracite," 68–78.

28. See reports of social problems in mining communities in the *Miners' Journal,* March 29, 1851; see also Yearley, "Enterprise and Anthracite," 172–73, 179.

29. *Miners' Journal,* July 27, 1850, Jan. 11, 1851.

30. *Luzerne, Lackawanna and Wyoming Counties, Pennsylvania,* 328, 449.

31. Berthoff, *British Immigrants in Industrial America*, 49.

32. *Peoria County, Illinois*, 874.

33. Conway, "Welsh Emigration to the United States," 234–35, 239; Berthoff, "Welsh," 1012; Berthoff, *British Immigrants in Industrial America*, 53–54; Gottlieb, "The Regulation of the Coal Mining Industry in Illinois," 52–53.

34. Yearley, "Enterprise and Anthracite," 168–70.

35. Morris and Williams, *The South Wales Coal Industry*, 218–19; see also Dalziel, *The Collier's Strike in South Wales*, 8.

36. For data, see Van Vugt, "Welsh Emigration," table 4, 555. On miners' relatively high wages and how they acquired their maximum wage rates while in their late teens and early twenties, see Hunt, *Regional Wage Variations in Britain*, 73; and Morris and Williams, *The South Wales Coal Industry*, 140.

37. Morris and Williams, *The South Wales Coal Industry*, 237ff. See also Benson, *British Coalminers in the Nineteenth Century*, 121–23; and Hodges, "The Peopling of the Hinterland and the Port of Cardiff," esp. 5–8.

38. Morris and Williams, *The South Wales Coal Industry*, 38.

39. Conway, "Welsh Emigration to the United States," 226. For the "land hungry" Welsh miners in particular, see Conway, ed., *The Welsh in America*, 119; and Berthoff, "Welsh," 1012.

40. Mining and stone-quarrying were common methods by which Britons in America earned enough capital to buy their farms. Erickson, *Invisible Immigrants*, 42–43.

41. For examples of this happening among the Welsh, see Conway, ed., *The Welsh in America*, 199.

42. *Columbia County, Wisconsin*, 845.

43. Williams, *The Welsh Community of Waukesha County*, 28–29, 32–38.

44. Bradsby, *Vigo County, Indiana*, 790. For similar cases of Welsh miners becoming farmers in America, see the story of Isaac Richards in *Luzerne, Lackawanna and Wyoming Counties, Pennsylvania*, 438R.

45. Long, *Where the Sun Never Shines*, 128–29; *Schuylkill County, Pennsylvania*, 2:736. See the also the cases of Jenkins Jones, *Luzerne and Lackawanna Counties, Pennsylvania*, 344B; of Reese Evans, ibid., facing 433; and of Thomas Williams, *Portage and Summit Counties, Ohio*, 956.

46. *Schuylkill County, Pennsylvania*, 287.

47. *Trumbull and Mahoning Counties* [Ohio], 236–39.

48. Smith, *A People's History of the Post-Reconstruction Era*, 224.

49. Berthoff, *British Immigrants in Industrial America*, 146.

50. Jones, *Wales in America*, 3–14, 31–35, 51–60.

51. *Census of Great Britain* (1851), vol. 1/2, div. 11, 33.

52. *Cornwall Royal Gazette*, June 29, 1851. Six Welsh quarriers on the 1851 ship lists provided a more precise origin, and all of them were from "North Wales" (table B10, Appendix B).

53. *Cornwall Royal Gazette*, June 29, 1851; *The Welshman*, June 27, 1851.

54. Van Vugt, "Welsh Emigration," table 4, 555.

55. *Columbia County, Wisconsin*, 1084; a similar case was that of William Owen (1053).

56. *Iowa County, Wisconsin*, 894; *Dodge County, Wisconsin*, 683–84; *Racine and Kenosha Counties, Wisconsin*, 627; *Columbia County, Wisconsin*, 1052.

57. Van Vugt, "Welsh Emigration," table 2, 549.

58. Ibid., 558.

59. William Chambers's *The Emigrant's Manual* (1851) warned of the possible glut on some skilled labor in some American regions, although unskilled labor was still in great demand. See chapter 4 of this volume.

60. *Cardiff and Merthyr Guardian,* Jan. 8, 15, 22, 1848; *Monmouthshire Merlin,* Jan. 8, 1848.

61. *Cardiff and Merthyr Guardian,* Jan. 29, Feb. 12, July 1, 1848.

62. *Cardiff and Methyr Guardian,* Feb. 12, July 22, 1848.

63. *Carmarthen Journal,* Jan. 28, 1848; *Monmouthshire Merlin,* Jan. 29, Feb. 5, March 4, April 1, May 20, 1848.

64. *Census of Great Britain* (1851), vol. 1/2, div. 11, 17.

65. Ibid., 25ff.

66. Swank, *Introduction to a History of Ironmaking and Coal Mining in Pennsylvania,* 100–101; Paskoff, *Industrial Revolution,* 91. On the effect of the end of the railway building boom on Pennsylvania's iron industry, see Temin, *Iron and Steel in Nineteenth-Century America,* 119.

67. Temin, *Iron and Steel in Nineteenth-Century America,* 119. Although conditions in South Wales's iron industry were reported in 1851 as being still generally "depressed," there were also hopeful reports in January and November, as a few new orders for iron were coming in. *The Cambrian,* Jan. 17, 1851; *Swansea and Glamorgan Herald,* Jan. 1, Nov. 26, 1851.

68. Part of the continued problems in South Wales's coal industry in 1851 seems to have been due to the competition of highly productive collieries in Northumberland and Durham, which were less dependent on the iron industry. Benson, *British Coalminers in the Nineteenth Century,* 25–27, 76–80.

69. Jones, "From the Old Country to the New," 99–100.

70. The work of Friedlander and Roshier shows that comparatively little migration occurred from Wales to parts of England. See "A Study of Internal Migration in England and Wales," esp. 252.

71. The Welsh who settled in Waukesha County, Wisconsin, chose hilly areas where they could feel "at home" and be reminded of Wales. Williams, *The Welsh Community of Waukesha County,* 11–12.

Chapter 7: The Elite

1. In addition to the epigraph from *Hillsdale County, Michigan,* ed. Reynolds, 225, see *Stark County, Ohio,* 133; *Adams County, Illinois,* 425; *Will County, Illinois,* 495; and *Portrait of Jo Daviess and Carroll Counties, Illinois,* 630.

2. These figures are for males only; for a discussion of women professionals, see chapter 8. Van Vugt, "Who Were the Women Immigrants?" table 13.2, 165.

3. *Foster's Work and Wages,* 1–3. The report from *The Times*'s correspondent was quoted in the *Doncaster Chronicle,* Oct. 25, 1850. A similar report discouraging clerks from emigrating was printed in the *Somerset County Gazette,* April 20, 1850.

4. Erickson, *Invisible Immigrants,* 429; *Montreal Emigration Agency Annual Report for 1860,* 21.

5. Anderson, *Victorian Clerks,* 129. Orchard, *The Clerks of Liverpool,* 12–18, 37–38, 54,

cites the declining standard of living among clerks and predicts increasing emigration of them to the colonies.

6. By this time, clerks composed 5.6 percent of the emigrants and 3.7 percent of the British labor force. Erickson, *Leaving England,* table 3.6, 106.

7. For bleak reports from Australia, see the *Inverness Courier,* Aug. 22, 1850; *Bedford Mercury,* Sept. 7, 1850; *Thirteenth General Report of the Colonial Land and Emigration Commissioners,* 40:76ff; and *Tenth General Report of the Colonial Land and Emigration Commissioners,* 40:45.

8. *Minutes of Evidence Taken before the Select Committee on the Passenger Acts,* 19:74.

9. Erickson, *Invisible Immigrants,* 395–96. Thomas Petingale was another immigrant clerk concerned about status. Ibid., 395, 433ff.

10. *Morgan and Scott Counties, Illinois,* 302.

11. *Waukesha County, Wisconsin,* 923–24. English immigrant John Shortney acquired a clerkship in Wisconsin in 1850 with ease, apparently because he had been well educated in a London private school. *The Counties of Rock, Green, Grant, Iowa, and Lafayette, Wisconsin,* 25–26.

12. *Morgan and Scott Counties, Illinois,* 482. For a similar story of an accomplished clerk who left a good position to clerk in America until he could take up farming, see that of John Porter in *Peoria County, Illinois,* 640.

13. For examples and discussion of these attitudes among British immigrants at this time, see Erickson, *Invisible Immigrants,* 395–96, 399. These immigrants did not always use a network for their migration. Dunae, *Gentlemen Emigrants,* 5–6; Athearn, *Westward the Briton.*

14. Reader, *Professional Men,* ch. 3, 4. Not until the Medical Act of 1858, for example, were standards and discipline strengthened within the medical profession. See also Young, *The Rise of the Meritocracy.*

15. Musgrove, *The Migratory Elite* (a work primarily concerned with the post-1860 period).

16. See also Hyde, *Cunard and the North Atlantic,* 64, as well as chapter 1 of this volume.

17. *History of Washtenaw County, Michigan,* 1046; *Randolph, Jackson, Perry, Monroe Counties, Illinois,* 561.

18. Numbers, "The Fall and Rise of the American Medical Profession," 51–53.

19. For these cases see, respectively, *Waukesha County, Wisconsin,* 964; *Macomb County, Michigan,* 872; and *Oakland County, Michigan,* 866. See also the case of Dr. Charles Loftus Martin, a well-educated veterinarian surgeon who also bought a farm in Wisconsin. *Rock County, Wisconsin,* 714–15.

20. *Columbia County, Wisconsin,* 961.

21. *Dane County, Wisconsin,* 709; Parker, *Albany County, New York,* 363. Some British immigrants had unique educational experiences and exposure to high culture. William Brummitt, for example, became a page to the daughter of the Duke of Newcastle and "traveled with the Rothchilds" throughout Europe for three years, an experience that seems to have inspired his migration to America in 1855. Soon he was directing art galleries in New York and Philadelphia and then became a real estate speculator and the owner of a gallery in Pontiac, Michigan. *Oakland County, Michigan,* 521–22.

22. Bloomfield, "Law," 35–36.

23. *DeKalb County, Indiana*, 626, 722–23.

24. See the case of William Slatter in *Dane County, Wisconsin*, 818; see also the account of David Hughes in Williams, *The Welsh Community of Waukesha County*, 48.

25. *Eighteenth General Report of the Colonial Land and Emigration Commissioners*, 24:Appendix 6, 78; *Sixteenth General Report of the Colonial Land and Emigration Commissioners*, 24:Appendix 6, 62. For passenger list figures, see the note for table A2, Appendix A.

26. McFarlane, "The Fairmont Colony in Martin County Minnesota."

27. Rubinstein, "The British," 119.

28. Shepperson, *British Emigration to North America*, 35–36, 57–61.

29. Forsythe, "The English Colony at Victoria."

30. Stratton, *Pioneer Women*, 93–94, 223–27.

Chapter 8: Women

1. Of these British women, 67 percent were English, 28 percent were Scottish, and 5 percent were Welsh. There was no significant variation among the three subgroups. Throughout this chapter, then, women are referred to collectively as "British," although the predominance of the English should be kept in mind.

2. See the example of the widow Sarah Jewell, who "determined to emigrate with her family" of seven children in the late 1840s. Her eldest son preceded them by three years. *Portrait of Jo Daviess and Carroll Counties, Illinois*, 302–5. See also the story of Susannah Boddy in *Morgan and Scott Counties, Illinois*, 199–200.

3. Erickson, *Leaving England*, 242.

4. *The Counties of Rock, Green, Grant, Iowa, and, Lafayette, Wisconsin*, 460.

5. *Dane County, Wisconsin*, 287.

6. As Henry Squier wrote to his uncle, Edwin Kimberley, on January 2, 1854, "We also hear that Mr. Barwell has abandoned all thoughts of coming to America, as his wife is averse to it." Edwin Oscar Kimberley Papers.

7. [Mother] to William Candler, June 14, 1853, Henry Ernest Candler Papers.

8. Thomas, *Research Memorandum on Migration Differentials*.

9. For data, see Van Vugt, "Who Were the Immigrant Women?" 166.

10. Ibid., table 13.4, 167.

11. Quoted from Erickson, *Invisible Immigrants*, 184.

12. In spite of historians' generalizations about large surpluses of males on the American frontier, in new farming areas that surplus was small. It was virtually impossible to run farms without women. Walsh, *The American Frontier Revisited*, 63.

13. Erickson, *Invisible Immigrants*, 175–77.

14. *Will County, Illinois*, 370.

15. *Portrait of Jo Daviess and Carroll Counties, Illinois*, 325–26.

16. For the sources, see "Birth and Marriage Certificates" in the Bibliography.

17. Jeffrey, *Frontier Women*.

18. *Portrait of Jo Daviess and Carroll Counties, Illinois*, 373–75.

19. Weatherford, *Foreign and Female*, 239–40.

20. *The Counties of Rock, Green, Grant, Iowa, and Lafayette, Wisconsin*, 223.

21. Rowe, *The Hard-Rock Men*, 56.

22. Van Vugt, "Who Were the Immigrant Women?" table 13.4, 167.

23. These women were all traveling without husbands. The sample also included five more miners and three more shoemakers who had arrived with husbands listed as having the same occupation. Possibly the women were the wives of miners and shoemakers, although the 1851 census did enumerate three thousand female coal miners and thirty-one thousand female shoemakers. Clapham, *An Economic History of Modern Britain*, 2:24.

24. The census of 1851 reported 272,000 female cotton workers and 113,000 female wool workers. Clapham, *An Economic History of Modern Britain*, 2:24ff.

25. Green, *Holyoke, Massachusetts*, 49.

26. The 1851 census enumerated 60,588 needlewomen (or seamstresses) twenty and above (four-fifths of the women surveyed) and 12,352 under twenty. *Census of Great Britain* (1851), *Population Tables*, pt. 2, vol. 1, 87, cxvii–cxxi and ccxvii–ccxxi; Van Vugt, "Who Were the Immigrant Women?" 166.

27. *Northampton Mercury*, March 2, 1850; see also Hammerton, *Emigrant Gentlewomen*, 99.

28. *Cornwall Royal Gazette*, Jan. 18, 1850; *Stirling Observer*, Jan. 24, 31, 1850; *Northampton Mercury*, June 29, 1850; *Liverpool Chronicle*, June 1, 1850; *West Briton and Cornwall Advertiser*, April 25, 1851.

29. For complete data, see Van Vugt, "Who Were the Immigrant Women?" 166–68.

30. The importance of needlewomen's income is illustrated by the letters of two London housepainters whom their parish had assisted in emigrating to Wisconsin. Hoping the parish would also assist their wives who remained in England, they warned them in 1849, "Do not let the parish know that you can work at the Needle, as they would say you could earn your own living." "'God Raised Us Up Good Friends,'" 226.

31. Erickson, *Invisible Immigrants*, 315; for other examples, see 254, 291, and the letter of an English potter in Foreman, "Settlement of English Potters in Wisconsin," 385.

32. *History of Washtenaw County, Michigan*, 1219.

33. *Census of Great Britain* (1851), vol. 2/1, table 53. Of the 188 servants in the sample, 145 were twenty and above.

34. Hunt, *Regional Wage Variations in Britain*, 131, 140; Dawes, *Not in Front of the Servants*, 114ff.

35. Van Vugt, "Who Were the Immigrant Women?" 166–68.

36. Schrier, *Ireland and the American Emigration*, 75ff; Adams, *Ireland and Irish Emigration to the New World*, 223–24.

37. Jones, *American Immigration*, 130; Taylor, *Distant Magnet*, 174; Wittke, *The Irish in America*, 43–44.

38. *Cornwall Royal Gazette*, Oct. 4, 1850. For examples of colonial reports stating the great demand for servants in Australia, see *Papers Relative to Emigration to the Australian Colonies* (1850), 40:44–45, and (1852), 36:116, 133, 418ff. According to a popular emigrants' guide, *Foster's Work and Wages*, female servants in America could earn $4–8 per month, although $5–6 (equal to £12–14 per year) a month was more usual.

39. Hammerton, *Emigrant Gentlewomen*, ch. 4.

40. Roughly a thousand female servants were assisted to Australia each year at mid-century. *Papers Relative to Emigration to the Australian Colonies* (1852), 36:12, 74–75, and (1852–53), 68:163; *Stirling Observer*, Jan. 31, 1850.

41. *Bedford Mercury*, June 1, 1850; *Bristol Mirror*, April 13, 1850.

42. American-born women migrating to the American frontier between 1840 and 1880 were also more active in the migration process than some historians have assumed. They,

too, contributed to family income by working as seamstresses and domestic servants. Jeffrey, *Frontier Women*, 30–36, 60, 94.

43. For an assessment of Irish women immigrants, see Diner, *Erin's Daughters in America*, 50, 54, 70, and Miller, *Emigrants and Exiles*, 315, 318–19. See also Blessing, "Irish," esp. 531; Conzen, "Germans," 405–25; and Köllmann and Marschalk, "German Emigration to the United States," 499–545, esp. 530–31.

Chapter 9: Becoming Americans

1. *Primitive Methodist Magazine* 10 (1852): 369.
2. *Primitive Methodist Magazine* 16 (1858): 568.
3. *The Doctrines and Discipline of the Primitive Methodist Connexion*, 3–9; Alderson, "The Origin of the Primitive Methodist Connexion in the Middlewest." See also Werner, *The Primitive Methodist Connexion*, xi, 44–47, 94–95, 135; and Clark, *The Making of Victorian England*, 182–87.
4. County histories often recorded changes in a subject's religious affiliation, which allows certainty on pre-migratory religion. For those that only recorded current affiliation in America, denominational loyalty is assumed.
5. Thompson, "The 1851 Religious Census," 87–97; Best, *Mid-Victorian Britain*, 179.
6. Thistlethwaite, "Migration from Europe Overseas"; Swierenga, "Religion and Immigration Behavior"; Bratt, *Dutch Calvinism in Modern America*, ch. 1.
7. This was also true of Methodists during the years immediately before the American Revolution. Bailyn, *Voyagers to the West*, 378, 420.
8. Inglis, *Churches and the Working Classes in Victorian England*; Vincent, *Literacy and Popular Culture*.
9. Knowles, *Calvinists Incorporated*, 228–29.
10. Mathias, *The First Industrial Nation*, 142; Inglis, *Churches and the Working Class in England*, 73.
11. *History of Dearborn, Ohio, and Switzerland Counties, Indiana*, 461–62, 560, 986; Shaw, ed., *History of Dearborn County, Indiana*, 212–15, 227. At least twenty-two Yorkshire families followed the Ewbanks to this corner of Indiana.
12. Erickson, *Invisible Immigrants*, 74. The extent to which British immigrants intermarried with native-born Americans is, according to the county histories, impressionably high when compared to other European immigrants but impossible to determine accurately. The nationality of marriage partners in America is not always clear, and young immigrants were more likely to marry Americans than widowers, for example. Generally, between a quarter and half of the British immigrants who married in America chose American-born partners, according to sampling in *The Past and Present of Lake County, Illinois; Randolph, Jackson, Perry, and Monroe Counties, Illinois, Portrait of Jo Daviess and Carroll Counties, Illinois;* and *Iowa County, Wisconsin.*
13. *Primitive Methodist Magazine* 16 (1858): 568.
14. Taylor, "Why Did British Mormons Emigrate?"; Erickson, *Leaving England*, 60. On the Mormon missions and their voyages to America, see Sonne, *Saints on the Seas*.
15. This "large number" followed eighty of their co-religionists who had left Swansea the previous week. *Cardiff and Merthyr Guardian*, April 12, 1851; *Bristol Times and Bath Advocate*, May 17, 1851; *Monmouthshire Merlin*, May 16, 1851; *Liverpool Chronicle*, May 17, 1851. See also Taylor, *Expectations Westward*, 101.
16. Taylor, "Why Did British Mormons Emigrate?" 252–53, 259–65. Bliss speculates that

Matthew Walker from Yorkshire converted from Methodism to Mormonism because that was the cheapest way to get to America. *Merchants and Miners in Utah,* 36. Walker died in St. Louis on his way west, but his sons proceeded west and became owners of a mining and banking empire in Utah.

17. *Doncaster Chronicle,* April 28, 1854; see also the *Sheffield and Rotherham Independent,* Jan. 1, Jan. 4, 1851. Charles Dickens, in contrast, referred to the Mormon emigrants as the "pick and flower of England." Bliss, *Merchants and Miners in Utah,* 40.

18. *Primitive Methodist Magazine* 10 (1852): 287.

19. *Branch County, Michigan,* 200–202. For more examples, see Taylor, "Why Did British Mormons Emigrate?" 268. The Walker brothers had long been disaffected by the church by the time they were excommunicated in the 1870s. Bliss, *Merchants and Miners in Utah,* 212.

20. Goddard, "The Road to a Promised Land," pts. 1–2.

21. Ibid., pt. 1, 11.

22. Shipps, *Mormonism.*

23. Harrison, *Drink and the Victorians,* 101–4.

24. Berthoff, *British Immigrants in Industrial America,* 146–47.

25. *Portrait of Jo Daviess and Carroll Counties, Illinois,* 788. See, too, the case of Thomas Reed from Cornwall, a prominent advocate of prohibitionism, on page 576 of the same volume.

26. *Racine and Kenosha Counties, Wisconsin,* 704.

27. *Waukesha County, Wisconsin,* 922–23. See also *Morgan and Scott Counties, Illinois,* 229–30, for the case of the Robert Hills family, well known as temperance people.

28. *Columbia County, Wisconsin,* 1051.

29. Rohrbough, *The Trans-Appalachian Frontier,* 61.

30. Harrison, *Drink and the Victorians,* 101.

31. E. Chapman to John Cooper, January 1852, E. Chapman Letters.

32. Cooke and Ramadhyani, comps., *Indians and a Changing Frontier.* For more details of these events, see McKee, ed., *The Trail of Death,* 106; Madison, *The Indiana Way,* 124–25; and Edmunds, "'Designing Men, Seeking a Fortune,'" 109–22.

33. Van Vugt, "An English Shoemaker in Indiana," 43–45. Generally sympathetic views toward Native Americans by English immigrants and travelers can also be seen in Stein, "Indian Removal as Seen by European Travelers in America"; and "'God Raised Us Up Good Friends,'" 231. Yet Billington found that some elite travelers and writers from Britain believed that the American frontier was meant to be exploited by the whites at the cost of Native Americans. See *Land of Savagery, Land of Promise,* 46.

34. Diary entry for Nov. 17, 1845, Matthew Dinsdale Papers.

35. E. Chapman to J. C. Gotch, May 1, 1850, E. Chapman Letters.

36. John Wood to Wheatley Wood, Jan. 30, 1853.

37. Henry Squier to Edwin Kimberley, Jan. 2, 1854, Edwin Oscar Kimberley Papers.

38. Clark, *The Making of Victorian England,* 37.

39. Bolt, *Victorian Attitudes to Race,* 29.

40. Thistlethwaite, *The Anglo-American Connection,* 108.

41. *Sheffield and Rotherham Independent,* May 25, 1847; see also Maurer, "'Punch' on Slavery and Civil War in America," 5–28; and Thistlethwaite, *The Anglo-American Connection,* 119.

42. Lillibridge, *Beacon of Freedom*, 46.

43. Briggs, *Victorian People*, 171; Bolt, *Victorian Attitudes to Race*, 33.

44. Briggs, *Victorian People*, 202, 223–24. Briggs quotes the words of Victorian historian John Morely. The influence of American politics in Britain is explored in Lillibridge, *Beacon of Freedom*.

45. Erickson, *Invisible Immigrants*, 75. Only a minority were racist, as is indicated by the comments of one Welsh miner in 1868: "Almost all the Welshmen are on the radical [Republican] ticket and I would be so myself except for the nigger equality which does not agree with my views that the Creator never intended them to be equal to the white man." Conway, ed., *The Welsh in America*, 182.

46. *Randolph, Jackson, Perry, and Monroe Counties, Illinois*, 625; Erickson, *Invisible Immigrants*, 251; *Portrait and Biographical Album of Lake County, Illinois*, 343. That slavery repulsed British settlers can also be seen in the early example of Matthew Foster, an immigrant from Durham who passed through Indiana in 1817 on his way to St. Louis but was so disturbed by the agitation to make Missouri a slave state that he returned to Indiana. "The Pike County Indiana Ancestors of John Foster Dulles."

47. *Racine and Kenosha Counties, Wisconsin*, 370.

48. Ibid., 627; see also case of William Reid, *Waukesha County, Wisconsin*, 1005–6.

49. Parker, *Albany County, New York*, 8. See also the case of Daniel Dawson, who had lived in Arkansas and Kentucky before coming to Illinois, in *Randolph, Jackson, Perry, and Monroe Counties, Illinois*, 443–44.

50. As a girl, Henrietta Ramsden had sold the first book in England that told of the life of Frederick Douglass, *Album of Genealogy and Biography, Cook County, Illinois*, 766.

51. Poucher, "An English Colony in Floyd County," 213–14.

52. *Grant County, Wisconsin*, 900.

53. Lonn, *Foreigners in the Union Army and Navy*, 577–79.

54. *Lincoln, Rutland and Stamford Mercury*, July 31, 1863.

55. Lonn, *Foreigners in the Confederacy*, 198–99. Stanley (whose original name was John Rowlands) later returned to Britain, established a reputation as an explorer of Africa, was knighted, and served two terms in the House of Commons. See Stanley, *The Autobiography of Sir Henry Morton Stanley*; and Symons, *H. M. Stanley*.

56. Burton, *Melting Pot Soldiers*, 66; Lonn, *Foreigners in the Union*, 5.

57. Crawford, *The Anglo-American Crisis of the Mid-Nineteenth Century*.

58. Riley, "A Social and Economic History of La Fayette County," 46.

59. See the case of Samuel Clark in *History of McHenry County, Illinois*, 646–47.

60. For examples, see *Morgan and Scott Counties, Illinois*, 346; *Peoria County, Illinois*, 293, 534, 606; *Allen County, Indiana*, 135; and *Randolph, Jackson, Perry, and Monroe Counties, Illinois*, 556.

61. Quoted from Erickson, *Invisible Immigrants*, 350. Crawshaw also reported that he was paid $13 per month, "sufficient for spending money," and a month later he told his father, "But you must bear in mind that I am for a good cause or I shouldn't be carrying a rifle." Ibid., 351.

62. *Randolph, Jackson, Perry, and Monroe Counties, Illinois*, 221.

63. *Biographical History of Tippecanoe, White, Jasper, Newton, Benton, Warren, and Pulaski Counties, Indiana*, 1:451–52. See also the case of Jeremiah Winter (2:868), who immigrated in 1858 and fought for the Union. Such a response by recent English immi-

grants also occurred during the Mexican-American War. William Cook left Boston in Lincolnshire in 1846 and still served in the quartermaster's department of the American army, and Henry Erredge left London in 1845 and joined the army early enough to go all the way to Mexico City in 1847. *Columbia County, Wisconsin*, 1003; *Waukesha County, Wisconsin*, 853.

64. Bahmer, *Coshocton County, Ohio*, 1:40–43. See also the case of Thomas Blackburn, who emigrated in 1859 and still served. *Portage and Summit Counties, Ohio*, 600. William Stockdale immigrated during the war and still served. William Stockdale Letters.

65. *The Counties of Rock, Green, Grant, Iowa, and Lafayette, Wisconsin*, 376–78; for other examples, see Lonn, *Foreigners in the Union*, 255–56.

66. *Racine and Kenosha, Wisconsin*, 661–62. See 663 for the case of Reuben North, who served at age fifty-five.

67. See the examples in *LaSalle County, Illinois*, 699; *Madison County* [Illinois], 355; *Peoria County, Illinois*, 534. *Tompkins County, New York*, 202; and *Ottawa County, Michigan*, 117.

68. *Ottawa County, Michigan*, 70.

69. *Biographical History of Tippecanoe, White, Jasper, Newton, Benton, Warren, and Pulaski Counties, Indiana*, 1:487–88; Blanchard, ed., *Counties of Clay and Owen, Indiana*, 472; *History of Dearborn, Ohio, and Switzerland Counties, Indiana*, 744; *Portrait and Biographical Record of Montgomery, Parke and Fountain Counties, Indiana*, 615–16; *Portrait and Biographical Album of Lake County, Illinois*, 698; *The Past and Present of Lake County, Illinois*, 418; *Peoria County, Illinois*, 293.

70. Blanchard, ed., *Counties of Morgan, Monroe, and Brown, Indiana*, 633–34; Lane, *City of the Century*, 15–16; *Peoria County, Illinois*, 298–99. Far fewer British immigrants served in the Confederacy, though some served with distinction as officers. See Lonn, *Foreigners in the Confederacy*, 464, 482–88, 494–95.

71. *Biographical History of Tippecanoe, White, Jasper, Newton, Benton, Warren and Pulaski Counties, Indiana*, 2:868; *McHenry County, Illinois*, 535; *Tompkins County, New York*, 160; *History of Washtenaw County, Michigan*, 1333; *Oneida County, New York*, 566–67.

72. *Will County, Illinois*, 495. For another case of a Scottish immigrant raising a regiment and becoming captain, see that of James B. White in *Allen County, Indiana*, 134–35. White was twice captured during the war.

73. *Kane County, Illinois*, 707; Summers, ed., *Genealogical and Family History of Eastern Ohio*, 479–80. Three of Cartwright's four brothers also survived the war.

74. [Father] to William Stockdale, April 28, 1867, William Stockdale Letters.

75. Jewel, *Cornish in America* , 40–41.

76. Berthoff, *British Immigrants in Industrial America*, 161–64.

77. Lipson, *Freemasonry in Federalist Connecticut*, chs. 1–2.

78. Berthoff, *British Immigrants in Industrial America*, 167–69.

79. Conway, ed., *The Welsh in America;* Berthoff, *British Immigrants in Industrial America*, 172–75.

80. Berthoff, *British Immigrants in Industrial America*, 143.

81. Ibid., 147–48.

82. Wilcox, "Sport and the Nineteenth Century Immigrant Experience," 182.

83. Seymour, *Baseball*, 4–14.

84. *Dane County, Wisconsin*, 286–88.
85. Gordon, *The Orange Riots*.
86. Kleppner, *The Third Electoral System*, 61, 64, 147–48, 163–65.

Conclusion

1. *Randolph, Jackson, Perry, and Monroe Counties, Illinois*, 370. William Jewell crossed the Atlantic nine times. See *Portrait of Jo Daviess and Carroll Counties, Illinois*, 304.

2. For examples, see *McHenry County, Illinois*, 904; *Portrait of Jo Daviess and Carroll Counties, Illinois*, 382; *Peoria County, Illinois*, 412–13; *Morgan and Scott Counties, Illinois*, 200, 413, 471; *Randolph, Jackson, Perry, and Monroe Counties, Illinois*, 561; and Signor, ed., *Orleans County, New York*, 172.

3. Baines, *Migration in a Mature Economy*, 140.

4. Fischer, *Albion's Seed*.

5. Bailyn, *Voyagers to the West*, esp. 160, 172, 203, 233, 285.

6. Gerber, *The Making of an American Pluralism*, xv, 93–95, 107.

7. Diary entry for March 17, 1847, Matthew Dinsdale Papers.

Appendix A: Sources

1. On the nature of county histories and "mug books" and their potential use by historians, see Hanna, "Everyman His Own Biographer," and Chudacoff, "The S. J. Clarke Publishing Company."

2. See "U.S. County Histories" in the Bibliography for full references.

3. *Census of Great Britain* (1851), vol. 1/1, cxxxv, cxlii.

4. The classic study of English and Scottish immigrant letters is Erickson, *Invisible Immigrants;* for the Welsh, see Conway, ed., *The Welsh in America*.

5. For a convenient discussion of the passenger lists and some of the important studies that have used them, see Swierenga, "List upon List."

6. The method used here is based on a study conducted by Charlotte Erickson that determined the best sampling methods for the study of emigration from the United Kingdom ("The Uses of Passenger Lists," 88–116). The result is a one-in-ten sample of all the lists of ships carrying six or more British emigrants. Statistical tests on four variables indicate that the sample accurately reflects the entire body of ship lists. In "The Occupations of English Immigrants," Cohn made his own estimates of the occupational makeup of English immigrants based on a nonrandom sample of passenger lists. He originally drew the sample, which included lists with extensive ditto marks under "labourer," for a study of mortality on immigrant ships from 1836 to 1853. He then used the same lists to investigate occupations. Predictably, such results will show more laborers than samples that do not include lists marred by extensive dittos and imprecise occupational headings.

7. This occupational scheme is based on the one Erickson used in "Who Were the English and Scots Emigrants to the United States in the Late Nineteenth Century?" An excellent discussion and guide to the nature of Victorian occupations is found in Samuel, "Workshop of the World."

Bibliography

Primary Sources

Manuscripts

Alderson, James. "The Origin of the Primitive Methodist Connexion in the Middlewest." Microfilm 40, article 3d. University of Wisconsin, Platteville.

George and Nanny Ainley Letters. Ms. 1156/Add./1. West Yorkshire Archaeological Society, Leeds.

Ralph Ashworth Letters, 1849–1850. SC 39. University of Wisconsin, Platteville.

Bewick, Stephenson C. L. "Recollections of Pioneer Life in Wisconsin." Stephenson C. L. Bewick Papers. SC 2651. State Historical Society of Wisconsin, Madison.

Bryson Collection. D/B/119C(41). Department of Archives, Merseyside County Museum, Liverpool.

George W. Buxton Papers. Wis. Ms. SC1158. State Historical Society of Wisconsin, Madison.

Henry Ernest Candler Papers. Bentley Historical Library, University of Michigan, Ann Arbor.

E. Chapman Letters. GK 1038, 1039. Northamptonshire Record Office, Northampton.

Collection of Immigrant Letters. [9 boxes.] British Library of Political and Economic Science, London School of Economics.

John Curtis to Richard Cobden, May 8, 1844. M87/2/2/25. Manchester Central Library, Manchester.

Matthew Dinsdale Papers. Wis. Ms. DL. State Historical Society of Wisconsin, Madison.

"The Pike County, Indiana Ancestors of John Foster Dulles." SC 587. Indiana Historical Society, Indianapolis.

James Finlay Letters. Ancaster Estate Papers. 3 Anc. 59/70 (May 31–Nov. 30, 1849 [Lindsey Coast Estate]) and 59/56 (May 31–Nov. 30, 1859). Lincolnshire County Archives, Lincoln.

Robert Gorst Papers. Wis. Ms. BZ. State Historical Society of Wisconsin, Madison.

Joseph Hurst Diary. Ms. 910.4 H1. Manchester Central Library, Manchester.

Jenkin, Alfred. "The Cornish Emigration," ca. 1965. Bentley Historical Library, University of Michigan, Ann Arbor.

Edwin Oscar Kimberley Papers, 1840–1919. State Historical Society of Wisconsin, Madison.

William Moore Letter, Aug. 25, 1854. Ms. 1156/3. Yorkshire Archaeological Society, Leeds.

Page, Margaret Robinson. "History of the Welsh Baptist Church, Town of Aurora, 1857–1916, Waushara County, Wisconsin." Wis. Ms. SC 455. State Historical Society of Wisconsin, Madison.

Spencer, Mable K. "Biographical Sketch of John Spencer." SC 1976. State Historical Society of Wisconsin, Madison.

William Stockdale Letters. SC 1412. Indiana Historical Society, Indianapolis.

Isaac Taylor Letter, Dec. 20, 1848. Isaac Taylor (1811–1887) Letters, 1848–85. Bentley Historical Library, University of Michigan, Ann Arbor.

Thorpe Letters and Poems, 1838, 1850, 1879. Kent State University Library, Kent, Ohio.

Jane Trattles Letters, 1854–68. Bentley Historical Library, University of Michigan, Ann Arbor.

Wilson Family Papers, 1848–1902. Bentley Historical Library, University of Michigan, Ann Arbor.

John Wood Letter, Jan. 30, 1853. Z109. West Yorkshire Archive Service, Wakefield.

Birth and Marriage Certificates

[All certificates—other than that of John Noble in the British Public Record Office—are in St. Catherine's House, London. In this listing, place names are followed by date and volume, page numbers, and a short citation referring to the "U.S. County Histories" section of this bibliography. Names in parentheses are the certificate-holder's children who are featured in county histories.]

Adams, Robert (Joseph)	Great Wilbrahim, Cambridgeshire, 1841, H0107/72/7; see *Waukesha County, Wisconsin*, 882.
Allen, Edwin	Beaminster, Dec. 1842, 8/19; see *Waukesha County, Wisconsin*, 922.
Amos, W. H.	St. George Hanover Square, June 1840, 1/5; see *Racine and Kenosha Counties, Wisconsin*, 565.
Bainbridge, Matthew	Teesdale, Sept. 1846, 24/351; marriage: M[ay?] 1868, 10a/271; see *The Counties of Rock, Green, Grant, Iowa, and Lafayette, Wisconsin*, 618.
Banks, Francis	Malton, Yorkshire, Dec. 1840, 24/406; see *Racine and Kenosha Counties, Wisconsin*, 634.
Barber, Seth	Camberwell, June 1846, 4/49; see *Album of Genealogy and Biography, Cook County, Illinois*, 438.
Beckley, Eli	Birmingham, Jan. 1853, GD/123; see *Randolph, Jackson, Perry, and Monroe Counties, Illinois*, 370–71.
Blackler, John (Thomas)	Ashburton, March 1840, 10/147; see *Album of Genealogy and Biography, Cook County, Illinois*, 457.
Bouch, Joseph	Holbeach, March 1840, 14/537; see *Album of Genealogy and Biography, Cook County, Illinois*, 767.
Brain, Moses Aaron	Bristol, Jan. 1841, 11/244; see *Waukesha County, Wisconsin*, 932.

Bray, Robert   Glanford, March 1853, 7a/601; see *Waukesha County,*
                                      Wisconsin, 932.
Burden, John   Launceston, Dec. 1842, 9/202; see *Waukesha County,*
                                      Wisconsin, 895.
Chapman, E. F. A. (William)   Marlyebone, Aug. 1845, 1/288; see *Randolph, Jackson,*
                                      Perry, and Monroe Counties, Illinois, 676.
Chapman, F. W.   Marlyebone, Sept. 1845, 1/288; see *La Fayette County,*
                                      Wisconsin, 716.
Clementson, Joseph (George)   Richmond, Yorkshire, March 1842, 24/461; see *Grant*
                                      County, Wisconsin, 887–88.
Cooper, Joseph   Glanford P., Jan. 1852, 7a/1282; see *Waukesha County,*
                                      Wisconsin, 934.
Cotton, George (James)   Wellington, Dec. 1841, 18/177; see *Portrait and Bio-*
                                      graphical Album of Jackson County, Michigan, 412–13.
Danby, William   Wakefield, Dec. 1844, 22/674; see *Will County, Illinois,*
                                      526–27.
Davis, William   Wolverhampton, Dec. 1839, 17/383; see *Trumbull and*
                                      Mahoning Counties [Ohio], 246–47.
Dinsdale, Matthew (John)   Askrigg, April 1853, M.B. 427/149; see *The Counties of*
                                      Rock, Green, Grant, Iowa, and Lafayette, Wisconsin, 111–
                                      12.
Dixon, John   Lincoln, June 1842, 14/775; see *Waukesha County, Wis-*
                                      consin, 961.
Foreman, George (William)   Faversham, Sept. 1839, 5/153; see *Racine and Kenosha*
                                      Counties, Wisconsin, 661–62.
Fox, Samuel   Banbury, [n.d.], 16/30; see *Waukesha County, Wiscon-*
                                      sin, 934–35.
Froggatt, John   Worksop, March 1849, 15/841; see *Dane County, Wis-*
                                      consin, 302–3.
Hall, Samuel   Chesterfield, Dec. 1843, 19/459; see *Dane County, Wis-*
                                      consin, 358–59.
Hardy, James   Ecclesfield, Dec. 1840, 22/128; see *Waukesha County,*
                                      Wisconsin, 969.
Harnden, Marsh   Poothing, March 1844, 5/7; see *Rock County, Wisconsin,*
                                      751.
Jackson, Samuel (William)   Stockport, June 1838, 19/231; see *Album of Genealogy*
                                      and Biography, Cook County, Illinois, 680.
Lyth, John   York, Oct. 1843, 23/755; see Smith, ed., *History of the*
                                      City of Buffalo and Erie County [New York],
Marshall, William   Retford, March 1843, 15/607; see *Kane County, Illinois,*
                                      770.
Moulding, Thomas (Charles)   Warrington, Dec. 1842, 20/792; see *Kane County, Illi-*
                                      nois, 436.
Newman, John   Bishops Stortford, Jan. 1842, 6/474; see *Kane County,*
                                      Illinois, 420.
Noble, John (Joseph)   Raistrick, Yorkshire, [n.d.], PRO/RG4/2749; see *Racine*
                                      and Kenosha Counties, Wisconsin, 647.

Phillips, Henry J. (John)	Cripplegate, Jan. 1840, 2/211; see *Rock County, Wisconsin*, 875.
Pound, John	Devizes, March 1842, 8/39; see *Oakland County, Michigan*, 891.
Rudge, George	Upton, March 1852, 6c/273; see *Trumbull and Mahoning Counties* [Ohio], 476–77.
Rundell, Samuel (William)	Little Petherick, March 1848, 9/69; see *Grant County, Wisconsin*, 921.
Smailes, William	Bridlington, June 1842, 23/24; see *Kane County, Illinois*, 515.
Smith, William	Kingston Upon Hull, June 1841, 22/407; see Andrews, ed., *History of Marietta and Washington County, Ohio*, 1072–75.
Snashall, Caleb (James)	Yalding, Maidstone, May 1840, 5/306; see *Rock County, Wisconsin*, 867.
Spriggs, John (Jabez)	J. S. Kettering, Sept. 1845, 15/401; see *Racine and Kenosha Counties, Wisconsin*, 674.
Sturman, William	W. S. Southam, March 1845, 16/455; see *Oakland County, Michigan*, 200–201.
Sumpter, John	H. Boston, Aug. 1841, 14/331; see *Racine and Kenosha Counties, Wisconsin*, 674.
Sutton, John	Preston, Dec. 1839, 21/338; see *Oakland County, Michigan*, 582–83.
Turner, George	Manchester, Dec. 1846, 20/429; see *Trumbull and Mahoning Counties* [Ohio], 472.
Webb, William (Alfred)	Wallingford, Jan. 1842, 6/252; see *Oakland County, Michigan*, 597.
Winkley, Henry	Long Sutton, Sept. 1858, 7a/370; Holbeach, March 1864, 7a/370; see *Rock County, Wisconsin*, 840.
Wood, John	Brighton, June 1850, 7/429; see *Rock County, Wisconsin*, 881.
Varley, Thomas	Pocklington, Dec. 1844, 23/145; see *Will County, Illinois*, 399–400.

Parliamentary Papers

Census of Great Britain, vol. 1/1, 1/2. London: Her Majesty's Printing Office, 1851.

Census of Great Britain, Population Tables, pt. 2, *Ages, Civil Condition, Occupations, and Birth-place of the People*, vol. 1, *England and Wales*. London: Her Majesty's Printing Office, 1851.

Eighteenth General Report of the Colonial Land and Emigration Commissioners, vol. 24. London: Her Majesty's Printing Office, 1858.

Fourth Annual Report of the Poor Law Board, vol. 23. London: Her Majesty's Printing Office, 1851 [1852].

Minutes of Evidence Taken before the Select Committee on the Passenger Acts, vol. 19. London: Her Majesty's Printing Office, 1851.

Montreal Emigration Agency Annual Report for 1860, vol. 40. London: Her Majesty's Printing Office, 1860.

Papers Relative to Emigration to the Australian Colonies, vols. 40, 34, 68. London: Her Majesty's Printing Office, 1850, 1852, 1852–53.

Papers Relative to Emigration, Return of the Trades or Callings of the Emigrants Who Arrived at the Ports of Quebec and Montreal, vol. 40. London: Her Majesty's Printing Office, 1851.

Sixteenth General Report of the Colonial Land and Emigration Commissioners, vol. 24. London: Her Majesty's Printing Office, 1858.

Tenth General Report of the Colonial Land and Emigration Commissioners, vol. 40. London: Her Majesty's Printing Office, 1850.

Thirteenth General Report of the Colonial Land and Emigration Commissioners, vol. 40. London: Her Majesty's Printing Office, 1852–53.

Thirty-third General Report of the Colonial Land and Emigration Commissioners, vol. 18. London: Her Majesty's Printing Office, 1873.

Twelfth General Report of the Colonial Land and Emigration Commissioners, vol. 22. London: Her Majesty's Printing Office, 1862.

Newspapers and Periodicals

Bristol Times and Bath Advocate; Bucks Herald; Cambrian; Cardiff and Merthyr Guardian; Carmarthan Journal; Constitutional and Perthshire Agricultural and General Advertiser; Cornwall Royal Gazette; Daily American; Devizes and Wiltshire Gazette; Doncaster Chronicle and Farmer's Journal; Harrogate Herald; Lincolnshire, Boston, and Spalding Free Press; Liverpool Chronicle; Mark Lane Express; Miners' Journal; Monmouthshire Merlin; Morning Chronicle; Northampton Chronicle; Northampton Herald; Northampton Mercury; North British Agriculturalist; North Wales Chronicle; Pennsylvania Telegraph; Perthshire Courier; Plymouth, Devonport, and Stonehouse Herald; Plymouth Journal; Potters' Examiner and Workman's Advocate; Primitive Methodist Magazine; Salisbury and Wiltshire Herald; Somerset County Gazette; Somerset Country Herald; Somerset Observer; Sussex Agricultural Express; Swansea and Glamorgan Herald; Times; Welshman; West Briton and Cornwall Advertiser; West of England Conservative; York Herald

U.S. County Histories

Illinois

Adams County. *Portrait and Biographical Record of Adams County, Illinois, Containing Biographical Sketches of Prominent and Representative Citizens.* Chicago: Chapman Brothers, 1892.

Album of Genealogy and Biography, Cook County, Illinois. Chicago: Calumet Book and Engraving, 1895.

Andreas, A. T. *History of Cook County, Illinois. From the Earliest Period to the Present Time.* Chicago: A. T. Andreas Publishing, 1884.

Dyson, Howard, ed. *History of Schuyler County.* Chicago: Munsell Publishing, 1908.

Hancock, McDonough, and Henderson Counties. *Portrait and Biographical Record of Hancock, McDonough and Henderson Counties Illinois, Containing Biographical*

Sketches of Prominent and Representative Citizens of the County. Chicago: Lake City Publishing, 1894.

Jo Daviess and Carroll Counties. *Portrait and Biographical Album of Jo Daviess and Carroll Counties, Illinois, Containing Full-Page Portraits and Biographical Sketches of Prominent and Representative Citizens of the County.* Chicago: Chapman Brothers, 1889.

Kane County. *Biographical and Historical Record of Kane County, Illinois, Containing Full-Page Portraits and Biographical Sketches of Prominent and Representative Citizens of the County.* Chicago: Beers, Leggett, 1888.

Lake County. *The Past and Present of Lake County, Illinois.* Chicago: William Le Baron, 1877.

————. *Portrait and Biographical Album of Lake County, Illinois, Containing Full-Page Portraits and Biographical Sketches of Prominent and Representative Citizens of the County.* Chicago: Lake City Publishing, 1891.

LaSalle County. *History of LaSalle County, Illinois, Together with Sketches of its Cities, Villages and Towns, Educational, Religious, Civil, Military, and Political History, Portraits of Prominent Persons, and Biographies of Representative Citizens.* Chicago: Inter-State Publishing, 1886.

Madison County. *Portrait and Biographical Record of Madison County, Containing Biographical Sketches of Prominent and Representative Citizens of the County.* Chicago: Biographical Publishing, 1894.

McHenry County. *History of McHenry County, Illinois, Together with Sketches of Its Cities, Villages and Towns, Educational, Religious, Civil, Military, and Political History, Portraits of Prominent Persons, and Biographies of Representative Citizens.* Chicago: Inter-State Publishing, 1885.

Morgan and Scott Counties. *Portrait and Biographical Album of Morgan and Scott Counties, Illinois, Containing Full-Page Portraits and Biographical Sketches of Prominent and Representative Citizens of the County.* Chicago: Chapman Brothers, 1889.

Partridge, Charles A., ed. *Historical Encyclopedia of Illinois, and History of Lake County.* Chicago: Munsell Publishing, 1902.

Peoria County. *Portrait and Biographical Album of Peoria County, Illinois, Containing Full-Page Portraits and Biographical Sketches of Prominent and Representative Citizens of the County.* Chicago: Biographical Publishing, 1890.

Portrait and Biographical Record of Cook and Dupage Counties, Illinois. Chicago: Lake City Publishing, 1894.

Randolph, Jackson, Perry, and Monroe Counties. *Portrait and Biographical Record of Randolph, Jackson, Perry and Monroe Counties, Illinois, Containing Biographical Sketches of Prominent and Representative Citizens of the Counties.* Chicago: Biographical Publishing, 1894.

Scott County. *Atlas Map of Scott County, Illinois.* Davenport: Andreas, Lyter, 1873.

St. Clair County. *Portrait and Biographical Record of St. Clair County, Illinois, Containing Biographical Sketches of Prominent and Representative Citizens.* Chicago: Chapman Brothers, 1892.

Will County. *Portrait and Biographical Album of Will County, Illinois, Containing Full-Page Portraits and Biographical Sketches of Prominent and Representative Citizens of the County.* Chicago: Chapman Brothers, 1890.

Winnebago County. *Portrait and Biographical Record of Winnebago and Boone Counties,*

Illinois, Containing Biographical Sketches of Prominent and Representative Citizens. Chicago: Biographical Publishing, 1892.

Indiana

Allen County. *History of Allen County, Indiana, with Illustrations and Biographical Sketches of Some of Its Prominent Men and Pioneers.* Chicago: Kingman Brothers, 1880.

Alvord, Samuel E. *Alvord's History of Noble County, Indiana.* Logansport: B. F. Bowen, Publishers, 1902.

Birch, Jesse S. *History of Benton County and Historic Oxford.* Oxford, Ind.: Craw and Craw, 1928.

Blanchard, Charles, ed. *Counties of Clay and Owen, Indiana, Historical and Biographical.* Chicago: F. A. Battey, 1884.

———. *Counties of Morgan, Monroe, and Brown, Indiana, Historical and Biographical.* Chicago: F. A. Battey, 1884.

Bradsby, H. C. *History of Vigo County, Indiana, with Biographical Selections.* Chicago: S. B. Nelson Publishers, 1891.

Clark County. *Biographical and Historical Souvenir for the Counties of Clark, Crawford, Harrison, Floyd, Jefferson, Jennings, Scott and Washington, Indiana.* Chicago: Printing, 1889.

Elliot, Joseph P. *A History of Evansville and Vanderburgh County, Indiana. A Complete and Concise Account from the Earliest Times to the Present, Embracing Reminiscences of the Pioneers and Biographical Sketches of the Men Who Have Been Leaders in Commercial and Other Enterprises.* Evansville: Keller Printing, 1897.

Esarey, Logan. *History of Indiana from Its Exploration to 1922, also an Account of St. Joseph County.* 3 vols. Dayton: Dayton Historical Publications Company, 1923.

History of Dearborn, Ohio, and Switzerland Counties, Indiana. From Their Earliest Settlement, Containing a History of the Counties; Their Cities, Townships, Towns, Villages, Schools, and Churches; Reminiscences, Extracts, etc.; Local Statistics; Portraits of Early Settlers and Prominent Men; Biographies; Preliminary Chapters on the History of the North-West Territory, the State of Indiana, and the Indians. Chicago: F. E. Weakley, Publishers, 1885.

LaGrange and Noble Counties. *Counties of LaGrange and Noble, Indiana. Historical and Biographical.* Chicago: F. A. Battey, Publishers, 1882.

Porter and Lake Counties. *Counties of Porter and Lake, Indiana, Historical and Biographical.* Chicago: F. A. Battey, Publishers, 1882.

Portrait and Biographical Record of Montgomery, Parke, and Fountain Counties, Indiana. Chicago: Chapman Brothers, 1893.

Posey County. *History of Posey County Indiana. From the Earliest Time to the Present; with Biographical Sketches, Reminiscences, Notes, etc.; Together with an Extended History of the Northwest, the Indiana Territory and the State of Indiana.* Chicago: Goodspeed Publishing, 1886.

Shaw, Archibald, ed. *History of Dearborn County, Indiana: Her People, Industries and Institutions.* Indianapolis: B. F. Bowen, 1915.

Sulgrove, B. R. *History of Indianapolis and Marion County, Indiana.* Philadelphia: L. H. Everts, 1889.

Warrick, Spencer, and Perry Counties. *History of Warrick, Spencer, Perry Counties, Indi-*

ana, from the Earliest Time to the Present; Together with Interesting Biographical Sketches, Reminiscences, Notes, etc. Chicago: Goodspeed Brothers, Publishers, 1885.
White and Warren Counties. *Biographical History of Tippecanoe, White, Jasper, Newton, Benton, Warren, and Pulaski Counties, Indiana.* Vols. 1–2. Chicago: Lewis Publishing, 1899.

Michigan

Beakes, Samuel W. *Past and Present of Washtenaw County, Michigan, Together with Biographical Sketches of Many of Its Prominent and Leading Citizens and Illustrious Dead.* Chicago: S. J. Clarke Publishing, 1906.
Bonner, R. I., and W. A. Whitney, comps. *History and Biographical Record of Lenawee County, Michigan, Containing a History of the Organization and Early Settlement of the County, Together with a Biographical Record of Many of the Oldest and Most Prominent Settlers and Present Residents, Obtained from Personal Interviews with Themselves or Their Children.* Vol. 1. Adrian: W. Stearns, 1876.
Branch County. *Portrait and Biographical Album of Branch County, Michigan, Containing Full-Page Portraits and Biographical Sketches of Prominent and Representative Citizens of the County.* Chicago: Chapman Brothers, 1888.
Fisher, Ernest B., ed. *Grand Rapids and Kent County Michigan: Historical Account of Their Progress from First Settlement to the Present Time.* Vol. 2. Chicago: Robert O. Law, 1918.
Genesee County. *History of Genesee County, Michigan. With Illustrations and Biographical Sketches of Its Prominent Men and Pioneers.* Philadelphia: Everts and Abbott, 1879.
Ionia and Montcalm Counties. *Portrait and Biographical Album of Ionia and Montcalm Counties, Michigan, Containing Full-Page Portraits and Biographical Sketches of Prominent and Representative Citizens of the County.* Chicago: Chapman Brothers, 1891.
Jackson County. *Portrait and Biographical Album of Jackson County, Michigan, Containing Full-Page Portraits and Biographical Sketches of Prominent and Representative Citizens of the County.* Chicago: Chapman Brothers, 1890.
Kalamazoo, Allegan, and Van Buren Counties. *Portrait and Biographical Record of Kalamazoo, Allegan and Van Buren Counties, Michigan, Containing Biographical Sketches of Prominent and Representative Citizens.* Chicago: Chapman Brothers, 1892.
Lapeer County. *History of Lapeer County Michigan, with Illustrations and Biographical Sketches of Some of Its Prominent Men and Pioneers.* Chicago: H. R. Page, 1884.
Macomb County. *History of Macomb County, Michigan, Containing an Account of Its Settlement, Growth, Development and Resources; an Extensive and Minute Sketch of Its Cities, Towns and Villages—Their Improvements, Industries, Manufactories, Churches, Schools and Societies; Its War Record, Biographical Sketches, Portraits of Prominent Men and Early Settlers.* Chicago: M. A. Leeson, 1882.
Muskegon County. *History of Muskegon County, Michigan, with Illustrations and Biographical Sketches of Some of Its Prominent Men and Pioneers.* Chicago: H. R. Page, 1882.
Oakland County. *Portrait and Biographical Album of Oakland County, Michigan, Containing Full-Page Portraits and Biographical Sketches of Prominent and Representative Citizens of the County.* Chicago: Chapman Brothers, 1891.
Ottawa County. *History of Ottawa County, Michigan, with Illustrations and Biographical Sketches of Some of Its Prominent Men and Pioneers.* Chicago: H. R. Page, 1882.

Reynolds, Elon G., ed. *Compendium of History and Biography of Hillsdale County, Michigan.* Chicago: A. W. Bowen, 1903.

Washtenaw County. *History of Washtenaw County, Michigan; Together with Sketches of Its Cities, Villages, and Townships, Educational, Religious, Civil, Military, and Political History; Portraits of Prominent Persons, and Biographies of Representative Citizens.* Chicago: Charles C. Chapman, 1881.

Wayne County. *Wayne County Historical and Pioneer Society Chronography of Notable Events in the History of the Northwest Territory and Wayne County, Together with Biographical Sketches of the Early Explorers and Pioneers.* Detroit: O. S. Gulley, Bornman, 1890.

Wing, Talcott E., ed. *History of Monroe County, Michigan.* New York: Munsell, 1890.

New York

Conover, George S., ed. *History of Ontario County, New York, with Illustrations and Family Sketches of Some of the Prominent Men and Families.* Comp. Lewis Cass Aldrich. Syracuse: D. Mason, 1893.

Cowles, George W., ed. *Landmarks of Wayne County, New York.* Syracuse: D. Mason, 1895.

Everts, L. H., and J. M. Holcomb. *History of St. Lawrence Co., New York. With Illustrations and Biographical Sketches of Some of Its Prominent Men and Pioneers.* Philadelphia: L. H. Everts, 1878.

Hardin, George A., ed. *History of Herkimer County, New York, Illustrated with Portraits of Many of Its Citizens.* Frank H. Willard, assistant ed. Syracuse: D. Mason, 1893.

Merrill, Georgia D., ed. *History of Chautauqua County, New York.* Boston: W. A. Fergusson, 1894.

Oneida County. *History of Oneida County, New York, with Illustrations and Biographical Sketches of Some of Its Prominent Men and Pioneers.* Philadelphia: Everts and Fariss, 1878.

Parker, Amasa J. *Landmarks of Albany County New York.* Syracuse: D. Mason, 1897.

Signor, Isaac S., ed. *Landmarks of Orleans County, New York.* Syracuse: D. Mason, 1894.

Smith, H. Perry, ed. *History of the City of Buffalo and Erie County, with Illustrations and Biographical Sketches of Some of Its Prominent Men and Pioneers.* Syracuse: D. Mason, 1884.

Tompkins County. *Landmarks of Tompkins County, New York, Including a History of Cornell University.* Syracuse: D. Mason, 1894.

Ohio

Andrews, Martin T., ed. *History of Marietta and Washington County, Ohio, and Representative Citizens.* Chicago: Biographical Publishing, 1902.

Bahmer, William J. *Centennial History of Coshocton County, Ohio.* Vol. 1. Chicago: S. J. Clarke, 1909.

Delaware County. *History of Delaware County and Ohio.* Chicago: L. Baskin, Historical Publishers, 1880.

Erie County, *History of Erie County, Ohio, with Illustrations and Biographical Sketches of Some of Its Prominent Men and Pioneers.* Syracuse: D. Mason, 1889.

Lawrence and Gallia Counties. *Historical Hand-Atlas Illustrated . . . Map of Gallia County and Histories of Lawrence and Gallia Counties, Ohio. Illustrated, Containing a Condensed History of the County: Biographical Sketches.* Chicago: H. H. Hardesty, 1882.

Marion County. *Portrait and Biographical Record of Marion and Hardin Counties, Ohio, Containing Portraits and Biographical Sketches of Prominent and Representative Citizens of the Counties.* Chicago: Chapman Publishing, 1895.

Meigs County. *Hardesty's Historical and Geographical Encyclopedia, Illustrated, Containing . . . Outline Map and History of Meigs County, Ohio, Containing a Condensed History of the County; Biographical Sketches; General Statistics; Miscellaneous Matters, etc.* Chicago: H. H. Hardesty, 1883.

Portage and Summit Counties. *A Portrait and Biographical Record of Portage and Summit Counties, Ohio, Containing Biographical Sketches of Many of Its Prominent and Representative Citizens.* Logansport: A. W. Bowen, 1898.

Summers, Ewing, ed. *Genealogical and Family History of Eastern Ohio, Illustrated.* New York: Lewis Publishing, 1903.

Stark County. *Portrait and Biographical Record of Stark County, Ohio, Containing Biographical Sketches of Prominent and Representative Citizens.* Chicago: Chapman Brothers, 1892.

Trumbull and Mahoning Counties. *History of Trumbull and Mahoning Counties, with Illustrations and Biographical Sketches.* 2 vols. Cleveland: H. Z. Williams, 1882.

Pennsylvania

Luzerne, Lackawanna, and Wyoming Counties. *History of Luzerne, Lackawanna and Wyoming Counties, Pennsylvania, with Illustrations, and Biographical Sketches of Some of Their Prominent Men and Pioneers.* New York: W. W. Munsell, 1880.

Schuylkill County. *Schuylkill County, Pennsylvania, Genealogy—Family History—Biography, Containing Historical Sketches of Old Families and of Representative and Prominent Citizens, Past and Present.* Vols. 1 and 2. Chicago: J. H. Beers, 1916.

Wisconsin

Columbia County. *The History of Columbia County, Wisconsin, Containing . . . Biographical Sketches, Portraits of Prominent Men and Early Settlers.* Chicago: Western Historical Company, 1880.

Dane County. *History of Dane County, Wisconsin, Biographical and Genealogical.* Madison: Western Historical Association, 1906.

Dodge County. *The History of Dodge County, Wisconsin, Containing . . . Biographical Sketches, Portraits of Prominent Men and Early Settlers, etc.* Chicago: Western Historical Company, 1880.

Fond Du Lac County. *Portrait and Biographical Album of Fond Du Lac County, Wisconsin, Containing Full-Page Portraits and Biographical Sketches of Prominent and Representative Citizens of the County.* Chicago: Acme Publishing, 1889.

Grant County. *History of Grant County Wisconsin, Containing . . . Biographical Sketches, Portraits of Prominent Men and Early Settlers.* Chicago: Western Historical Company, 1881.

Green Lake, Marquette, and Waushara Counties. *Portrait and Biographical Album of Green Lake, Marquette and Waushara Counties.* Chicago: Acme Publishing, 1890.

Iowa County. *History of Iowa County, Wisconsin, Containing . . . Biographical Sketches, Portraits of Prominent Men and Early Settlers.* Chicago: Western Historical Company, 1881.

Jefferson County. *The History of Jefferson County, Wisconsin, Containing . . . Biographical Sketches, Portraits of Prominent Men and Early Settlers, etc.* Chicago: Western Historical Company, 1879.

La Crosse County. *History of La Crosse County, Wisconsin, Containing . . . Biographical Sketches, Portraits of Prominent Men and Early Settlers.* Chicago: Western Historical Company, 1881.

La Fayette County. *History of La Fayette County, Wisconsin, Containing . . . Biographical Sketches, Portraits of Prominent Men and Early Settlers.* Chicago: Western Historical Company, 1881.

Lyman, Frank H. *The City of Kenosha and Kenosha County Wisconsin: A Record of Settlement, Organization, Progress and Achievement.* Vols. 1 and 2. Chicago: S. J. Clarke, 1916.

Racine and Kenosha Counties. *The History of Racine and Kenosha Counties, Wisconsin, Containing . . . Biographical Sketches, Portraits of Prominent Men and Early Settlers.* Chicago: Western Historical Company, 1879.

Rock County. *The History of Rock County, Wisconsin, Containing . . . Biographical Sketches, Portraits of Prominent Men and Early Settlers, etc.* Chicago: Western Historical Company, 1879.

Rock, Green, Grant, Iowa, and Lafayette Counties. *Commemorative Biographical Record of the Counties of Rock, Green, Grant, Iowa and Lafayette, Wisconsin.* Chicago: J. H. Beers, 1901.

Sauk County. *The History of Sauk County, Wisconsin, Containing . . . Biographical Sketches, Portraits of Prominent Men and Early Settlers.* Chicago: Western Historical Company, 1880.

Walworth County. *History of Walworth County, Wisconsin, Containing . . . Biographical Sketches, Portraits of Prominent Men and Early Settlers.* Chicago: Western Historical Company, 1882.

Watrous, Jerome A., ed. *Memoirs of Milwaukee County. From the Earliest Historical Times Down to the Present, Including a Genealogical and Biographical Record of Representative Families in Milwaukee County.* Vol. 2. Madison: Western Historical Association, 1909.

Waukesha County. *The History of Waukesha County, Wisconsin, Containing . . . Biographical Sketches, Portraits of Prominent Men and Early Settlers.* Chicago: Western Historical Company, 1880.

Secondary Sources

Adams, William F. *Ireland and Irish Emigration to the New World, from 1815 to the Famine.* New Haven: Yale University Press, 1932.

Albion, Robert G. *The Rise of New York Port, 1815–1860.* New York: C. Scribner's Sons, 1939.

Allen, G. C. *British Industries and Their Organization.* 3d ed. New York: Longmans, Green, 1956.

America and England Contrasted; or, The Emigrant's Hand-Book and Guide to the United States (n.p.: 1845).

Anderson, Gregory. *Victorian Clerks.* Manchester: Manchester University Press, 1976.

Anderson, Michael. *Family Structure in Nineteenth-Century Lancashire.* Cambridge: Cambridge University Press, 1971.

———. "Sociological History and the Working Class Family: Smelser Revisited." *Social History* 1 (Oct. 1976): 317–34.

Armstrong, W. A. "The Influence of Demographic Factors on the Position of the Agricultural Labourer in England and Wales, c. 1750–1914." *Agricultural History Review* 29 (1981): 71–82.

Arnold, Rollo. *The Farthest Promised Land: English Villagers, New Zealand Immigrants of the 1870s.* Wellington: Victoria University Press with Price Melburn, 1981.

Athearn, Robert G. *Westward the Briton.* New York: Scribner, 1953.

Bailyn, Bernard. *Voyagers to the West: A Passage in the Peopling of America on the Eve of the Revolution.* New York: Knopf, 1986.

Baines, Dudley. *Emigration from Europe, 1815–1930.* New York: Cambridge University Press, 1995.

———. *Migration in a Mature Economy: Emigration and Internal Migration in England and Wales, 1861–1900.* New York: Cambridge University Press, 1985.

Barker, J. L. "The Lead Miners of Swaledale and Arkengarthdale in 1851." *Northern Mine Research Society* 2 (1992): 1–9.

Barney, William L. *The Passage of the Republic.* Lexington, Mass.: D. C. Heath, 1987.

Baron, Hal S. *Those Who Stayed Behind: Rural Society in Nineteenth-Century New England.* New York: Cambridge University Press, 1984.

Batty, Margaret. *Gunnerside Chapel and Gunnerside Folk.* Barnard Castle: Teesdale Mercury Press, 1976.

———. *A View of Arkengarthdale.* Barnard Castle: Teesdale Mercury Press, 1982.

Beijbom, U. "Swedes." In *Harvard Encyclopedia of American Ethnic Groups,* ed. Stephen Thernstrom, 971–81. Cambridge: Harvard University Press, 1980.

Benson, John. *British Coalminers in the Nineteenth Century: A Social History.* London: Gill and Macmillan, 1980.

Berthoff, Rowland T. *British Immigrants in Industrial America, 1790–1950.* 1953. Reprint. New York: Russell and Russell, 1968.

———. "Welsh." In *Harvard Encyclopedia of American Ethnic Groups,* ed. Stephen Thernstrom, 1011–17. Cambridge: Harvard University Press, 1980.

Best, Geoffrey F. *Mid-Victorian Britain, 1851–1875.* London: Fontana Press, 1971.

Bidwell, Percy W., and John I. Falconer. *History of Agriculture in the Northern United States, 1620–1860.* Washington: Carnegie Institution of Washington, 1925.

Billington, Ray. *Land of Savagery, Land of Promise: The European Image of the American Frontier in the Nineteenth Century.* New York: Harper and Brothers, 1981.

Birch, Alan. *The Economic History of the British Iron and Steel Industry, 1784–1879.* New York: A. M. Kelly, 1967.

Birch, Brian P. "The Editor and the English, George Sheppard and English Immigration to Clinton County." *Annals of Iowa* 47 (Spring 1985): 622–42.

———. "From Southwest England to Southwest Wisconsin: Devonshire Hollow, Lafayette County." *Wisconsin Magazine of History* 69 (Winter 1985–86): 129–49.

Birbeck, Morris. *Notes on a Journey in America from the Coast of Virginia to the Territory of Illinois.* London: Severn and Redington for Ridgeway, 1818.

Blaug, Mark. "The Myth of the Old Poor Law and the Making of the New." *Journal of Economic History* 23 (1963): 151–84.

———. "The Poor Law Report Re-examined." *Journal of Economic History* 24 (1964): 229–45.

Blessing, P. J. "Irish." In *Harvard Encyclopedia of American Ethnic Groups*, ed. Stephen Thernstrom, 524–45. Cambridge: Harvard University Press, 1980.

Bliss, Jonathan. *Merchants and Miners in Utah: The Walker Brothers and Their Bank*. Salt Lake City: Western Epics, 1983.

Bloomfield, Maxwell H. "Law: The Development of a Profession." In *The Professions in American History*, ed. Nathan O. Hatch, 33–49. Notre Dame: University of Notre Dame Press, 1988.

Bogue, Allen. *From Prairie to Corn Belt: Farming on the Illinois and Iowa Prairies in the Nineteenth Century*. Chicago: University of Chicago Press, 1963.

Bolt, Christine. *Victorian Attitudes to Race*. Boston: Routledge and Kegan Paul, 1971.

Boston, Ray. *British Chartists in America, 1839–1900*. Totowa: Roman and Littlefield, 1971.

Bowen, Eli, ed. *The Coal Regions of Pennsylvania*. Pottsville: E. N. Carvalho, 1848.

Bratt, James D. *Dutch Calvinism in Modern America*. Grand Rapids: Eerdmanns, 1984.

Briggs, Asa. *The Age of Improvement*. 1959. Reprint. New York: David McKay, 1962.

———. *Victorian People: A Reassessment of Persons and Themes*. New York: Harper, 1955.

Brown, William. *America: A Four Years' Residence in the United States and Canada*. Leeds: Kemplay and Bolland, 1849.

Buchanan, R. A. "Gentleman Engineers: The Making of a Profession." *Victorian Studies* 26 (Summer 1983): 407–29.

Burnley, James. *Two Sides of the Atlantic*. London: Simpkin, Marshall, 1880.

Burn, William L. *The Age of Equipoise: A Study of the Mid-Victorian Generation*. London: George Allen and Unwin, 1964.

Burton, William L. *Melting Pot Soldiers: The Union's Ethnic Regiments*. Ames: Iowa State University Press, 1988.

Bythell, Duncan. *The Handloom Weavers: A Study in the English Cotton Industry during the Industrial Revolution*. New York: Cambridge University Press, 1969.

———. *The Sweated Trades: Outwork in Nineteenth-Century Britain*. New York: St. Martin's Press, 1978.

Caird, James. *English Agriculture in 1850–51*. London: Longman, Brown, Green, and Longmans, 1852.

———. *High Farming under Liberal Covenants, the Best Substitute for Protection*. 4th ed. Edinburgh: Blackwood, 1849.

Cairncross, Alec K. *Home and Foreign Investment, 1870–1913: Studies in Capital Accumulation*. New York: Cambridge University Press, 1953.

Cairncross, Alec K., and B. Weber. "Fluctuations in Building in Great Britain, 1785–1849." *Economic History Review* 92 (Dec. 1956): 283–97.

Carrothers, William A. *Emigration from the British Isles*. London: P. S. King and Son, 1929.

Carter, Mrs. Fremont. *New Diggings Is an Old Diggings*. New Diggings, Wis.: C. L. Lacke, 1948.

Carter, Margaret S. "New Diggings on the Fever River, 1824–1860." Benton, Wis.. Published privately, 1959.

Chambers, W. *The Emigrants' Guide to the United States and the Dominion of Canada*. N.p.: N.p., 1872.

———. *The Emigrant's Manual: British America and the United States of America*. Edinburgh: W. and R. Chambers, 1851.

Chambers, Jonathan D., and G. E. Mingay. *The Agricultural Revolution, 1750–1880*. 1966. Reprint. London: Batsford, 1968.

Chase, Malcolm. *The People's Farm: English Radical Agrarianism.* New York: Oxford University Press, 1988.

Chudacoff, Howard. "The S. J. Clarke Publishing Company and the Study of Urban History." *The Historian* 49 (Feb. 1987): 184–93.

Church, Roy A. *The Great Victorian Boom, 1850–1873.* London: Macmillan, 1975.

——. *The History of the British Coal Industry.* 3 vols. New York: Oxford University Press, 1986.

Clapham, John H. *An Economic History of Modern Britain.* Vol 2: *Free Trade and Steel, 1850–1886.* New York: Cambridge University Press, 1930.

——. *The Woollen and Worsted Industries.* London: Methuen, 1907.

——. "Work and Wages." In *Early Victorian England, 1830–1865,* ed. George M. Young. Vol. 1, 1–76. New York: Oxford University Press, 1934.

Clark, George Kitson. *The Making of Victorian England.* Cambridge: Harvard University Press, 1962.

Clements, R. V. "Trade Unions and Emigration, 1840–1880." *Population Studies* 9 (Nov. 1955): 167–80.

Cohn, Raymond. "The Occupations of English Immigrants to the United States, 1836–1853." *Journal of Economic History* 52 (June 1992): 377–86.

Cole, Donald B. *Immigrant City: Lawrence, Massachusetts, 1845–1921.* Chapel Hill: University of North Carolina Press, 1963.

Coleman, Terry. *Passage to America: A History of Emigrants from Great Britain and Ireland to America in the Nineteenth Century.* London: Pimlico, 1972.

Collins, Terry. "Harvest Technology and Labour Supply in Britain, 1790–1870." *Economic History Review* 22 (Dec. 1969): 453–73.

——. "Migrant Labour in British Agriculture in the Nineteenth Century." *Economic History Review* 29 (Feb. 1976): 38–59.

Conway, Alan. "Welsh Emigration to the United States." In *Perspectives in American History.* Vol. 4, 177–271. Cambridge: Harvard University Press, 1973.

——, ed. *The Welsh in America: Letters from the Immigrants.* Minneapolis: University of Minnesota Press, 1961.

Conzen, Kathleen N. "Germans." In *Harvard Encyclopedia of American Ethnic Groups,* ed. Stephen Thernstrom, 405–25. Cambridge: Harvard University Press, 1980.

Cooke, Sarah, and Rachel Ramadhyani, comps. *Indians and a Changing Frontier: The Art of George Winter.* Indianapolis: Indiana Historical Society, 1993.

Cooney, E. W. "Long Waves of Building in the British Economy of the Nineteenth Century." In *British Economic Fluctuations, 1790–1939,* ed. D. H. Aldcroft and P. Pearson, 220–34. London: Macmillan, 1972.

Copeland, Louis A. "The Cornish in Southwestern Wisconsin." *Collections of the State Historical Society of Wisconsin* 14 (1898): 301–17.

Cowan, Helen. *British Emigration to British North America: The First Hundred Years.* 1928. Revised and enlarged. Toronto: University of Toronto Press, 1961.

Crawford, Martin. *The Anglo-American Crisis of the Mid-Nineteenth Century: "The Times" and America, 1850–1862.* Athens: University of Georgia Press, 1987.

Curti, Merle. *The Making of an American Community: A Case Study of Democracy in a Frontier County.* Stanford: Stanford University Press, 1959.

Curti, Merle, and K. Birr. "The Immigrant and the American Image in Europe, 1860–1914." *Mississippi Valley Historical Review* 37 (Sept. 1950): 203–30.

Dalziel, Alexander. *The Collier's Strike in South Wales.* Cardiff: Western Mail, 1871.

Danhof, Clarence. *Change in Agriculture: The Northern United States, 1820–1870.* Cambridge: Harvard University Press, 1969.

Davidoff, Lenore. "Domestic Service in the Working Class Life Cycle." *Society for the Study of Labour History* 26 (Spring 1973): 10–13.

———. "Mastered for Life: Servant and Wife in Victorian and Edwardian England." *Journal of Social History* 7 (Summer 1974): 406–28.

Davies, Maud F. *Life in an English Village: An Economic and Historical Survey of the Parish of Corsley in Wiltshire.* London: T. F. Unwin, 1909.

Davies, Phillips G. "The Welsh in Ohio: Thomas's *Hanes Cymry America.*" *Old Northwest* 3 (Sept. 1977): 289–318.

———. "The Welsh in Wisconsin: Thomas's *Hanes Cymry America.*" *Old Northwest* 5 (Fall 1979): 269–89.

Dawes, Frank V. *Not in Front of the Servants: Domestic Service in England 1850–1939.* London: Wayland Publishers, 1973.

Diner, Hasia R. *Erin's Daughters in America: Irish Immigrant Women in the Nineteenth Century.* Baltimore: Johns Hopkins University Press, 1983.

"Doctrines and Discipline of the Primitive Methodist Connexion." *Annual Conference Proceedings May 19–24, 1852.* Mineral Point, Wis.: N.p., 1852.

Donaldson, Gordon. "Scots." In *Harvard Encyclopedia of American Ethnic Groups,* ed. Stephen Thernstrom, 908–16. Cambridge: Harvard University Press, 1980.

———. *The Scots Overseas.* London: R. Hale, 1966.

Dunae, Patrick A. *Gentlemen Emigrants: From the British Public Schools to the Canadian Frontier.* Vancouver: Douglas and McIntyre, 1981.

Edwards, Everette E., ed. *The Early Writings of Frederick Jackson Turner.* Madison: University of Wisconsin Press, 1938.

Edmunds, R. David. "'Designing Men, Seeking a Fortune': Indian Traders and the Potawatomi Claims Payment of 1836." *Indiana Magazine of History* 77 (June 1981): 109–22.

Engels, Friedrich. *The Condition of the Working Class in England.* New York: Penguin Books, 1987.

Erickson, Charlotte J. "Agrarian Myths of English Immigrants." In *In the Trek of the Immigrants,* ed. Oscar F. Ander, 59–80. Rock Island: Augustana College Library, 1964.

———. *American Industry and the European Immigrant, 1860–1885.* 1957. Reprint. New York: Russell and Russell, 1967.

———. "British Immigrants in the Old Northwest, 1815–1860." In *The Frontier in American Development,* ed. D. Ellis, 323–56. Ithaca: Cornell University Press, 1969.

———. *British Industrialists: Steel and Hosiery, 1850–1950.* Cambridge: Cambridge University Press, 1959.

———. "Emigration from the British Isles to the U.S.A. in 1831." *Population Studies* 35 (1981): 175–97.

———. "Emigration from the British Isles to the U.S.A. in 1841, Part 1." *Population Studies* 43 (1989): 347–67.

———, ed. *Emigration from Europe, 1815–1914: Select Documents.* London: A. and C. Black, 1976.

———. "The Encouragement of Emigration by British Trade Unions, 1850–1900." *Population Studies* 3 (1949): 248–73.

————. "English." In *Harvard Encyclopedia of American Ethnic Groups,* ed. Stephen Thernstrom, 319–36. Cambridge: Harvard University Press, 1980.

————. *Invisible Immigrants: The Adaptation of English and Scottish Immigrants in Nineteenth-Century America.* Leicester: Leicester University Press, 1972.

————. *Leaving England: Essays on British Emigration in the Nineteenth Century.* Ithaca: Cornell University Press, 1994.

————. "The Uses of Passenger Lists for the Study of British and Irish Emigration." In *Migration across Time and Nations: Population Mobility in Historical Contexts,* ed. Ira Glazier and Luigi de Rosa, 318–35. New York: Holmes and Meier, 1986.

————. "Who Were the English and Scots Emigrants to the United States in the Late-Nineteenth Century?" In *Population and Social Change,* ed. D. V. Glass and R. Revelle, 347–81. London: Edward Arnold, 1972.

Fairlie, S. "The Corn Laws and British Wheat Production, 1829–1876." *Economic History Review* 22 (April 1969): 88–116.

————. "The Nineteenth-Century Corn Law Reconsidered." *Economic History Review* 18 (Dec. 1965): 562–75.

Farnie, D. A. "The Cotton Famine in Great Britain." In *Great Britain and Her World, 1750–1914,* ed. B. M. Ratcliffe, 313–23. Manchester: Manchester University Press, 1975.

Fawcett, Edward R. *Lead Mining in Swaledale.* Roughlee, Burnley: Faust, 1985.

Fay, Charles R. *The Corn Laws and Social England.* New York: Cambridge University Press, 1932.

————. *Round about Industrial Britain, 1830–1860.* Toronto: University of Toronto Press, 1952.

Fender, Stephen. *Sea Changes: British Emigration and American Literature.* New York: Cambridge University Press, 1992.

Fischer, David Hackett. *Albion's Seed: Four British Folkways in America.* New York: Oxford University Press, 1989.

Fletcher, T. W. "The Great Depression of English Agriculture 1873–1896." *Economic History Review* 13 (April 1961): 417–32.

Flower, George. *History of the English Settlement in Edwards County, Illinois.* Vol. 1. Chicago: Chicago Historical Society's Collection, 1882.

Foerster, Robert F. *The Italian Emigration of Our Times.* Cambridge: Harvard University Press, 1919.

Fogel, R. W. *Railways and American Economic Growth: Essays in Economic History.* Baltimore: Johns Hopkins University Press, 1964.

Foreman, Grant. "Settlement of English Potters in Wisconsin." *Wisconsin Magazine of History* 21 (June 1938): 375–96.

Forsythe, James L. "The English Colony at Victoria, Another View." *Kansas History: A Journal of the Central Plains* 12 (Autumn 1989): 175–84.

Foster, John. *Class Struggle and the Industrial Revolution: Early Industrial Capitalism in Three English Towns.* 1974. Reprint. New York: St. Martin's Press, 1975.

Foster's Work and Wages; or, The Penny Emigrant's Guide to the United States and Canada. London: W. and F. G. Cash, 1854.

Fox, A. W. "Agricultural Wages in England and Wales during the Last Fifty Years." *Journal of the Royal Statistical Society* 64 (1903): 273–348.

Friedlander, D. and R. J. Roshier. "A Study of Internal Migration in England and Wales: Part 1." *Population Studies* 19 (March 1966): 239–79.

Fussell, G. E. "Four Centuries of Lincolnshire Farming." *Reports and Papers of the Lincolnshire Architectural and Archaeological Society* 4 (1952): 1–44.

Gale, Walter K. V. *The British Iron and Steel Industry: A Technical History.* Devon, England: David and Charles, 1967.

Gates, Paul W. *The Farmer's Age: Agriculture, 1815–1860.* New York: Holt, Rinehart and Winston, 1960.

———. *The Illinois Central and Its Colonization Work.* Cambridge: Harvard University Press, 1934.

Gayer, Arthur D., Walter W. Rostow, and A. J. Schwartz. *The Growth and Fluctuation of the British Economy, 1790–1850.* 2 vols. New York: Oxford University Press, 1953.

Gerber, David. *The Making of an American Pluralism: Buffalo, New York, 1825–1860.* Urbana: University of Illinois Press, 1989.

Gitelman, Howard M. *Workingmen of Waltham, Mobility in American Urban Industrial Development 1850–1890.* Baltimore: Johns Hopkins University Press, 1974.

Goddard, J. R. "The Road to a Promised Land." *Family Tree* 4 (Oct. 1988): 11 and 5 (Nov. 1988): 4–5.

"'God Raised Us Up Good Friends': English Immigrants in Wisconsin." *Wisconsin Magazine of History* 47 (Spring 1964): 224–37.

Gordon, Michael, A. *The Orange Riots: Irish Political Violence in New York City, 1870 and 1871.* Ithaca: Cornell University Press, 1993.

Gottlieb, Amy Z. "Immigration of British Coal Miners in the Civil War Decade." *International Review of Social History* 23 (1978): 357–75.

———. "The Influence of British Trade Unionists on the Regulation of the Mining Industry in Illinois, 1872." *Labor History* 19 (Summer 1978): 397–415.

———. "The Regulation of the Coal Mining Industry in Illinois, with Special Reference to the Influence of British Miners and British Precedents, 1870–1911." Ph.D. diss., London School of Economics, 1975.

Gould, J. D. "European Inter-Continental Emigration, 1815–1914: Pattern and Causes." *Journal of European Economic History* 8 (Winter 1979): 593–679.

Graham, Peter A. *The Rural Exodus: The Problem of the Village and the Town.* London: Methuen, 1892.

Gray, M. "Scottish Emigration: The Social Impact of Agrarian Change in the Rural Lowlands, 1775–1875." In *Perspectives in American History.* Vol. 7, 95–174. Cambridge: Harvard University Press, 1973.

Green, Constance M. *Holyoke Massachusetts: A Case History of the Industrial Revolution in America.* New Haven: Yale University Press, 1934.

Gregg, Pauline. *A Social and Economic History of Britain, 1760–1965.* 1950. 5th ed., revised. New York: Pegasus, 1965.

Guillet, Edwin C. *The Great Migration: The Atlantic Crossing by Sailing Ships since 1770.* Toronto: Thomas Nelson and Sons, 1937.

Habukkuk, H. J. *American and British Technology in the Nineteenth Century: The Search for Labour-Saving Inventions.* New York: Cambridge University Press, 1967.

———. "Fluctuations in House-Building in Britain and the United States in the Nineteenth Century." In *British Economic Fluctuations 1790–1939,* ed. D. H. Aldcroft and P. Fearon, 236–67. London: Macmillan, 1972.

Hammerton, A. J. *Emigrant Gentlewomen, Genteel Poverty and Female Emigration, 1830–1914.* New York: St. Martin's Press, 1979.

Hanna, Archibald, Jr. "Every Man His Own Biographer." *Proceedings of the American Antiquarian Society* 80, no. 2 (1970): 291–98.

Hansen, Marcus L. *The Atlantic Migration, 1607–1860.* Cambridge: Harvard University Press, 1940.

———. *The Immigrant in American History.* Cambridge: Harvard University Press, 1941.

Harley, C. K. "The Shift from Sailing Ships to Steamships, 1850–1890: A Study in Technical Change and Its Diffusion." In *Essays on a Mature Economy,* ed. Donald McCloskey 215–34. Princeton: Princeton University Press, 1971.

Harrison, Brian H. *Drink and the Victorians: The Temperance Question in England 1815–1872.* Pittsburgh: University of Pittsburgh Press, 1971.

Hartmann, Edward G. *Americans from Wales.* Boston: Christopher Publishing House, 1967.

Hasbach, Wilhelm. *A History of the English Agricultural Labourer.* London: P. S. King and Son, 1908.

Hedges, James B. *Building the Canadian West: The Land and Colonization Policies of the Canadian Pacific Railway.* New York: Macmillan, 1939.

———. "The Colonization Work of the Northern Pacific Railroad." *Mississippi Valley Historical Review* 13 (1926): 311–42.

Henderson, William O. "The Cotton Famine in Scotland and the Relief of Distress, 1862–1864." *Scottish Historical Review* 30 (Oct. 1951): 154–66.

———. *The Lancashire Cotton Famine, 1861–1865.* Manchester: Manchester University Press, 1934.

Historical Statistics of the United States: Colonial Times to 1957. Washington: Bureau of the Census, 1976.

Hitchins, Fred H. *The Colonial Land and Emigration Commission.* Philadelphia: University of Pennsylvania Press, 1931.

Hobsbawm, Eric J. *Labouring Men: Studies in the History of Labour.* New York: Basic Books, 1964.

Hodges, T. M. "The Peopling of the Hinterland and the Port of Cardiff (1801–1914)." In *Industrial South Wales 1750–1914: Essays in Welsh Economic History,* ed. W. E. Minchinton, 3–18. London: L. Cass, 1969.

Hogland, Arthur W. *Finnish Immigrants in America 1880–1929.* Madison: University of Wisconsin Press, 1960.

Horn, Henry H. *An English Colony in Iowa.* Boston: Christopher Publishing House, 1931.

Horn, Pamela. *Joseph Arch (1826–1919): The Farm Workers' Leader.* Kineton: Roundwood Press, 1971.

———. *Labouring Life in the Victorian Countryside.* Dublin: Gill and Macmillan, 1976.

Howell, D. W. "The Agricultural Labourer in Nineteenth-Century Wales." *Welsh History Review* 6 (June 1973): 262–87.

Howkins, Alun. "Labour History and the Rural Poor, 1850–1980." *Rural History* 1 (1990): 113–22.

Hughes, Jonathan R. T. *American Economic History.* Glenview: Scott, Foresman, 1983.

———. *Fluctuations in Trade, Industry and Finance: A Study of British Economic Development, 1850–1860.* New York: Oxford University Press, 1960.

Hunt, C. J. *The Lead Mines of the Northern Pennines.* Manchester: Manchester University Press, 1970.

Hunt, Edward H. *Regional Wage Variations in Britain, 1850–1914.* New York: Oxford University Press, 1973.

Hunter, Louis C. "Influence of the Market upon Technique in the Iron Industry in Western Pennsylvania up to 1860." *Journal of Economic and Business History* 1 (Feb. 1929): 241–81.

Hvidt, Kristian. *Flight to America: The Social Background of Three Hundred Thousand Danish Emigrants.* New York: Academic Press, 1975.

Hyde, C. K. *Technical Change and the British Iron Industry, 1700–1870.* Princeton: Princeton University Press, 1977.

Hyde, Francis E. *Cunard and the North Atlantic, 1840–1973: A History of Shipping and Financial Management.* London: Macmillan, 1975.

Imlah, Albert H. *Economic Elements in the Pax Britannica.* Cambridge: Harvard University Press, 1958.

Inglis, Kenneth S. *Churches and the Working Classes in Victorian England.* Boston: Routledge and Kegan Paul, 1963.

James, J. *History of the Worsted Manufactures in England from the Earliest Times.* London: Longman, Brown, Green, Longmans, and Roberts, 1857.

Jeffrey, Julie Roy. *Frontier Women: The Trans-Mississippi West, 1840–1880.* New York: Hill and Wang, 1979.

Jeremy, David. "British Technological Transmission to the United States, the Philadelphia Experience, 1770–1820." *Business History Review* 47 (1973): 23–52.

———. *Transatlantic Industrial Revolution: The Diffusion of Textile Technologies between Britain and America, 1790–1830s.* Oxford: Basil Blackwell, 1981.

Jerome, Harry. *Migration and the Business Cycle.* New York: National Bureau of Economic Research, 1926.

Jewell, Jim. *Cornish in America: Linden, Wisconsin: A Historical Glimpse at Immigrants from Cornwall England Who Settled in the Mining Region of Southwest Wisconsin.* Linden: Cornish Miner Press, 1990.

John, Arthur H. *The Industrial Development of South Wales, 1750–1850.* Cardiff: University of Wales Press, 1950.

Johnson, Hugh J. M. *British Emigration Policy, 1815–1830: "Shovelling Out Paupers."* New York: Oxford University Press, 1972.

Johnston, Stanley C. *Emigration from the United Kingdom to North America, 1763–1912.* 1913. Reprint. London: F. Cass, 1966.

Jones, Eric L. "The Agricultural Labour Market in England, 1793–1872." *Economic History Review* 7 (May 1964): 322–38.

———. "The Changing Basis of English Agricultural Prosperity, 1853–1873." *Agricultural History Review* 10 (1962): 102–19.

———. *Development of English Agriculture.* London: Macmillan, 1968.

Jones, Maldwyn A. *American Immigration.* Chicago: University of Chicago Press, 1960.

———. "The Background to Emigration from Great Britain in the Nineteenth Century." In *Perspectives in American History.* Vol. 7, 3–92. Cambridge: Harvard University Press, 1973.

———. *Destination America.* London: Book Club Association, 1976.

———. "From the Old Country to the New: The Welsh in Nineteenth-Century America." *Flintshire Historical Society Publications* 27 (1975–76): 85–100.

————. "The Role of the United Kingdom in the Transatlantic Emigrant Trade, 1815–1875." Ph.D. diss., University of Oxford, 1956.

Jones, William D. *Wales in America: Scranton and the Welsh, 1860–1920.* Cardiff: University of Wales Press, 1993.

Joyce, Patrick. *Work, Society and Politics: The Culture of the Factory in Later Victorian England.* New Brunswick: Rutgers University Press, 1980.

Kebbel, T. E. *The Agricultural Labourer: A Short Summary of His Position.* London: W. H. Allen, 1887.

Kemp, Betty. "Reflections on the Repeal of the Corn Laws." *Victorian Studies* 5 (March 1962): 189–204.

Kerr, Barbara. "The Dorset Agricultural Labourer, 1750–1850." *Proceedings of the Dorset Natural History and Archaeological Society* 84 (1962): 158–77.

Kirk, Dudley. *Europe's Population in the Interwar Years.* Geneva: League of Nations, 1946.

Kittle, William. *History of the Township and Village of Mazomanie.* Madison: State Journal Printing Co., 1900.

Kleppner, Paul. *The Third Electoral System, 1853–1892: Parties, Voters, and Political Cultures.* Chapel Hill: University of North Carolina Press, 1979.

Köllmann, W., and P. Marschalk. "German Emigration to the United States." *Perspectives in American History* 7 (1973): 499–554.

Knowles, Anne Kelly. *Calvinists Incorporated: Welsh Immigrants on Ohio's Industrial Frontier.* Chicago: University of Chicago Press, 1997.

Lamphere, Louise. *From Working Daughters to Working Mothers: Immigrant Women in a New England Industrial Community.* Ithaca: Cornell University Press, 1987.

Lane, James B. *City of the Century: A History of Gary, Indiana.* Bloomington: University of Indiana Press, 1978.

Lasslet, Peter, ed. *Household and Family Ties in Times Past.* New York: Cambridge University Press, 1974.

Laurie, Bruce, Theodore Hershberg, and George Alter. "Immigrants and Industry: The Philadelphia Experience, 1850–1880." In *Immigrants in Industrial America, 1850–1920,* ed. Richard L. Ehrlich, 123–50. Charlottesville: University Press of Virginia, 1977.

Lebergott, Stanley. *The Americans: An Economic Record.* New York: W. W. Norton, 1984.

Lee, Clive H. *British Regional Employment Statistics, 1841–1971.* New York: Cambridge University Press, 1979.

Leeson, Robert A. *Travelling Brothers: The Six Centuries' Road from Craft Fellowship to Trade Unionism.* London: G. Allen and Unwin, 1979.

Lewis, Evan D. *The Rhondda Valleys: A Study in Industrial Development, 1800 to the Present Day.* London: Phoenix House, 1959.

Lewis, W. A., and P. J. O'Leary. "Secular Swings in Production and Trade, 1870–1913." *Manchester School of Economic and Social Studies* 20 (1955): 113–52.

Lichtenberg, Robert M. *One-Tenth of a Nation: National Forces in the Economic Growth of the New York Region.* Cambridge: Harvard University Press, 1960.

Lillibridge, George D. *Beacon of Freedom: The Impact of American Democracy upon Great Britain, 1830–1870.* 1955. Revised. New York: A. S. Barnes, 1961.

Lindert, P. H., and J. G. Williamson. "English Workers' Living Standards during the Industrial Revolution: A New Look." *Economic History Review* 36 (Feb. 1983): 1–25.

Lindsay, Donald, and E. S. Washington. *A Portrait of Britain between the Exhibitions, 1851–1951.* New York: Oxford University Press, 1952.

Lipson, Dorothy Ann. *Freemasonry in Federalist Connecticut.* Princeton: Princeton University Press, 1977.

Loehr, Rodney C. "The Influence of English Agriculture on American Agriculture, 1775–1825." *Agricultural History* 11 (Jan. 1937): 3–15.

Long, Priscilla. *Where the Sun Never Shines: A History of America's Bloody Coal Industry.* New York: Paragon House, 1991.

Lonn, Ella. *Foreigners in the Confederacy.* Gloucester: Peter Smith, 1965.

———. *Foreigners in the Union Army and Navy.* 1951. Reprint. New York: Greenwood Press, 1969.

MacDonagh. Oliver. *A Pattern of Government Growth, 1800–1860: The Passenger Acts and Their Enforcement.* London: MacGibbon and Kee, 1961.

Madison, James H. *The Indiana Way: A State History.* Bloomington: Indiana University Press, 1986.

Mageean, Deirdre. "Pre and Post Famine Migrant Families: Patterns and Change." Presented at the annual meeting of the Social Science History Association, 1981.

Margrave, Richard D. *The Emigration of Silk Workers from England to the United States of America in the Nineteenth Century.* New York: Garland, 1986.

Marshall, J. D. "Nottinghamshire Labourers in the Early Nineteenth Century." *Transactions of the Thoroton Society of Nottinghamshire.* Vol. 64, 56–73. Nottingham: The Thoroton Society, 1960.

———. "Some Aspects of the Social History of Nineteenth-Century Cumbria: Migration and Literacy." *Transactions of the Cumberland and Westmorland Antiquarian and Archeological Society.* Vol. 69, 280–307. Cumberland and Westmorland Antiquarian and Archeological Society, 1969.

Mathias, Peter. *The First Industrial Nation: An Economic History of Britain, 1700–1914.* London: Methuen, 1969.

Matthews, Robert C. O. *The Trade Cycle.* New York. Cambridge University Press, 1959.

Maurer, Oscar. "'Punch' on Slavery and Civil War in America, 1841–1865." *Victorian Studies* 1 (Sept. 1957): 5–28.

McCormack, Ross. "Cloth Caps and Jobs: The Ethnicity of English Immigrants in Canada 1900–1914." In *Ethnicity, Power and Politics in Canada,* ed. Jorgan Dahlie and Tissa Fernando, 38–55. New York: Methuen, 1981.

McFarlane, Larry A. "The Fairmont Colony in Martin County, Minnesota in the 1870s." *Kansas History: A Journal of the Central Plains* 12 (Autumn 1989): 166–74.

McKee, Irving, ed. *The Trail of Death: Letters of Benjamin Marie Petit.* Vol. 14. Indianapolis: Indiana Historical Society Publications, 1941.

Miller, Kirby A. *Emigrants and Exiles: Ireland and the Irish Exodus to North America.* New York: Oxford University Press, 1985.

Mitchell, Brian R., and Phyllis Deane. *Abstract of British Historical Statistics.* New York. Cambridge University Press, 1962.

Mitchell, Thomas. *Monmouthshire Iron and Steel, Labour and Wages Sixty Years Ago.* Newport: John E. Southall, 1904.

Mokyr, Joel. *Why Ireland Starved: A Quantitative and Analytical History of the Irish Economy, 1780–1850.* Boston: Allen and Unwin, 1983.

Moore, D. C. "The Corn Laws and High Farming." *Economic History Review* 18 (Dec. 1965): 544–61.

Morris, David. *Dalesman of the Mississippi River.* York: William Sessions, 1989.

Morris, John H., and Lawrence J. Williams. *The South Wales Coal Industry, 1841–1875.* Cardiff: University of Wales Press, 1958.

Morton, J. C. *Hand Book of Farm Labour.* London: Bradbury, Agnew, 1868.

Munch, P. A. "Norwegians." In *Harvard Encyclopedia of American Ethnic Groups,* ed. Stephen Thernstrom, 750–61. Cambridge: Harvard University Press, 1980.

Murphy, M. J. *Cambridge Newspapers and Opinion, 1780–1850.* New York: Cambridge University Press, 1977.

Musgrove, Frank L. E. H. *The Migratory Elite.* London: Heinemann, 1963.

Numbers, Ronald L. "The Fall and Rise of the American Medical Profession." In *The Professions in American History,* ed. Nathan O. Hatch, 51–72. Notre Dame: University of Notre Dame Press, 1988.

Oberley, James. *Sixty Million Acres: American Veterans and the Public Lands before the Civil War.* Kent: Kent State University Press, 1990.

Olsson, Nils W. *Swedish Passenger Arrivals.* Stockholm: P. A. Nortstadt and Soners, 1967.

Orchard, B. G. *The Clerks of Liverpool.* Liverpool: J. Collinson, 1871.

Ostergren, Robert C. *A Community Transplanted: The Trans-Atlantic Experience of a Swedish Immigrant Settlement in the Upper Middle West, 1835–1915.* Madison: University of Wisconsin, 1988.

Overton. *Burlington West: A Colonization History of the Burlington Railroad.* Cambridge: Harvard University Press, 1941.

Parmet, Robert D. *Labour and Immigration in Industrial America.* Boston: Twayne, 1981.

Paskoff, Paul F. *Industrial Revolution: Organization, Structure, and Growth of the Pennsylvania Iron Industry 1750–1860.* Baltimore: Johns Hopkins University Press, 1983.

Perloff, Harvey S. *Regions, Resources, and Economic Growth.* Baltimore: Johns Hopkins University Press, 1960.

Phillips, A. D. M. *The Underdraining of Farmland in England during the Nineteenth Century.* New York: Cambridge University Press, 1989.

Pooley, William V. "The Settlement of Illinois from 1820 to 1850." *Bulletin of the University of Wisconsin* 1, no. 4 (1908): 287–595.

Potter, James. "Atlantic Economy, 1815–60: The U.S.A. and the Industrial Revolution in Britain." In *Studies in the Industrial Revolution,* ed. L. S. Pressnell, 236–80. London: University of London, 1960.

Poucher, John. "An English Colony in Floyd County." *Indiana Magazine of History* 11 (Sept. 1915): 122–15.

Prothero, E. R. *English Farming Past and Present.* 3d ed. London: Longmans, Green, 1922.

Quaife, Milo M. *Wisconsin: Its History and Its People, 1634–1924.* 4 vols. Chicago: S. J. Clark, 1924.

Raistrick, Arthur, and Bernard Jennings. *A History of Lead Mining in the Pennines.* London: Longmans, 1965.

Reader, William J. *Professional Men: The Rise of the Professional Classes in Nineteenth-Century England.* London: Weidenfield and Nicolson, 1966.

Redford, Arthur. *Economic History of England.* London: Longmans, Green, 1931.

Reed, Mary J. "A Population Study of the Driftless Hill Land during the Pioneer Period, 1832–1860." Ph.D. diss., University of Wisconsin, 1941.

Reynolds, Lloyd G. *The British Immigrant: His Social and Economic Adjustment in Canada.* New York: Oxford University Press, 1935.

Rickard, T. A. *A History of American Mining.* New York: McGraw Hill, 1932.

Riley, Martha. "A Social and Economic History of LaFayette County." M.A. thesis, Marquette University, 1934.

Robertson, A. J. "The Decline of the Scottish Cotton Industry, 1860–1914." *Business History* 7 (July 1970): 116–28.

Robertson, Ross M. *History of the American Economy.* 4th ed. New York: Harcourt Brace Jovanovich, 1979.

Robinson, Charles Alexander. *Ancient History: From Prehistoric Times to the Death of Justinian.* New York: Macmillan, 1951.

Rohrbough, Malcolm J. *The Trans-Appalachian Frontier: People, Societies, and Institutions, 1775–1850.* New York: Oxford University Press, 1978.

Rose, Gregory S. "Indiana's Ethnicity in the Context of Ethnicity in the Old Northwest in 1850." In *Peopling Indiana: The Ethnic Experience,* ed. Robert M. Taylor, Jr., and Connie A. McBirney, 616–44. Indianapolis: Indiana Historical Society, 1996.

Rosen, Carol J. "Images of Wisconsin's Settlement Frontier." Ph.D. diss., University of Wisconsin, Milwaukee, 1990.

Rostow, Walt W. *British Economy of the Nineteenth Century.* 1948. Reprint. New York: Oxford University Press, 1961.

Rothstein, Morton. "America in the International Rivalry for the British Wheat Market, 1860–1914." *Mississippi Valley Historical Review* 47 (1960): 401–18.

Rowe, John. *The Hard-Rock Men: Cornish Immigration and the North American Mining Frontier.* Liverpool: Liverpool University Press, 1974.

Rubinstein, Sarah P. "The British," In *They Chose Minnesota: A Survey of the State's Ethnic Groups,* ed. June Drenning Holmquist, 111–29. St. Paul: Minnesota Historical Society Press, 1981

Runblom, Harald, and Hans Norman, eds. *From Sweden to America: A History of the Migration.* Minneapolis: University of Minnesota Press, 1977.

Ruoff, Henry W. *The Century Book of Facts.* Springfield, Mass.: King Richardson, 1906.

Samuel, Raphael. "Workshop of the World: Steam Power and Hand Technology in Mid-Victorian Britain." *History Workshop* 3 (Spring 1977): 6–72.

Saul, S. B. "Housebuilding in England, 1890–1914." *Economic History Review* 15 (Aug. 1962): 119–37.

———. *The Myth of the Great Depression, 1873–1896.* New York: Macmillan, 1969.

Saville, John. *Rural Depopulation in England and Wales, 1851–1951.* Boston: Routledge and Kegan Paul, 1957.

Schafer, Joseph. *The Wisconsin Lead Region.* Madison: State Historical Society of Wisconsin, 1932.

Schrier, Arnold. *Ireland and the American Emigration, 1850–1900.* Minneapolis: University of Minnesota Press, 1958.

Semmingsen, Ingrid. *Norway to America: A History of the Migration.* Minneapolis: University of Minnesota Press, 1978.

———. "Norwegian Emigration in the Nineteenth Century." *Scandinavian Economic History Review* 8 (1960): 150–60.

Seymour, Harold. *Baseball: The Early Years.* New York: Oxford University Press, 1960.

Shepperson, Wilbur S. *British Emigration to North America: Projects and Opinions in the Early Victorian Period.* New York: Blackwell, 1957.

————. *Emigration and Disenchantment: Portraits of Englishmen Repatriated from the United States*. Norman: University of Oklahoma Press, 1965.

Shipps, Jan. *Mormonism: The Story of a New Religious Tradition*. Urbana: University of Illinois Press, 1987.

Simon, R. D. "The Birds of Passage in America, 1865–1914." M.A. thesis, University of Wisconsin, 1966.

Smith, Page. *A People's History of the Post-Reconstruction Era*. Vol. 6: *The Rise of Industrial America*. New York: McGraw-Hill, 1984.

Snow, C. E. "Emigration from Great Britain." In *International Migrations*. Vol. 2. Ed. Imre Ferenczi and Walter Willcox. New York: National Bureau of Economic Research, 1931.

Sonne, Conway B. *Saints on the Seas: A Maritime History of Mormon Migration, 1830–1890*. Salt Lake City: University of Utah Press, 1983.

Stanley, Henry Morton. *The Autobiography of Sir Henry Morton Stanley*. 2d ed. Boston: Houghton Mifflin, 1909.

The Statistical History of the United States: From Colonial Times to the Present. Washington: U.S. Bureau of the Census, 1976.

Stein, Gary C. "Indian Removal as Seen by European Travelers in America." *Chronicles of Oklahoma* 51 (Winter 1973–74): 399–410.

The Story of Mineral Point, 1827–1941. 1941. Reprint. Mineral Point: Mineral Point Historical Society, 1979.

Stott, Richard B. *Workers in the Metropolis: Class, Ethnicity, and Youth in Antebellum New York City*. Ithaca: Cornell University Press, 1990.

Stratton, Joanna L. *Pioneer Women: Voices from the Kansas Frontier*. New York: Simon and Schuster, 1981.

Sturgess, R. W. "The Agricultural Revolution on the English Clays." *Agricultural History Review* 14 (1966): 104–21.

Swank, James M. *Introduction to a History of Ironmaking and Coal Mining in Pennsylvania*. Philadelphia: Published privately, 1878.

Swierenga, Robert P. "The Delayed Transition from Folk to Labor Migration: The Netherlands, 1880–1920." *International Migration Review* 27 (Summer 1993): 406–24.

————. "Dutch Immigrant Demography, 1820–1880." *Journal of Family History* 5 (Winter 1980): 390–405.

————. "Ethnicity and American Agriculture." *Ohio History* 89 (Summer 1980): 323–44.

————. "List upon List: The Ship Passenger Records and Immigration Research." *Journal of American Economic History* 10 (Spring 1991): 42–53.

————. "Religion and Immigration Behavior: The Dutch Experience." In *Belief and Behavior: Essays in New Religious History*, ed. Philip R. Vandermeer and Robert P. Swierenga, 164–88. New Brunswick: Rutgers University Press, 1991.

————. "Under-Reporting of Dutch Immigration Statistics: A Recalculation." *International Migration Review* 21 (Winter 1987): 1596–99.

Swierenga, Robert P., and Harry S. Stout. "Dutch Immigration in the Nineteenth Century, 1820–1877: A Quantitative Overview." *Indiana Social Studies Quarterly* 28 (Autumn 1975): 7–34.

Sykes, J. D. "Agriculture and Science." In *The Victorian Countryside*, ed. G. E. Mingay, 260–72. Boston: Routledge and Kegan Paul, 1981.

Symons, Alphons J. A. *H. M. Stanley*. London: Falcon Press, 1950.

Taylor, A. J. "Labour Productivity and Technological Innovation in the British Coal Industry, 1850–1914." *Economic History Review* 14 (Aug. 1961): 48–70.

Taylor, Clare. "Paddy's Run: A Welsh Community in Ohio." *Welsh History Review* 11 (June 1983): 302–16.

Taylor, Phillip A. M. *The Distant Magnet.* New York: Harper and Row, 1971.

———. *Expectations Westward: The Mormons and the Emigration of the British Converts in the Nineteenth Century.* Edinburgh: Oliver and Boyd, 1965.

———. "Why Did British Mormons Emigrate?" *Utah Historical Quarterly* 22 (July 1954): 249–70.

Temin, Peter. *Iron and Steel in Nineteenth-Century America: An Economic History.* Cambridge: MIT Press, 1964.

Thistlethwaite, Frank. *The Anglo-American Connection in the Early Nineteenth Century.* New York: Russell and Russell, 1959.

———. "The Atlantic Migration of the Pottery Industry." *Economic History Review* 9 (Dec. 1958): 264–78.

———. "Migration from Europe Overseas in the Nineteenth and Twentieth Centuries." In *A Century of European Migrations, 1830–1930,* ed. Rudolph J. Vecoli and Suzanne M. Sinke, 17–49. Urbana: University of Illinois Press, 1991.

Thomas, Brinley. "Demographic Determinants of British and American Building Cycles, 1870–1913." In *Essays on a Mature Economy: Britain after 1840,* ed. Deirdre N. McCloskey, 39–74. Princeton: Princeton University Press, 1971.

———. *Migration and Economic Growth.* New York: Cambridge University Press, 1954.

———. *Migration and Urban Development: A Reappraisal of British and American Long Cycles.* London: Methuen, 1972.

———. "Wales and the Atlantic Economy." *Scottish Journal of Political Economy* 6 (Nov. 1959): 169–92.

Thomas, D. S. *Research Memorandum on Migration Differentials.* Bulletin 43. New York: Social Science Research Council, 1938.

Thomas, William I., and Florian Znanieki. *The Polish Peasant in Europe and America.* 2 vols. Chicago: University of Chicago Press, 1920.

Thompson, David M. "The 1851 Religious Census: Problems and Possibilities." *Victorian Studies* 11 (Sept. 1967): 87–97.

Thompson, Francis M. L. *English Landed Society in the Nineteenth Century.* Boston: Routledge and Kegan Paul, 1963.

———. "The Second Agricultural Revolution, 1815–1880." *Economic History Review* 21 (April 1968): 62–77.

Tiratsoo, Nick. "Coventry's Ribbon Trade in the Mid-Victorian Period: Some Social and Economic Responses to Industrial Development and Decay." Ph.D. diss., University of London, 1980.

Todd, Arthur Cecil. *The Cornish Miner in America: The Contribution to the Mining History of the United States by Emigrant Cornish Miners—the Men Called "Cousin Jacks."* Cornwall: Barton, Clark, 1967.

Tweedale, Geoffrey. *Sheffield Steel and America: A Century of Commercial and Technological Interdependence, 1830–1930.* New York: Cambridge University Press, 1987.

Vamplew, Wray. "The Protection of English Cereal Producers: The Corn Laws Reassessed." *Economic History Review* 33 (Aug. 1980): 382–95.

Vander Zee, Jacob. *The British in Iowa*. Iowa City: Athens Press, 1922.

Van Vugt, William E. "British Emigration during the Early 1850s, with Special Reference to Emigration to the U.S.A." Ph.D. diss., University of London, 1986.

————. "English Emigrant Guidebooks and Pamphlets, 1860–1899: The Image of America." Master's thesis, Kent State University, 1981.

————. "An English Shoemaker in Indiana: The Story of Samuel Fowler Smith." *Indiana Magazine of History* 91 (March 1995): 16–56.

————. "Prosperity and Industrial Emigration from Britain to the U.S.A. during the Early 1850s." *Journal of Social History* 20, no. 2 (1988): 339–54.

————. "Running from Ruin? The Emigration of British Farmers to the U.S.A. in the Wake of the Repeal of the Corn Laws." *Economic History Review* 16, no. 3 (1988): 411–28.

————. "Welsh Emigration to the United States in the Mid-Nineteenth Century." *Welsh History Review* 15, no. 4 (1991): 545–61.

————. "Who Were the Women Immigrants from Britain in the Mid-Nineteenth Century?" In *Immigration and Ethnicity: American Society, "Melting Pot" or "Salad Bowl"?* ed. Michael D'Innocenzo and Joseph P. Sirefman, 163–75. Westport: Greenwood Press, 1992.

The Victoria History of the Counties of England: A History of the County of Lincolnshire. 2 vols. London: A. Constable, 1906.

The Victoria History of the Counties of England: A History of the County of Staffordshire. 2 vols. London: A. Constable, 1906.

The Victoria History of the Counties of England: A History of the County of Suffolk. London: A. Constable, 1907.

The Victoria History of the Counties of England: A History of the County of Yorkshire. 2 vols. London: A. Constable, 1907.

Vincent, David. *Literacy and Popular Culture, England, 1750–1914*. New York: Cambridge University Press, 1989.

Walker, Mack. *Germany and the Emigration, 1816–1885*. Cambridge: Harvard University Press, 1964.

Walsh, Margaret. *The American Frontier Revisited*. London: Macmillan, 1980.

Walsh, Timothy, ed. "The Voyage of an Iowa Immigrant." *Annals of Iowa* 44 (Fall 1977): 137–45.

Ware, Caroline F. *The Early New England Cotton Manufacture: A Study in Industrial Beginnings*. Boston: Houghton Mifflin, 1931.

Warner, Sam B. "Innovation and the Industrialization of Philadelphia 1880–1850." In *The Historian and the City*, ed. Oscar Handlin and J. Burchard, 63–69. Cambridge: MIT Press, 1963.

"'We Are Yankeys Now': Joseph Hartley's Transplanting from Brighouse Wood, Yorkshire, Old England to Lockport, New York, Told by Himself and His Wife in Letters Home." *New York History* 45 (July 1964): 222–64.

Werner, Julia S. *The Primitive Methodist Connexion: Its Background and Early History*. Madison: University of Wisconsin Press, 1984.

Wetherford, Doris. *Foreign and Female: Immigrant Women in America, 1840–1930*. New York: Schocken Books, 1986.

Wilcox, Ralph C. "Sport and the Nineteenth Century Immigrant Experience," In *Immigration and Ethnicity: American Society, "Melting Pot" or "Salad Bowl"?* ed. Michael D'Innocenzo and Joseph P. Sirefman, 177–89. Westport: Greenwood Press, 1992.

Williams, David. *A History of Modern Wales.* 1950. Reprint. London: J. Murray, 1962.

———. "Some Figures Relating to Emigration from Wales." *Bulletin of the Board of Celtic Studies* 7 (May 1935): 396–415.

Williams, David Jenkins. *The Welsh Community of Waukesha County.* Columbus: Hann and Adair, 1926.

Williamson, Harold F., ed. *The Growth of the American Economy.* 2d ed. New Jersey: Prentice-Hall, 1951.

Williamson, Jeffrey. "The Impact of the Corn Laws Just Prior to Repeal." *Explorations in Economic History* 27 (1990): 123–56.

Williamson, J. G. *Late-Nineteenth-Century Economic Development.* Cambridge: Harvard University Press, 1974.

Winther, Oscar. "English Migration to the American West, 1865–1900." In *In the Trek of the Immigrants,* ed. Oscar F. Ander, 115–25. Rock Island: Augustana College Library, 1964.

———. "Promoting the American West in England, 1865–1890." *Journal of Economic History* 16 (Dec. 1956): 506–13.

Wittke, Carl F. *The Irish in America.* 1956. Reprint. New York: Russell and Russell, 1970.

Wright, James E. *The Galena Lead District: Federal Policy and Practice, 1824–1847.* Madison: University of Wisconsin Press, 1966.

Yearley, Clifton K. *Britons in American Labor.* Baltimore: Johns Hopkins University Press, 1957.

———. *Enterprise and Anthracite: Economics and Democracy in Schuylkill County, 1820–1875.* Baltimore: Johns Hopkins University Press, 1961.

Young, Michael. *The Rise of the Meritocracy, 1870–2033: An Essay on Education and Equality.* Harmonsworth, England: Penguin Books, 1965.

Zevin, R. B. "The Growth of Cotton Textile Production after 1851." In *The Reinterpretation of American Economic History,* ed. Robert Fogel and Stanley Engerman, 122–47. New York: Harper and Row, 1971.

Index

Aberdeen, Scotland, 137
Aberystwyth, Wales, 113
abolitionism, 61, 139–44
Addenbrooke, William, 116
age: of British immigrants, 17–18, 63; of women, 122–24, 127; *see also specific occupations*
agrarian myth, 50–55, 119–21, 124, 154
agricultural conditions: in Britain, 21–34, 181n53; in the United States, 35–59; in Wales, 194n13
agricultural distress, 22, 25, 31–32, 34, 43, 180n27
agricultural laborers, 34–42; wages of, 42–45, 48, 50
agriculture: American methods of, 30, 181n4; English methods of, 30–32, 37–38; *see also* Corn Laws; land
alcohol consumption, 61–62, 84, 103, 106, 119, 121; *see also* temperance
Alderson, Edward, 82
Alderson, Jonathan, 82, 83
Anderson, Gregory, 112
Anderson, Michael, 63
Anderton, George, 113
Angel, Samuel, 144
Ann Arbor, Mich., 115, 116
Applegarth, Robert, 142
apprentices, 16, 37, 46, 47, 52, 54, 67, 113
Argyleshire, 48
Arizona, 87
Arkansas, 124

Armstrong, W. A., 41
artisans, 51–52, 61, 72; *see also specific occupations*
assisted immigration, 44, 127, 129, 184n49
Ashburton, Devonshire, 43
Ashworth, Ralph, 88
assimilation, 38, 146, 148–52
Australia, 8, 10, 87, 112, 127, 129
Ayrshire, 39, 91, 95

Bailey, Charles, 65
Bailyn, Bernard, 5
bakers, 71, 91–92
baseball, 148, 151
Bath, 116
Bedford, John, 50
Bedfordshire, 32, 33
Berkshire, 32
Berthoff, Rowland, 4
Birkbeck, Morris, 38
Birkett, Thomas, 74
Birmingham, 52, 116
Birtwhistle, Mr., 24, 26
blacksmiths, 52, 71–75, 88, 186n83, 190n62
boilermakers, 66
bookbinders, 126
Borland, Thomas, 39
Boston, 44
Bouch, Joseph, 53
Briggs, Asa, 9, 143
Bright, John, 142
Brighton, Sussex, 74

Bristol, 143
British Emigration Temperance Society, 56–57, 137
Broadhead, William, 64
Brooks, Mary, 125
Brown, William, 55
Building Trades Workers, 69–71, 184n52; see also specific trades
Burden, John, 46
Burn, W. L., 9
Burns, Robert, 149
butchers, 71
Butterworth, Rebecca, 124

cabinetmakers, 71, 73, 126
Caird, James, 22, 27, 29–33, 41, 42, 65, 178n4
calico printers, 188n26
California, 1, 11, 71, 87, 89, 90, 91, 92, 93, 101, 154
Calvinist Methodists, 98, 105, 133, 148
Campbell, John, 71
Cambridgeshire, 32, 50, 70
Cambridge University, 120
Canada, 10, 17, 58, 79, 118
capital investment, 12, 32–33, 181n50
Carbondale, Pa., 91, 93, 95, 103
Cardiff, Wales, 109
Cardiganshire, Wales, 98, 105
Carnarvonshire, Wales, 105, 107, 108
Carnegie, Andrew, 64
carpenters, 52, 69–71, 88, 189n56
Carrothers, W. A., 4
Chadwick, Jane, 19, 125
chain migration, 2, 44, 46, 65, 80, 83, 93, 98, 103, 132, 134, 135–36, 155; see also immigrant letters
Chapman, E., 140, 153
Cheshire, 32
Chester, 49
Chicago, Ill., 19, 45
children, 17, 48–50, 63, 70, 124
Christmas celebrations, 150
Church, Roy, 176n3
Cincinnati, Ohio, 19, 91
Civil War (U.S.), 3, 92, 116, 142, 144–48
Clark, Jonathan, 45
Clavering, Essex, 52
clay soil, 31–32, 181n47
clerks, 52, 53, 111, 112–14, 155, 198n12; wages in America, 52

Cleveland, Ohio, 19, 66
cloth finishers, 188n33
clothiers, 54
coal miners, 93–95, 96, 101, 104, 154
coal mining: in America, 93–95; in Britain, 78–79
Cobden, Richard, 61, 143
Colorado, 87, 121
Columbus, Ohio, 19
Conkling, Roscoe, 117
Connecticut, 95
Conway, Alan, 5, 99, 105, 109
coopers, 65
Copeland, Louis, 83
copper mining, 44, 54
Cornish. See Cornwall
Corn Laws, 3, 21, 27, 29, 33, 36, 40, 41, 51, 58, 59, 100, 143, 153, 156
Cornwall, 1, 43, 56, 70, 78, 80, 81, 86, 87, 93, 123, 125, 126, 154; Cornish language and culture in America, 83–85
cotton bleachers, 64
Cowan, Helen, 4
Cox, Henry S., 116
craftsmen, 58, 60–61, 69–77, 154; see also specific occupations
cricket, 120, 151
Crimean War, 34, 54, 101, 146, 154
Cumberland, 32, 74
Curtis, John, 61
cutlers, 126

Daniels, John, 45
Darwin, Charles, 9
Davis, David, 116
Delaware, 143
depopulation, 69–70, 71, 72, 73, 154, 189nn50,51
Derbyshire, 46
Detroit, Mich., 19, 123
Devonshire, 43, 45, 47, 49, 64, 70, 83, 117
Dinsdale, Matthew, 1–2, 15, 40, 140, 157, 175n1
doctors, 52, 88, 113, 115–16, 127
domestic servants, 11, 128–29
Doncaster, South Yorkshire, 24
Dorset, 39
Douglass, Frederick, 141, 142
drainage, 27, 31, 33, 36–38, 59, 90, 180nn32,41, 182n14
dressmakers, 16, 125
druggists, 52

Dubuque, Iowa, 81
Dundee, Scotland, 67
Durham, 32, 79
The Dutch, 37, 132, 178n37
dyers, 10

East Sussex, 42
economics: relationship between Britain and
    America, 3, 4, 9–12
Edinburgh, Scotland, 115, 116, 137, 146
Edwards, D. L., 113
egalitarianism: in America, 12
eisteddfod competitions, 150
Elliott, Henry, 67
emigration schemes, 56–58; see also individual
    group names
Engels, Friedrich, 21
engineers, 10, 11, 66–69, 188n40
engravers, 52, 54
Erickson, Charlotte, 4–5, 148
Essex, 31, 43, 52
Ewbank, John, 134

Fairlie, Susan, 27
Fairmont, Minn., 118–20
farm laborers, 14, 22–23, 35, 39, 40–48, 105, 153,
    184nn55,58
farmers, 11, 12, 35–40, 99, 105, 114, 124, 138, 153
farmers' sons, 1, 48–50, 185n70
farming conditions. See agriculture
Fell, James, 47
Fender, Stephen, 48
Fifeshire, Scotland, 52, 75, 137
Fischer, David Hacket, 5
Fisher, Charlotte, 123
flax hacklers, 187n22
foundry workers, 54, 66; wages in America, 50
Fourier, Charles, 57
foxhunting, 119
free trade, 3, 9, 21, 22, 25, 27, 31, 32, 35, 39, 43–
    44, 48, 61, 103; see also Corn Laws
Freeman, Job, 94
Freeman, Richard, 94
Froggat, John, 46
fullers, 64

Garrison, William Lloyd, 144
gentlemen, 118–21
Geraghty, J. P., 144
Germans, 7, 18, 99, 121, 130

Gilkeson, Annie, 121
Glasgow, Scotland, 54, 65, 70, 95
Gloucestershire, 32, 93
Goalby, William, 94
gold mining. See Gold Rush
Gold Rush, 58, 87, 89–93
Gorst, Robert, 57
Graham, Peter Anderson, 69–70
Grant, George, 120–21
Great Exhibition of 1851, 9, 176n3
"Great Victorian Boom," 9, 175n3
grocers, 54
group migration, 24, 57, 58, 83, 120, 191n16,
    192n19
gunmakers, 52, 189n44

Hadaway, Samuel, 44
Hampshire, 32
handloom weavers, 62–64, 77, 187n10
Hansen, Marcus, 4, 22, 41
Hardie, George, 50
hard-rock miners, 80–93
Hasbach, Wilhelm, 41
hatters/milliners, 52, 125, 126
Herbert, Lewis, 105
Herbert, Sydney, 126
Hopkins, Benjamin, 138
Hopkins, Thomas, 39
Hughes, J. R. T., 9

Illinois, 1, 11, 19, 38, 46, 47, 49, 50, 52, 53, 54, 67, 70,
    71, 75, 80, 82, 86, 88, 91, 92, 93, 94, 95, 97, 103,
    113, 114, 115, 124, 125, 132, 137, 141, 143, 147, 155
immigrant letters, 1, 2, 4, 10, 12, 13, 55, 58, 75,
    82, 83, 103, 105, 124
Indiana, 17, 36, 38, 52, 75, 94, 97, 105, 117, 134,
    139, 144
industry: in America, 10–11, 60–62, 90–91,
    106–7; in Britain, 9–11, 60, 62–67; see also
    specific occupations
instrument makers, 51
Inverneshire, Scotland, 34
Iowa, 58, 80, 91, 92, 120, 125, 136
Iowa Emigration Society, 57–58
Irish, 9, 17, 42, 99, 128, 130, 151
iron foundry, 186n1
iron mining, 54
ironworkers, 10, 11, 66–69, 96, 108–10, 154,
    188n36; and farming in America, 68
Italians, 42

Jackson, John, 87
Jefferson, Thomas, 11
Jenkins, Martha, 123
Jeremy, David, 5, 11
Jewell, William, 92
Johnson, Stanley, 4
Jones, E. L., 42
Jones, James, 93
Jones, Maldwyn, 5, 99

Kansas, 16, 114, 120, 143
Kansas-Nebraska Act, 143
Kent, 42, 146
Kentucky, 93
Kimberley, Edwin O., 26, 141
Kistle, Philippa, 125

laborers, 16–17, 72, 108, 154; see also agricultural laborers
labor migration, 18, 20, 77, 178n37
lacemakers, 64
Lanarkshire, Scotland, 49, 147
Lancashire, 30, 31, 33, 53, 56, 62, 63, 64, 65, 88, 94, 124, 127
Lancastershire, 54
land: clearing of, 40; prices of, 11–12, 42, 53; selection of, 65, 105; see also agriculture
landlords: in Britain, 25, 26, 27, 32, 33, 44, 134
lawyers/attorneys, 35, 53, 116–17
lead mining: in America, 80–83, 87–88; in Britain, 72, 80
Leeds, West Yorkshire, 31, 54
Leicestershire, 143
Lincoln, Lincolnshire, 89
Lincolnshire, 13, 25, 26, 30, 31, 33, 36, 42, 44, 45, 47, 49, 50, 53, 54, 57, 70, 91, 113, 141, 144, 185nn68,71, 204n63
linen manufacturers, 52
linen workers, 52, 188n33
literacy, 112, 114, 125, 181n6
Liverpool, 13, 15, 24, 56, 76, 124
lodges, 138, 149, 151
London, 51, 53, 54, 70, 113, 116, 121, 127, 146, 147
Long, Priscilla, 79, 94
Louisiana, 143

machinists, 10, 11, 67–68, 95
Madison, Wis., 116, 151
Manchester, 51, 61, 62, 65, 125, 147
Maryland, 93
Masons, 69–71

Massachusetts, 65, 126
Mazomanie, Wis., 56
McAndrew, Helen, 128
mechanics, 57, 146, 147
Medical Act of 1858, 198n14
medical profession, 116; see also doctors
merchants, 35, 52, 58, 88, 112–14, 155, 175n1
Methodist Episcopal Church, 1, 84, 125, 132
Methodists, 65, 133, 141, 144; see also Calvinist Methodists; Methodist Episcopal Church; Primitive Methodist Church
Mexborough, West Riding, Yorkshire, 43
Mexican-American War, 11, 204n63
Mexico, 87, 91, 123
Michigan, 11, 19, 39, 44, 45, 48, 49, 50, 51, 53, 54, 55, 74, 80, 87, 92, 93, 115, 116, 128, 136
Michigan State University, 128
Mid-Atlantic, 10, 19; see also specific states
millers, 71, 73–74
millwrights, 66
Milwaukee, Wis., 19, 47, 49, 54, 55, 67, 89, 113, 116
miners, 11, 78–95, 101–7, 126, 154, 200n23; and farming in America, 85–86, 88, 91; see also coal miners; hard-rock miners; quarrymen
Mineral Point, Wis., 1, 56, 80, 84, 95, 126
Minnesota, 40, 118–19
Missouri, 93, 146, 203n46
Monies, William, 91–92
Monmouthshire, 47, 91, 106
Montana, 87
Montreal, 89, 112
Mormons, 135–36
musical instrument makers, 52

Native Americans, 1, 11, 55, 87, 92, 126, 139–41, 148
Nebraska, 92
needlewomen, 71, 126–27, 128
The Netherlands. See The Dutch
Nevada, 87, 94
New England, 10, 19, 61, 63, 137; see also specific states
Newfoundland, 15
New Hampshire, 11
New Jersey, 87
New Orleans, 91, 123, 145
New York (city of), 44, 56, 61, 62, 113, 117, 128, 149, 150, 151
New York (port of), 1, 12, 13, 15, 16, 45, 46, 115, 144
New York (state of), 19, 37, 44, 47, 49, 54, 64, 65, 74, 95, 116, 134, 139, 144

New Zealand, 127
newspapers, 14, 23, 24, 25, 26, 31, 38, 42, 43, 44,
  45, 55, 76, 83, 101–2, 103, 105, 112, 120, 126,
  129, 135, 137, 140, 142, 144, 148; *Albion*, 149;
  Bristol Times, 42; *Cambridge Independent
  Press*, 25; *Carmarthen Journal*, 109;
  Doncaster Chronicle and Farmers' Journal,
  24; *Eastern Counties Herald*, 57; *Emigrant
  Colonial Gazette*, 22; *Lincoln, Rutland, and
  Stamford Mercury*, 89; *Lincolnshire, Boston,
  and Spalding Free Press*, 23; *Mark Lane Ex-
  press*, 22; *Mineral Point* (Wis.) *Democrat*,
  88; *Monmouthshire Merlin*, 109; *Morning
  Chronicle*, 126; *New York Herald*, 145;
  Northampton Herald, 25; *Plymouth Journal*,
  42; *Scottish-American Journal*, 149; *The
  Times*, 26, 43, 112; *Y Drych*, 148
Nicaragua, 92
Nicholas, Philip, 50
Nicol, Andrew, 95
Norfolk, 43, 45, 70, 74
North Riding, Yorkshire, 31
Northampton, 32
Northamptonshire, 139, 140
Northumberland, 79, 90
North Wales, 54, 107, 108
Norwegians, 7, 18, 25, 132
Nottingham, 32, 64, 123
Nottinghamshire, 49, 75

occupations. *See specific occupations*
Ohio, 19, 40, 50, 61, 97, 98, 144, 146, 194n10
Oldham, Lancashire, 63
The Old Northwest, 3, 10, 16, 19, 22, 36, 38, 39,
  45, 50, 54, 55, 59, 87, 97, 132, 145, 153; *see also
  specific states*
Oxfordshire, 22
Oxford University, 53, 117

painters, 126
Panama, 1, 87, 91
Panic of 1837, 3
Panic of 1857, 3, 86, 109
Panluna, Alexander, 88
passenger lists, 5, 16, 22, 23, 27, 29, 32, 42, 99,
  108, 118
Pembrokeshire, 107
Pennsylvania, 11, 19, 50, 63, 66, 80, 81, 88, 89, 91,
  92, 93, 94, 95, 101, 103, 104, 105, 106, 108, 109,
  137, 149
Peny, William, 86

Peoria, Ill., 53
Petherick, William, 53, 116
Philadelphia, Pa., 61, 63, 101
Pittsburgh, Pa., 68, 93
Platteville, Wis., 80, 81, 90, 93
Poles, 42
Polk, James, K., 145
poor laws, 41, 44, 63
Porter, John, 53
potters, 11, 75
Potters' Joint-Stock Emigration Society and
  Savings Fund, 75–76, 138
power looms. *See* textile industries
prairies, 38, 40, 47, 49, 56, 121
preachers, 1
Primitive Methodist Church, 57, 84, 90, 131–
  32, 133
printers, 126
Prothero, R. E., 22
pudlers. *See* ironworkers

Quaife, Milo, 37–38
quarrymen, 11, 79, 95, 101, 107–8
Quebec, 8, 14, 17, 47, 79
Queen Victoria, 149, 150

railroad conductors, 52, 54
railroads, 66, 120
Redford, Arthur, 9
religion 131–39; *see also specific denominations*
Renfrewshire, 55
renting, 11, 25, 26, 39, 46, 48, 49, 56, 75, 86, 91,
  114
return migration, 13, 40, 50, 51, 55, 58, 62, 76,
  80, 82, 88, 91, 104, 107, 114, 123, 147, 155
Rhode Island, 65
Roberts, Thomas, 105
Robertson, Donald, 116
Robertson, Matthew Henry, 116
Rose, Gregory, 19
Rowe, John, 126

Sacramento, Calif., 92
saddlers, 126
sailors, 52, 53
Salt Lake City, Utah, 135
San Francisco, Calif., 91
Schofield, John, 113
Scotland, 64, 66, 71; *see also individual counties*
Scott, Robert, 137
Scranton, Pa., 92, 106

seamstresses. *See* needlewomen
Shanks, William, 55
Sheffield, 67–68, 151
Sheppard, George, 57–58, 186n102
Sheppardsville, Iowa, 58
Shepperson, Wilbur, 4
ship lists. *See* passenger lists
shoemakers, 71, 73–75, 88, 126, 137 190n75,
    200n23
shopkeepers, 127
Shortney, John, 15–16
silk workers, 176n5, 189n56
smallpox, 41
Smith, Samuel Fowler, 75, 140
Snow, C. E., 176n4
Somerset, 49, 70
Somersetshire, 94
South Haven, Mich., 53
South Wales, 67, 94, 101, 105, 108, 109, 135
Spencer, Herbert, 9
Spencer, John, 65
spinners, 64
sports, 150; *see also specific sports*
squatters, 40, 76, 84, 182n26
Staffordshire, 54, 75, 94, 106, 138
Stanley, Henry Morton, 145, 203n55
stationers, 52
statistics: for America, 7–8, 16–17; for Britain,
    7, 16, 41, 118, 175n6; for Wales, 7, 99, 194n7
steamships. *See* voyage to America
Stevenson, George, 67
Steward, Dr. J., 115
Stirlingshire, 38
Stoddart, Thomas, 52
stonemasons, 52, 54, 88, 189n56
Stowe, Harriet Beecher, 142
Stubbs, Joseph, 54
Suffolk, 31, 32
Surrey, 30, 31, 33
Sussex, 55, 74
Swamp Land Act of 1850, 11
Swedes, 18, 132

tailors, 35, 71, 88, 137
Tangye, Joseph, 88
taxes, 12, 24, 107
teachers, 117, 127
temperance, 137–39
Tennessee, 120
textile industries: in America, 10, 63–63, 126;
    in Britain, 62–64, 126, 187n8

textile workers, 10, 11, 62–66, 154, 188n28; and
    farming in America, 65; *see also specific oc-
    cupations*
Thistlethwaite, Frank, 3
Thomas, Brinley, 99
tin-dressers, 88
toolmakers, 68
tradesmen, 56
Treasure, Walter, 103
Turner, James, 47

Ukraine, 54
Uncle Tom's Cabin, 141, 142
unemployment in Britain, 41, 43, 63, 64
Upper Mississippi River Valley, 19, 80, 81, 83,
    85–87, 88, 89, 91, 132, 148; *see also specific
    states*
Utah, 135, 136

Vamplew, Wray, 27, 29
Varley, Thomas, 46
Vermont, 11
veterinarians, 146, 198n19
Vickredge, James, 113
"Victorian Boom," 9, 61, 154
Virginia, 87, 93, 120
voyage to America, 13–16, 17, 48, 58, 115,
    123

wages: in America, 45, 52, 61, 88, 91–92, 104; in
    Britain, 14, 42–43, 69, 79, 109; *see also
    specific occupations*
wagon makers, 52
Wainman, Thomas, 117
Wales, 64, 75, 96–110
Wallers, Richard, 81
Walters, John, 47
Warwickshire, 70
Washington, D.C., 58
watch and instrument makers, 66
Watters, John, 81
Wearne, Richard, 88–89
Weatherby, Edward, 90
weavers, 35, 62, 65, 114, 126; *see also* handloom
    weavers
Welsh Congregationalists, 98, 148
Westmorland, 70
West Riding, Yorkshire, 31
wheelwrights, 71, 73, 190n63
Whittaker, Ann, 124, 125
Whittaker, James, 94

Williams, David, 101
Williamson, Jeffrey, 27
Willis, Robert, 49
Wiltshire, 22, 43, 136, 180n31
Winter, George, 139
Wisconsin, 1–2, 11, 13, 19, 26, 37, 38, 39, 40, 46,
    49, 52, 53, 54, 56, 64, 67, 71, 74, 75, 76, 79, 80,
    83, 84, 86, 87, 90, 91, 92, 93, 97, 103, 105, 107,
    108, 116, 123, 125, 131, 134, 137, 138, 140, 141,
    144, 148, 150, 151, 157

Wood, John, 74
woodworkers, 114, 190n68

Yearley, C. K., 104
York, 37, 46
Yorkshire, 1, 30, 31, 43, 48, 49, 52, 54, 56, 58, 62,
    64, 65, 74, 75, 78, 80, 81, 83, 87, 93, 120, 134,
    140, 141, 144, 145, 146, 147, 154, 157

William E. Van Vugt is professor of history at Calvin College in Grand Rapids, Michigan, where he teaches courses in American and English history and writes on the relationship between Britain and America during the nineteenth century. He earned a B.A. in history at Calvin College, an M.A. in history at Kent State University, and a Ph.D. in economic history at the London School of Economics.

Statue of Liberty–Ellis Island Centennial Series

The Immigrant World of Ybor City: Italians and Their Latin Neighbors in
    Tampa, 1885–1985   *Gary R. Mormino and George E. Pozzetta*
The Butte Irish: Class and Ethnicity in an American Mining Town,
    1875–1925   *David M. Emmons*
The Making of an American Pluralism: Buffalo, New York, 1825–60
    David A. Gerber
Germans in the New World: Essays in the History of Immigration
    Frederick C. Luebke
A Century of European Migrations, 1830–1930   *Edited by Rudolph J. Vecoli
    and Suzanne M. Sinke*
The Persistence of Ethnicity: Dutch Calvinist Pioneers in Amsterdam,
    Montana   *Rob Kroes*
Family, Church, and Market: A Mennonite Community in the Old and the
    New Worlds, 1850–1930   *Royden K. Loewen*
Between Race and Ethnicity: Cape Verdean American Immigrants,
    1860–1965   *Marilyn Halter*
Les Icariens: The Utopian Dream in Europe and America   *Robert P. Sutton*
Labor and Community: Mexican Citrus Worker Villages in a Southern
    California County, 1900–1950   *Gilbert G. González*
Contented among Strangers: Rural German-Speaking Women and Their
    Families in the Nineteenth-Century Midwest   *Linda Schelbitzki Pickle*
Dutch Farmer in the Missouri Valley: The Life and Letters of Ulbe Eringa,
    1866–1950   *Brian W. Beltman*
Good-bye, Piccadilly: British War Brides in America   *Jenel Virden*
For Faith and Fortune: The Education of Catholic Immigrants in Detroit,
    1805–1925   *JoEllen McNergney Vinyard*
Britain to America: Mid-Nineteenth-Century Immigrants to the United
    States   *William E. Van Vugt*

Typeset in 10/13 Minion
with Helvetica Neue display
Designed by Paula Newcomb
Composed by Jim Proefrock
at the University of Illinois Press
Manufactured by Cushing-Malloy, Inc.

7878